Academic Writing in a Second or Foreign Language

Also available from Continuum

Academic Writing: Maggie Charles, Diane Pecorari and Susan Hunston

Academic Writing and Genre: Ian Bruce

Analysing Academic Writing: Louise J. Ravelli and Robert A. Ellis

Academic Writing in a Second or Foreign Language

Issues and Challenges Facing ESL/EFL Academic Writers in Higher Education Contexts

Edited by
Ramona Tang

continuum

Continuum International Publishing Group

The Tower Building	80 Maiden Lane
11 York Road	Suite 704
London SE1 7NX	New York NY 10038

www.continuumbooks.com

British Library Cataloguing-in-Publication Data
A catalogue record for this book is available from the British Library.

ISBN: HB: 978-1-4411-1216-3

Library of Congress Cataloging-in-Publication Data
Academic writing in a second or foreign language : Issues and challenges facing ESL/EFL academic writers in higher education contexts/ [edited and compiled by] Ramona Tang.
    p. cm.
Includes bibliographical references.
ISBN 978-1-4411-1216-3
1. English language–Rhetoric–Study and teaching–Foreign speakers. 2. Academic writing–Study and teaching. 3. Second language acquisition.
I. Tang, Ramona.
PE1128.A2A23 2011
808'.0428071–dc23   2011025095

Typeset by Deanta Global Publishing Services, Chennai, India
Printed and bound in Great Britain

Contents

**Part Three: Identity Work and Professional Opportunities
in Academic Writing**

Afterword

Acknowledgements

It seems fitting to start by thanking a group of very special people without whom this book would not have come into existence. Although I have been working in the area of academic writing for many years, my interest in the issues facing EFL academic writers only developed after I had the pleasure of teaching and getting to know several cohorts of early-career lecturers from China who came to the National Institute of Education, Singapore, as scholars on our Postgraduate Diploma in English Language Teaching programme. Their immense enthusiasm for learning, their generous spirits, and their tenacity in the face of the exacting demands of our programme inspired me to want to find out more about the realities facing ELT professionals in non-English-dominant countries, and the issues faced by students and professional academics who immerse themselves in advanced academic work in a language which is not their first language. I would add that they have also made the last six years of my teaching a real joy.

My deep appreciation also goes to all the contributors who agreed to lend their voices to this volume. I am especially grateful to Theresa Lillis, who very graciously accepted the challenging task of pulling out common threads from the various chapters in order to stitch together an 'Afterword' for this volume.

I wish to thank Susan Hunston and Maggie Charles, who have been great blessings with their support and advice, and Gurdeep Mattu and Colleen Coalter at Continuum for their interest in this project and for their very efficient help along the way. My former student Paula Png also deserves a special mention for providing assistance for this project.

Much love and many thanks go to my dear parents for their love and support. And, above all, my deepest thanks go to God, my strength and my reason for living.

Contributors

Margaret Cargill is an applied linguist currently working as a consultant in publication skills development and researcher education in Australia and internationally. She also holds an adjunct senior lectureship in the School of Agriculture, Food and Wine at The University of Adelaide, South Australia. Her research and teaching centre on innovative collaborative methods for helping scientists from all language backgrounds develop high-level skills for communicating their research findings effectively in the international arena.

Christine Pearson Casanave lived and worked in Japan for many years, most of them at a Japanese university, but also as adjunct at Teachers College Columbia University in Tokyo and visiting professor and adjunct at Temple University's Japan campus. She has long been interested in writing and studying about writing (journal writing, academic writing, writing for publication), in the professional development of language teachers, and in narrative, case study, and qualitative inquiry. One of her long-term goals is to help expand the accepted styles of writing in the TESOL field, and another is to argue for more humanistic, less technology-driven second language education.

Giuliana Diani is a tenured researcher in English Language and Linguistics at the University of Modena and Reggio Emilia, Italy. She holds an MA in Language Studies at the University of Lancaster (UK) and a PhD in English Linguistics at the University of Pisa (Italy). She has worked and published on pragmatic aspects of spoken and written discourse, with special reference to academic discourse in specific genres and disciplines. Her recent work centres on language variation across academic genres, with particular attention to metadiscursive and evaluative language features. She is co-editor (with Ken Hyland) of *Academic Evaluation: Review Genres in University Settings* (Palgrave, 2009), and (with Julia Bamford and Silvia Cavalieri) of

Variation and Change in Spoken and Written Discourse: Perspectives from Corpus Linguistics (John Benjamins, forthcoming).

Guangwei Hu holds a PhD and is an associate professor of applied linguistics at the National Institute of Education, Nanyang Technological University, Singapore. His main research interests include academic writing, bilingual education, language policy, second language acquisition, and language teacher education. He has published on these research areas in such international journals as *British Journal of Educational Psychology, Instructional Science, Journal of Multilingual and Multicultural Development, Language Learning, Language Policy, Research in the Teaching of English, Review of Educational Research, Studies in Second Language Acquisition, Teachers College Record,* and *TESOL Quarterly.*

Suganthi John is a lecturer in the Department of English at the University of Birmingham. Her research is in the area of academic discourse and she is particularly interested in the linguistic representations of the academic identity, the role of the revision process in writing and the nature of research writing at postgraduate level. She is also interested in applying research insights into the development of teaching materials for academic writing courses.

Maria Leedham is a lecturer in the Centre for Language and Communication at the Open University, UK. Previously, she taught English for Academic Purposes and worked on teacher training courses at Oxford and Oxford Brookes Universities, and worked in Senior High Schools in northern Japan. Her chapter in this volume forms part of her PhD thesis (2011) entitled *A Corpus-Driven Study of Features of Chinese Students' Undergraduate Writing in UK Universities.* Her research interests include student writing, corpus linguistics, lexical chunks/formulaic language and digital literacies.

Jo Lewkowicz has been working and researching in Poland since 2004, first at the University of Warsaw and then at the Lingwistyczna Szoła Wyższa. Prior to coming to Warsaw she had a varied and interesting career working at tertiary level in Egypt, Kenya, China, Hong Kong and Armenia. Her research interest and publications cover two main areas of applied linguistics, that of academic literacy focusing on thesis and dissertation writing as well as language testing and evaluation.

Theresa Lillis is a senior lecturer in language and education in the Centre for Language and Communication, The Open University, UK. Her research interests are in academic and professional writing, particularly in relation to the politics of access, location and participation. Methodologically, she is interested in developing ethnographic and collaborative research methodologies. She authored *Student Writing: Access, Regulation and Desire* (Routledge, 2001) and co-authored with Mary Jane Curry, *Academic Writing in a Global Context* (Routledge, 2010). She has published articles in numerous journals, including *Language and Education, TESOL Quarterly, Written Communication, Revista Canaria de Estudios Ingleses, Journal of English for Academic Purposes,* and *English for Specific Purposes.*

Emma Moreton is a Senior Lecturer in the Department of English and Languages at Coventry University, UK. As an early career researcher she is building a publication record in the fields of Systemic Functional Linguistics, Stylistics and Corpus Linguistics. Emma teaches on both the language and literature strands of the undergraduate degree in English as well as the MA in English Language Teaching. Emma has a BA in English Literature from De Montfort University in Leicester and an MPhil(B) in Corpus Linguistics from the University of Birmingham; she is currently in the third year of a PhD in Corpus Linguistics, for which she is developing a corpus of immigrant writing.

Hilary Nesi is Professor in English Language in the Department of English and Languages at Coventry University, UK. She has a particular interest in the use of English for academic purposes in international contexts, and in the design and use of lexical reference tools. She was principal investigator for the project to create the *BASE* corpus of British Academic Spoken English (2001–2005), and for the *BAWE* corpus project 'An Investigation of Genres of Assessed Writing in British Higher Education' (2004–2007).

Patrick O'Connor is a research ecologist, environmental consultant and science educator whose recent work has focused on the use of scientific principles in designing and evaluating environmental programs for governments and statutory authorities in Australia. Patrick is a specialist in the design and implementation of market-based instruments for restoration of ecosystem services in developed areas. His research interests also include the detection of change in plant and animal communities.

Hanako Okada teaches academic writing to students from diverse linguistic and cultural backgrounds at Sophia University in Tokyo, Japan. As a Japanese national educated entirely in English medium international schools and universities, she feels called upon to problematize the still-existing overly simplistic views toward language and culture within the fields of SLA and Applied Linguistics. Her research interests also include bilingual identities, sociocognitive approaches to learning and culture, illness narratives, and other reflective personal narratives.

Brian Paltridge is Professor of TESOL at the University of Sydney. With Sue Starfield he is co-author of *Thesis and Dissertation Writing in a Second Language* (Routledge, 2007) and with his TESOL colleagues at the University of Sydney, *Teaching Academic Writing* (University of Michigan Press, 2009). With Aek Phakiti he edited the *Continuum Companion to Research Methods in Applied Linguistics* (Continuum, 2010) and with Ken Hyland the *Continuum Companion to Discourse Analysis*. His most recent book is *New Directions in English for Specific Purposes Research* (University of Michigan Press, 2011) edited with Diane Belcher and Ann Johns. He is currently editing the *Handbook of English for Specific Purposes* with Sue Starfield, to be published by Blackwell.

Hongwei Ren is a lecturer at the Foreign Language College of Hebei University, the People's Republic of China, where she teaches intensive English, listening, and oral English to English language undergraduates. She has an MA in applied linguistics from Nanyang Technological University, Singapore, and an MA in English Language and Literature from Hebei University. Her main research interests are English teaching, second language writing, and oracy in a second language.

Ramona Tang is an Assistant Professor in the English Language and Literature Academic Group at the National Institute of Education (NIE), Singapore, where she teaches a range of applied linguistics, writing, and teaching methodology courses at undergraduate and postgraduate level. She developed and now manages NIE's academic discourse skills course which is taken by all undergraduates at the university, and is also the programme coordinator of NIE's Postgraduate Diploma in English Language Teaching programme for university EFL lecturers from China. Her research interests centre on the academic literacy practices of students and professional scholars, and on exploring effective ways of teaching and learning in higher education.

Lindy Woodrow is a Senior Lecturer in TESOL at the University of Sydney where she teaches thesis and dissertation writing to doctoral students. She has published in *Modern Language Journal*, *Foreign Language Annals*, and

Language Learning. Lindy is the author of *Adaptive Second Language Learning* (VDM Verlag Dr. Müller, 2008). She is one of the authors of *Teaching Academic Writing* (University of Michigan Press, 2009) and contributed a chapter to the *Continuum Companion to Research Methods in Applied Linguistics* (edited by Paltridge and Phakiti, 2010). Lindy also has a chapter in Mercer, Ryan and Williams' *Psychology for Language Learning* (Palgrave, forthcoming).

Chapter 1

The Issues and Challenges Facing Academic Writers from ESL/EFL Contexts: An Overview

Ramona Tang

There are increasing numbers of academic writers around the world these days for whom English is not their first language, but for whom producing written academic work in English is either a necessity or a personal choice. Included in such a group are the many Asian and European undergraduate and postgraduate students studying in universities in English-dominant countries, and those choosing to study English at a university in their home countries. Also included are academics from English as a Second Language (ESL) or English as a Foreign Language (EFL) contexts now working within BANA (British, Australian and North American) academic institutions, as well as the many scholars who, while staying within their own non-native-English-speaking contexts, face increasing pressures to publish in English in order to establish a presence in the English-dominant international academic scene and to advance in their careers.

This volume seeks to explore some of the issues and challenges facing these academic writers, by pulling together the voices of academic writing researchers from a variety of different contexts and backgrounds. Some of the contributors appearing in this volume would describe themselves as native speakers of English, some would identify themselves as EFL scholars and writers, and some would probably try to question any such labelling. But across all the chapters, we see professionals who have devoted a significant part of their careers to working with non-native-English-speaking students and/or academics, engaging with issues that concern them, and studying the texts that they produce. In some chapters, we see a pedagogic and normative intent to demystify dominant Anglo-American discourse practices so as to make them accessible to those who wish, for whatever reason, to learn and to adopt them. In other cases, we note a more transformative intent, to problematise and challenge dominant discourse practices and to offer alternative ways of understanding and making meaning within academia.

The chapters in this volume thus offer perspectives from (or some might say 'windows into') different Asian and European contexts, and I hope that what comes across will be that the voices, experiences, and goals of those of us working in the area of ESL/EFL academic writing are varied, as are the voices, experiences, and goals of the people who populate our research. In seeking to better understand the issues and challenges facing non-native-English-speaking academic writers, it would be prudent to remember that we are by no means talking about a homogeneous group. The degree of linguistic relatedness between English and an EFL scholar's first language, the extent to which Anglo-American culture is prevalent in his/her home country, the field within which he/she is working or studying, the extent to which English is privileged over local/national languages in academic publication within a country, the societal perception of 'studying abroad', personal goals and perceptions of 'identity', the extent to which a person is influenced by intrinsic motivation versus extrinsic rewards – these and other factors have an impact on how ESL/EFL students and professionals approach academic writing in English. By and large, therefore, the individual chapters in this volume serve to highlight very particular concerns of ESL/EFL academic writers in a range of very specific contexts.

At the same time, however, the chapters as a collection also bring to the fore a number of issues which are central to the field of academic writing research (which I will take to encompass the related fields of Academic Literacies, English for Academic Purposes and Second Language Writing). These include:

- the privileged status of English as the international lingua franca of academic research,
- the different ways in which students and scholars learn to write for academic purposes,
- the challenges associated with 'transitioning' from one context to another,
- the identity work involved in academic writing,
- the creation of opportunities for 'novices' or 'outsiders' to participate in the wider disciplinary conversation, and
- the relation and/or contrast between personal motivations and institutional demands.

It is the recurring nature of these themes across the different chapters of this volume which ties the volume together, and gives this volume, and the field, its unity.

This chapter sets the stage for the rest of this volume by sketching out a backdrop against which the research reported in the subsequent chapters can be read.

1 The Privileged Status of English as the International Lingua Franca of Academic Research

One of the keys to understanding the impetus behind research on academic writing in English as a second or foreign language and to appreciating the pedagogic and research work reported in the chapters in this volume is to recognise the privileged status that English currently enjoys as the international lingua franca of academic research and scholarship. The work that we do to make sense of the issues and challenges facing non-native-English-speaking academic writers would hardly be as compelling if there did not exist real and strong reasons for non-native-English-speaking students and academics to write in English.

The privileged status of English as the international language of academia is, by now, widely acknowledged (e.g. Canagarajah, 2002; Ferguson et al., 2011; Flowerdew & Li, 2009; Hamp-Lyons, 2011; Hyland, 2009; Lillis & Curry, 2010; Swales, 2004). Despite some collective academic and nationalistic concern about whether such a phenomenon is desirable, around the world many individual ESL/EFL students and academics have come to the not unreasonable conclusion that, all other things being equal, an ability to participate in the academic endeavour in the English language could be advantageous for them in terms of their career prospects. Studies have shown, for instance, that in this age of the 'internationalisation' of higher education (e.g. Gu, 2009; Knight, 1999; Teichler, 2009), students from EFL backgrounds, if they choose to pursue higher education abroad, tend to favour English-speaking countries, and there has in recent years been an increased demand by such students for undergraduate and postgraduate degrees from English-speaking countries (Abubakar et al., 2010; Vandermensbrugghe, 2004). According to Vandermensbrugghe (2004), international students choose to study in English-speaking countries 'to acquire internationally recognised linguistic and cultural competencies, which can be very useful in a global context', and believe that their degree from a university in an English-speaking country could be their 'passport' to the world (p. 418).

For ESL/EFL academics looking to establish their careers and to get their voices heard within their chosen disciplinary communities, academic publication is likely to be foremost on their minds since this is the primary means by which knowledge is constructed, negotiated, and disseminated within academic discourse communities (e.g. Becher & Trowler, 2001; Hyland, 2000, 2009). Increasingly, as matters of employment, promotion and tenure within universities are tied to research output and publications (Becher & Trowler, 2001; Belcher, 2007; Burgess & Martín-Martín, 2008; Curry & Lillis, 2010; Flowerdew & Li, 2009; Lillis & Curry, 2010; Pérez-Llantada et al., 2011; Uzuner, 2008), the pressure on academic faculty not just to publish, but to publish in 'international' journals with a 'high impact' factor is growing stronger. At first glance, this seems to be a reasonable expectation – if a scholar wishes to establish his/her membership within the wider discourse community, then certainly it makes sense for his/her research to be published in an 'international' publication. However, as Swales (2004) has noted, the term 'international' in the context of academic publication typically means publishing in *English*. Thus, we see in research reported from countries such as Armenia (Sahakyan & Sivasubramaniam, 2008), China (Cargill & O'Connor, 2006, this volume; Flowerdew & Li, 2009), Indonesia (Adnan, 2009), Italy (Giannoni, 2008), Korea (Cho, 2009), Poland (Duszak & Lewkowicz, 2008), Spain (Ferguson et al., 2011; Pérez-Llantada et al., 2011), Sudan (ElMalik & Nesi, 2008) and Hungary, Slovakia, and Spain (Curry & Lillis, 2004), that there is considerable pressure on non-native-English-speaking academics to publish in English in order to achieve international visibility and institutional recognition (often, though not always, in that order). In some EFL countries, universities with an eye on raising the international profile of their faculty and institutions even offer monetary rewards for successful publication in top-tier, usually English-medium, journals (Adnan, 2009; Flowerdew & Li, 2009; Lillis & Curry, 2010).

Recognising that this 'English-dominant reality' is what many real, working non-native-English-speaking students and academics face on a daily basis is central to the work that we do as researchers and practitioners in the area of ESL/EFL academic writing. This does not mean, of course, that we do not recognise the problems inherent in such a state of affairs. While there are, no doubt, advantages to having a common language through which research ideas can be exchanged internationally, the marked dominance of English in this respect does raise concerns for some. There is the sense, for instance, that research *has* to be published in English in order to feature on the radar of the global disciplinary community, as considerable research output published around the world in languages other than English (e.g. Chinese, French, Portuguese, Russian, Spanish) sits 'lost' behind language barriers and unappreciated beyond national boundaries

(Meneghini & Packer, 2007). There are also concerns about the attrition of national languages in the academic sphere as English supersedes local languages as the medium of choice for the dissemination of research (Duszak & Lewkowicz, 2008; Ferguson et al., 2011; Giannoni, 2008). And there are concerns about issues of linguistic inequality as ESL/EFL scholars may find themselves disadvantaged, not due to the lack of rigour or interest-value of their research, but because of issues to do with academic discourse in English.

Acknowledging the privileged status of English as the international lingua franca of academic research, then, I would argue, is simply that. It is not tantamount to ignoring the potentially negative aspects of the dominance of English in the academic sphere. Neither, I would point out, is it necessarily tantamount to homogenising the experience of non-native-English-speaking students and scholars around the world. We note, for instance, that despite an undeniable general trend that privileges English as the academic lingua franca, the actual extent to which English is favoured over local languages for publication in specific contexts is still dependent on many other factors, including the discipline within which one works, the nature of the research being undertaken, the flexibility of institutional policies of academic recognition, the level of nationalistic pride in the local language(s), academics' own personal goals for their research and the readership perceived as potentially benefiting the most from the research findings. (For discussions of these factors, see Casanave (2002), Duszak and Lewkowicz (2008), Flowerdew and Li (2009), Giannoni (2008), Lillis and Curry (2010), Petersen and Shaw (2002) and Polo and Varela (2009).)

The fact that English is currently the international lingua franca of academia, then, does not *dictate* the practices of non-native-English-speaking academic writers. It is however an essential part of the context within which our research in the field of ESL/EFL academic writing needs to be situated.

2 Problems Faced by ESL/EFL Scholars and Students Writing in English

Underlying all the chapters in this volume is the notion that non-native-English-speaking academic writers face writing-related challenges. It is one of the distinct characteristics of research on academic writing in English as a second or foreign language that the 'problems' associated with this endeavour are what dominate our research agenda. A read through Belcher and Braine's seminal 1995 volume *Academic Writing in a Second Language*, for instance, reveals a similar preoccupation with diagnosing and addressing the problems in the teaching of academic writing to non-native-English-speaking students. The issues addressed in the current volume, then, can be seen as extending a long tradition of research in this area and can best be appreciated when read in the context of this tradition.

The particular challenges that have been identified over the years as being associated with ESL/EFL undergraduate and postgraduate student writers have included both linguistic problems observable through textual analysis, as well as mental or psychological issues (e.g. expectations, attitudes, culturally-informed schemas) unearthed through ethnographic, or ethnographically-related, approaches. We find, for example, discussions of linguistic difficulties to do with grammar, vocabulary and sentence construction (e.g. Chan, 2010; Qian & Krugly-Smolska, 2008; Santos, 1988; Zhou, 2009), studies highlighting students' difficulties with reporting verbs (e.g. John, this volume; Neff et al., 2003; Thompson & Ye, 1991) and reports detailing difficulties with cohesive devices (e.g. Hinkel, 2001; Mu & Carrington, 2007; Nesi & Moreton, this volume), and we find research reporting uncertainty about textual borrowing or citation practices and the concept of plagiarism (e.g. Chandrasoma et al., 2004; Deckert, 1993; Pecorari, 2006; Shi, 2010). We also find discussions of students' difficulties with translating declarative knowledge about academic writing requirements (e.g. the need to 'critically evaluate sources') into actual practice (Wang, 2010), accounts of non-native-English-speaking students' difficulties with using idiomatic, and not merely grammatically-correct, academic English (Mu & Carrington, 2007), and reports of students having an inadequate understanding of the demands of the genres expected of them at the university (e.g. Bitchener & Basturkmen, 2006; Lewkowicz, this volume).

Of particular interest to academic writing researchers have been those problems which, while having observable textual manifestations, may be the result of complex internal negotiations. Difficulties with drawing on, evaluating and transforming source texts to create new texts (e.g. Connor & Kramer, 1995; Shi, 2004; Wette, 2010) could be purely a matter of linguistic proficiency for some, but for others, there could be the added dimension of having to undergo a shift in mindset, being used to an academic tradition where a student's role is seen as primarily to reproduce knowledge, and not to critique or transform it. Asian students, particularly in less-recent research, have been singled out as having reproductive, unquestioning dispositions (e.g. Ballard & Clanchy, 1991; Samuelowicz, 1987), though it should be noted that there is an increasing amount of research which challenges such stereotyping (e.g. Chalmers & Volet, 1997; Floyd, 2011; Shi, 2006). Similarly, ESL/EFL students' difficulties with manipulating hedging and boosting devices in academic writing so as to convey an appropriate level of authority and negotiability (Hinkel, 2005; Hyland & Milton, 1997; Neff et al., 2003) could be the result of their unfamiliarity with discourse conventions, but could at least in part also stem from an ambivalence regarding the amount of 'authority' that is appropriate for a student to display. Likewise, ESL/EFL students' problems with organisational patterns may have cultural roots, since different academic traditions may value different styles and modes of argumentation. The 'direct' approach favoured in Anglo-American academic writing, for instance, where thesis statements or main ideas are announced clearly before being supported by evidence, is not intuitively a quality of 'good' writing for some ESL/EFL writers who may be accustomed to subtler and more indirect ways of 'revealing' ideas in writing (e.g. Burke, 2010; Hinkel, 1997; Matalene, 1985). It has been suggested, in research into academic writing and identity, that substantial changes to one's discourse practices can be construed as the taking on of a whole new identity (e.g. Burke, 2010; Gu, 2009; Ivanič, 1998; Shen, 1989; Spack, 1997). When non-native-English-speaking students face two very different ways of meaning-making, then, they are most certainly facing an issue of identity. It is not surprising therefore that some may feel a degree of ambivalence towards writing in the new ways demanded by the Anglo-American discourse community. At the very least, it might take time for students to decide on the extent to which they can and will take on vastly different new ways of writing and thinking, and what this means for how they view themselves, and how they wish others to view them.

The challenges faced by non-native-English-speaking professional academics, as reported in the literature over the years, have tended to centre around the enterprise of publishing in English. While Flowerdew (2001) has given an encouraging report of the views of the editors of international journals on submissions from non-native-English-speaking contributors, the fact remains that some ESL/EFL scholars still feel themselves to be at a disadvantage when submitting papers to international English-medium journals. Studies, for instance, have reported on ESL/EFL scholars' research papers being rejected or criticised by academic journals due to language problems (e.g. Cho, 2009; Curry & Lillis, 2004; Duszak & Lewkowicz, 2008; Flowerdew, 2000). Others have highlighted the related phenomenon of non-native-English-speaking scholars needing to work collaboratively with native-speaker language professionals (Koyalan & Mumford, 2011) as well as a range of other 'shapers' (Burrough-Boenisch, 2003; Li & Flowerdew, 2007) or 'literacy brokers' (Lillis & Curry, 2010), people such as colleagues, supervisors, friends and spouses who provide various forms of editorial help and input on their papers prior to journal submission. Time, too, is a factor that has been raised, with some EFL scholars reporting that writing an academic paper in English takes a significantly longer time than writing a paper in their own first language (Curry & Lillis, 2004; Flowerdew, 1999; Flowerdew & Li, 2009). Researchers have also found that non-native-English-speaking academics may need help in understanding the Anglo-American conception of an effective research article, as the genre expectations for different sections of the research article may differ in different academic traditions (Adnan, 2009; Cargill & O'Connor, 2006; ElMalik & Nesi, 2008). In addition, some of the specific language and discourse problems identified above as being troubling to EFL students (e.g. range of vocabulary, idiomatic English, use of modal expressions, discourse organisation) have also been highlighted as a cause for concern for EFL academics seeking publication (e.g. Cao, 2009; Flowerdew, 1999; Flowerdew & Li, 2009).

Other studies have highlighted non-linguistic hurdles which have an impact on the EFL scholar's quest for publication. For example, a lack of access to top-tier international journals and current research literature can seriously hamper an academic's ability to keep up-to-date with developments in his/her field of research and to situate his/her own work within the current discussions of the discourse community, and this in turn could affect the 'publishability' of his/her academic papers (Braine, 2005; Canagarajah, 2002; Duszak & Lewkowicz, 2008). The growing role that new technology plays in the world of academic research has also been highlighted as a possible obstacle for contributors from some developing countries (Salager-Meyer, 2008). Journals which only have a presence online, new multimedia modes of presenting and disseminating academic scholarship, the increasing reliance by many leading journals on electronic manuscript submission, powerful search engines that can scour the internet and locate, in a matter of seconds, information about books and journal articles relevant to whatever one happens to be researching at the time – these make the professional life of the 'connected' academic incredibly convenient, but could potentially disadvantage a scholar whose country's infrastructure does not support easy access to the internet.

Confronted with the many difficulties faced by non-native-English-speaking academic writers, I would suggest that there are at least two possible responses. The first response is 'pedagogic' in nature, taken in the broadest sense to mean an attempt to help non-native-English-speaking academic writers understand and acquire the dominant practices of the Anglophone academy by 'demystifying' its conventions. This, it will be noticed as we progress through the chapters in this volume, is the response taken by many of the contributors here. It is not, however, the only possible response. The second response is 'transformatory' in nature, in essence treating dominant discourse conventions as 'contested' and worthy of being challenged, particularly if they are seen as hindering the participation of some (see, for example, Lillis & Scott, 2007). An interesting blend of both these responses is found in Salager-Meyer (2008). Among the radical changes that she proposes for the academic landscape in the future are suggestions for sustained and formalised mentoring programmes by top journals to help non-native-English-speaking researchers with their language issues *prior* to entering their manuscripts into the peer review process, a greater tolerance for the 'linguistic peculiarities' of non-native English in English-medium publications (Ammon, 2001, cited in Salager-Meyer, 2008, p. 126), and institutional rewards systems for promotion and tenure which accept non-English-medium regional journals as valued publication outlets. The first of these suggestions, I would say, is 'pedagogic' in nature, and the latter two 'transformatory'.

While the pedagogic, normative response may appear to some to be simply a tool for perpetuating the linguistic hegemony of English, I would point out, as Belcher and Braine (1995) have, that not all non-native-English-speaking scholars view the dominance of English in the academic sphere as linguistic imperialism or desire to challenge its status. Some are quite happy 'to use the voices and codes of academic authority' (p. xv). Many of the EFL postgraduates that I teach, for instance, recognise that inequality exists, but want nevertheless to acquire the codes of the dominant, to have their academic work judged with exactly the same criteria as would be applied to anyone else (in the Anglophone world). I would be seen as doing them no favours if I suggested otherwise.

As I stated at the start of this chapter then, it is prudent for us to remember that non-native-English-speaking students and academics are not a homogeneous group. As a researcher and teacher in the area of Academic Literacies and English for Academic Purposes, my own position has been that it is vital to raise awareness of the politics inherent in academic discourse practices and to thus 'empower' by highlighting 'what the discourse conventions of the community are, where they come from and what their effects are' (Clark, 1992, p. 118). The response to that knowledge, however, is something I leave to individuals to decide upon for themselves, for if imposing dominant Anglo-American academic discourse conventions on others is viewed as potentially a form of linguistic imperialism, then to oblige someone to take a position of resistance to dominant academic discourse practices is to risk a different sort of hegemony. One's choice of preferred academic discourse practices, as we have already seen, is ultimately a declaration of one's chosen academic identity. This is not a decision we can make on behalf of others.

3 A Departure from the 'Deficit' Discourse

It will not have escaped the notice of anyone who has been in this field for a time that the dominant discourse on ESL/EFL students and scholars studying and working in English-dominant contexts has tended to be located within a deficit model. Thus, as I mentioned at the start of the previous section, it is the *problematic* nature of the non-native-English-speaker's participation in the disciplinary community that has taken up much of the disciplinary spotlight. My own feeling is that it is time to get a different kind of research on non-native-English-speaking students and academics on to our research agenda. Certainly, real challenges do exist for non-native-English-speakers seeking to write in English in academic contexts and we should not sweep these problems under the carpet. However, I firmly believe that our discussions in this area need to be supplemented by a more positive discourse that also appreciates and foregrounds the cultural and linguistic capital that ESL/EFL scholars have (see Tang, this volume, Chapter 11).

Among the few voices that have emerged with a recognition of this need is Tran (2010). She challenges the predisposition, in universities in English-dominant countries, to view the different learning styles and practices of international students as being a 'problem', and argues that the challenges faced by international students in their socialisation into the Australian university culture need to be seen alongside the ways in which these students enhance the discourse community:

> Currently there seems to be an unbalanced approach to constructing the image of international students within the institutional structure. While they are often acknowledged as significantly contributing to the university's financial revenue and campus culture, their presence in the classroom is often linked to concerns about problems emerging from cultural difference and diverse learning styles and characteristics. In particular,

their contributions to the learning environment are not adequately recognized and capitalized on. The diversity in skills, knowledge and experiences that international students bring to the learning context represents a great potential for all students and academics to learn and grow together academically and personally. ... Unfortunately such potentials remain largely overlooked due to the overriding concerns to deal with the complexities in working with a diverse classroom. (Tran, 2010, p. 160)

Also from the Australian context, Cadman (2000) describes an 'Integrated Bridging Programme' for international postgraduates and their supervisors at the University of Adelaide, where 'postgraduates, with their supervisors, begin to explore the cultural relativity of the skills they *bring*, as distinct from those they need' (p. 477, original emphasis). The emphasis here that is important to note is that the international scholars are recognised as 'needing' certain skills that they do not yet have, but at the same time also 'bringing' with them different, potentially equally-valued, skills to the research enterprise. This, I feel, is the way forward, not dismissing the problems that non-native-English-speaking professionals and students may have with academic writing in English, but at the same time making a concerted effort to also see the value that difference and diversity bring to the discourse community.

On a different note, it is also worth pointing out, amidst our discussion of the challenges faced by non-native-English-speaking students and academics, that academic writing is difficult for native speakers of English too. Ferguson et al. (2011) have argued that the 'native/non-native distinction' is a 'coarse and somewhat unsatisfactory criterion for distinguishing between the advantaged and disadvantaged' (p. 41). Indeed, the literature is full of accounts of native-English-speaking novice academic writers encountering difficulties when faced with the demands of academic discourse (e.g. Bartholomae, 1985; Ivanič, 1998; Ivanič & Simpson, 1992; Lillis, 2001; Lillis & Turner, 2001; Woodward-Kron, 2004), and some of the problems highlighted (such as difficulties with citation, academic conventions, genre expectations, argumentation, word choice, cohesion, sentence structure and writer identity) are not so very different from those encountered by ESL/EFL writers.

One useful way of understanding the challenges posed by academic discourse (to all writers, regardless of linguistic background) is to think of academic discourse as a form of social practice (Fairclough, 1989, 1992; Lillis, 2001). As Chase (1988) has pointed out, the academic discourse community is 'organized around the production and legitimation of particular forms of knowledge and social practices at the expense of others' (p. 13). Only certain ways of constructing knowledge and expressing opinions are recognised and valued within the academic discourse community, and these privileged ways of meaning-making have to be learned. Academic literacy, as Ferguson et al. (2011) so eloquently put it, 'is not part of the native speaker's inheritance' (p. 42). The process of negotiating through the specialised discourse of the academy, of deciding which of the new ways of meaning-making to embrace and which to resist, is as much a matter of identity negotiation for native-English-speaking novices as it is for non-native-English-speaking writers. It bears remembering therefore that some of the difficulties faced by ESL/EFL academic writers are not necessarily the result of their non-native-English-speaking status, but rather a consequence of the fact that 'academic discourse' is not the natural 'first language' of any writer.

4 An Overview of this Volume

This chapter has given a necessarily brief (and personal) overview of the wider research context within which the studies in this volume are situated. As a whole collection, the chapters in this volume reflect the central ongoing concerns within academic writing research, while at the same time highlighting various entry points into the study of ESL/EFL academic writing:

(i) Voices from many different countries are represented. The contributors hail from Australia, China, Italy, Japan, Poland, Singapore, the UK and the US, and the perspectives that they offer relate to ESL/ EFL writers from a wide range of Asian and European backgrounds. This allows us to see both the particular concerns of particular contexts as well as the commonalities that exist across the field.

(ii) Different groups of non-native-English-speaking academic writers are represented, from undergraduates (Chapters 3, 4, 7, 8) to postgraduates (Chapters 5, 6, 7, 9, 10, 11) to professionals (Chapters 2, 9, 11), from those who have remained within their own EFL contexts for academic study or work (Chapters 2, 3, 4, 6) to those who have crossed borders to study or work in English-dominant environments (Chapters 5, 7, 8, 10, 11) to those who have not crossed borders but who have had all their education in English-medium international schools within their home countries (Chapter 9).

(iii) A range of different methodologies and approaches are represented, showcasing a variety of possible lenses through which to view and explore the issues and challenges faced by non-native-English-speaking academic writers. The chapter by Cargill and O'Connor draws on qualitative coding and quantitative analysis of questionnaire data to provide insights into the challenges faced by Chinese scientists seeking publication in English and their reactions to an academic writing training workshop tailored for them. The chapter by Hu and Ren also draws on questionnaire data, to comment on various factors influencing EFL student writers' feedback preferences. The chapters by Lewkowicz and John feature qualitative text analysis of EFL postgraduates' writing. Lewkowicz analyses the structure of PhD thesis conclusions written in English in Poland, and John looks at writer identity through the citations employed by EFL students in their master's dissertations. Nesi and Moreton, and Leedham draw on corpus investigations, the former to comment on EFL students' use of shell nouns, and the latter to highlight EFL students' strategies of using of visuals in academic writing. Two chapters take an academic writing class as their focal point – the chapter by Paltridge and Woodrow centres around the qualitative analysis of course reflections produced by EFL postgraduates in an academic writing class in Australia, and the chapter by Diani demonstrates how corpus and discourse analytical methods have been integrated in an undergraduate class on English for Academic Purposes in Italy. And finally, my chapter and the one by Okada and Casanave revolve around narratives – I shine the spotlight on the lived experiences of eight EFL postgraduates and academics to highlight ways in which EFL scholars have the potential to greatly enhance the disciplinary conversation, and Okada and Casanave generously shine the spotlight on themselves, drawing on their own experiences to problematise labels (such as 'native' and 'non-native' English speakers) that are commonly in use but which may not adequately reflect the complex identities of the people they are applied to.

The volume closes with an Afterword by Theresa Lillis. A noted researcher well-known for her detailed and multi-faceted ethnographic work with multilingual EFL academic writers from various countries as well as student writers within UK universities, she brings her keen understanding of the landscape of research in academic writing and her customary perceptiveness to offer her own take on the themes running through this volume and to suggest two 'routes' through the chapters – one which is more accepting of the status quo within the disciplinary space she terms 'English medium writing for academic purposes' or 'EWAP', and the other which challenges and recognises the contingent nature of oft-taken-for-granted categorisations within our field. It is a thought-provoking and forward-looking concluding chapter, and an excellent note, I feel, on which to end this volume.

The scope of research in the area of academic writing in a second or foreign language is indeed wide, and I hope that this volume goes some way to help readers appreciate the exciting, evolving, and multi-faceted nature of this field.

References

Abubakar, B., Shanka, T., & Muuka, G. N. (2010). Tertiary education: An investigation of location selection criteria and preferences by international students – The case of two Australian universities. *Journal of Marketing for Higher Education, 20*(1), 49–68.

Adnan, Z. (2009). Some potential problems for research articles written by Indonesian academics when submitted to international English language journals. *The Asian EFL Journal, 11*(1), 107–125.

Ballard, B., & Clanchy, J. (1991). Assessment by misconception: Cultural influences and intellectual traditions. In L. Hamp-Lyons (Ed.), *Assessing second language writing in academic contexts* (pp. 19–35). Norwood, NJ: Ablex.

Bartholomae, D. (1985). Inventing the university. In M. Rose (Ed.), *When a writer can't write* (pp. 134–165). New York: The Guilford Press.

Becher, T., & Trowler, P. R. (2001). *Academic tribes and territories* (2nd ed.). Buckingham: The Society for Research into Higher Education and Open University Press.

Belcher, D. D. (2007). Seeking acceptance in an English-only research world. *Journal of Second Language Writing, 16*, 1–22.

Belcher, D., & Braine, G. (Eds.). (1995). *Academic writing in a second language.* Norwood, NJ: Ablex.

Bitchener, J., & Basturkmen, H. (2006). Perceptions of the difficulties of postgraduate L2 thesis students writing the discussion section. *Journal of English for Academic Purposes, 5*, 4–18.

Braine, G. (2005). The challenge of academic publishing: A Hong Kong perspective. *TESOL Quarterly, 39*(4), 707–716.

Burgess, S., & Martín-Martín, P. (2008). Introduction. In S. Burgess & P. Martín-Martín (Eds.), *English as an additional language in research publication and communication* (pp. 7–15). Bern: Peter Lang.

Burke, S. B. (2010). The construction of writer identity in the academic writing of Korean ESL students. (Doctoral dissertation). Indiana University of Pennsylvania, US. Retrieved from the Indiana University of Pennsylvania DSpace: http://hdl.handle.net/2069/306

Burrough-Boenisch, J. (2003). Shapers of published NNS research articles. *Journal of Second Language Writing, 12*, 223–243.

Cadman, K. (2000). 'Voices in the air': Evaluations of the learning experiences of international postgraduates and their supervisors. *Teaching in Higher Education, 5*(4), 475–491.

Canagarajah, A. S. (2002). *A geopolitics of academic writing.* Pittsburgh, PA: University of Pittsburgh Press.

Cao, F. (2009). Hedging and boosting in abstracts of academic articles: A comparative study of Chinese and international journals of Applied Linguistics. (Unpublished Masters dissertation). National Institute of Education, Singapore.

Cargill, M., & O'Connor, P. (2006). Developing Chinese scientists' skills for publishing in English: Evaluating collaborating-colleague workshops based on genre analysis. *Journal of English for Academic Purposes, 5,* 207–221.

Casanave, C. P. (2002). *Writing games.* Mahwah, NJ: Lawrence Erlbaum.

Chalmers, D., & Volet, S. (1997). Common misconceptions about students from South-East Asia studying in Australia. *Higher Education Research & Development, 16*(1), 87–99.

Chan, A. Y. W. (2010). Towards a taxonomy of written errors: Investigation into the written errors of Hong Kong Cantonese ESL learners. *TESOL Quarterly, 44*(2), 295–319.

Chandrasoma, R., Thompson, C., & Pennycook, A. (2004). Beyond plagiarism: Transgressive and nontransgressive intertextuality. *Journal of Language, Identity, and Education, 3*(3), 171–193.

Chase, G. (1988). Accommodation, resistance and the politics of student writing. *College Composition and Communication, 39*(1), 13–22.

Cho, D. W. (2009). Science journal paper writing in an EFL context: The case of Korea. *English for Specific Purposes, 28,* 230–239.

Clark, R. (1992). Principles and practice of CLA in the classroom. In N. Fairclough (Ed.), *Critical Language Awareness* (pp. 117–140). London: Longman.

Connor, U. M., & Kramer, M. G. (1995). Writing from sources: Case studies of graduate students in business management. In D. Belcher & G. Braine (Eds.), *Academic writing in a second language* (pp. 155–182). Norwood, NJ: Ablex.

Curry, M. J., & Lillis, T. (2004). Multilingual scholars and the imperative to publish in English. *TESOL Quarterly, 38*(4), 663–688.

Deckert, G. D. (1993). Perspectives on plagiarism from ESL students in Hong Kong. *Journal of Second Language Writing, 2,* 131–148.

Duszak, A., & Lewkowicz, J. (2008). Publishing academic texts in English: A Polish perspective. *Journal of English for Academic Purposes, 7,* 108–120.

ElMalik, A. T., & Nesi, H. (2008). Publishing research in a second language: The case of Sudanese contributors to international medical journals. *Journal of English for Academic Purposes, 7,* 87–96.

Fairclough, N. (1989). *Language and power.* London: Longman.

Fairclough, N. (1992). *Discourse and social change.* Cambridge: Polity Press.

Ferguson, G., Pérez-Llantada, C., & Plo, R. (2011). English as an international language of scientific publication: A study of attitudes. *World Englishes, 30*(1), 41–59.

Flowerdew, J. (1999). Problems in writing for scholarly publication in English: The case of Hong Kong. *Journal of Second Language Writing, 8*(3), 243–264.

Flowerdew, J. (2000). Discourse community, legitimate peripheral participation, and the nonnative-English-speaking scholar. *TESOL Quarterly, 34*(1), 127–150.

Flowerdew, J. (2001). Attitudes of journal editors to nonnative speaker contributions. *TESOL Quarterly, 35*(1), 121–150.

Flowerdew, J., & Li, Y. (2009). English or Chinese? The trade-off between local and international publication among Chinese academics in the humanities and social sciences. *Journal of Second Language Writing, 18,* 1–16.

Floyd, C. B. (2011). Critical thinking in a second language. *Higher Education Research & Development, 30*(3), 289–302.

Giannoni, D. S. (2008). Medical writing at the periphery: The case of Italian journal editorials. *Journal of English for Academic Purposes, 7,* 97–107.

Gu, Q. (2009). Maturity and interculturality: Chinese students' experiences in UK higher education. *European Journal of Education, 44*(1), 37–52.

Hamp-Lyons, L. (2011). English for academic purposes: 2011 and beyond. *Journal of English for Academic Purposes, 10,* 2–4.

Hinkel, E. (1997). Indirectness in L1 and L2 academic writing. *Journal of Pragmatics, 27,* 361–386.

Hinkel, E. (2001). Matters of cohesion in L2 academic texts. *Applied Language Learning, 12*(2), 111–132.

Hinkel, E. (2005). Hedging, inflating, and persuading in L2 academic writing. *Applied Language Learning, 15,* 29–53.

Hyland, K. (2000). *Disciplinary discourses.* London: Longman.

Hyland, K. (2009). *Academic discourse.* London: Continuum.

Hyland, K., & Milton, J. (1997). Qualification and certainty in L1 and L2 students' writing. *Journal of Second Language Writing, 6*(2), 183–205.

Ivanič, R. (1998). *Writing and identity.* Amsterdam: John Benjamins.

Ivanič, R., & Simpson, J. (1992). Who's who in academic writing? In N. Fairclough (Ed.), *Critical Language Awareness* (pp. 141–173). London: Longman.

Knight, J. (1999). Internationalisation of higher education. In H. de Wit & J. Knight (Eds.), *Quality and internationalisation in higher education* (pp. 13–28). Paris: Organisation for Economic Co-operation and Development.

Koyalan, A., & Mumford, S. (2011). Changes to English as an Additional Language writers' research articles: From spoken to written register. *English for Specific Purposes, 30,* 113–123.

Li, Y., & Flowerdew, J. (2007). Shaping Chinese novice scientists' manuscripts for publication. *Journal of Second Language Writing, 16,* 100–117.

Lillis, T. (2001). *Student writing.* London: Routledge.

Lillis, T., & Curry, M. J. (2010). *Academic writing in a global context.* London: Routledge.

Lillis, T., & Scott, M. (2007). Defining academic literacies research: Issues of epistemology, ideology and strategy. *Journal of Applied Linguistics, 4*(1), 5–32.

Lillis, T., & Turner, J. (2001). Student writing in higher education: Contemporary confusion, traditional concerns. *Teaching in Higher Education, 6*(1), 57–68.

Matalene, C. (1985). Contrastive rhetoric: An American writing teacher in China. *College English, 47,* 789–807.

Meneghini, R., & Packer, A. L. (2007). Is there science beyond English? *European Molecular Biology Organization (EMBO) Reports, 8*(2), 112–116.

Mu, C., & Carrington, S. (2007). An investigation of three Chinese students' English writing strategies. *TESL-EJ, 11*(1), 1–23.

Neff, J., Dafouz, E., Herrera, H., Martínez, F., Rica, J. P., Díez, M., Prieto, R., & Sancho, C. (2003). Contrasting learner corpora: The use of modal and reporting verbs in the expression of writer stance. In S. Granger & S. Petch-Tyson (Eds.), *Extending the scope of corpus-based research: New applications, new challenges* (pp. 211–230). Amsterdam/New York: Rodopi.

Pecorari, D. (2006). Visible and occluded citation features in postgraduate second-language writing. *English for Specific Purposes, 25,* 4–29.

Pérez-Llantada, C., Plo, R., & Ferguson, G. R. (2011). 'You don't say what you know, only what you can': The perceptions and practices of senior Spanish academics regarding research dissemination in English. *English for Specific Purposes, 30*(1), 18–30.

Petersen, M., & Shaw, P. (2002). Language and disciplinary differences in a biliterate context. *World Englishes, 21*(3), 357–374.

Polo, F. J. F., & Varela, M. C. (2009). English for research purposes at the University of Santiago de Compostela: A survey. *Journal of English for Academic Purposes, 8,* 152–164.

Qian, J., & Krugly-Smolska, E. (2008). Chinese graduate students' experiences with writing a literature review. *TESL Canada Journal, 26*(1), 68–86.

Sahakyan, T., & Sivasubramaniam, S. (2008). The difficulties of Armenian scholars trying to publish in international journals. *ABAC Journal, 28*(2), 31–51.

Salager-Meyer, F. (2008). Scientific publishing in developing countries: Challenges for the future. *Journal of English for Academic Purposes, 7,* 121–132.

Samuelowicz, K. (1987). Learning problems of overseas students: Two sides of a story. *Higher Education Research & Development, 6*(2), 121–133.

Santos, T. (1988). Professors' reactions to the academic writing of nonnative-speaking students. *TESOL Quarterly, 22*(1), 69–90.

Shen, F. (1989). The classroom and the wider culture: Identity as a key to learning English composition. *College Composition and Communication, 40*(4), 459–466.

Shi, L. (2004). Textual borrowing in second-language writing. *Written Communication, 21*(2), 171–200.

Shi, L. (2006). The successors to Confucianism or a new generation? A questionnaire study on Chinese students' culture of learning English. *Language, Culture and Curriculum, 19*(1), 122–147.

Shi, L. (2010). Textual appropriation and citing behaviors of university undergraduates. *Applied Linguistics, 31*(1), 1–24.

Spack, R. (1997). The acquisition of academic literacy in a second language: A longitudinal case study. *Written Communication, 14*(1), 3–62.

Swales, J. M. (2004). *Research genres: Exploration and applications.* Cambridge: Cambridge University Press.

Teichler, U. (2009). Internationalisation of higher education: European experiences. *Asia Pacific Education Review, 10*(1), 93–106.

Thompson, G., & Ye, Y. (1991). Evaluation in the reporting verbs used in academic papers. *Applied Linguistics, 12*(4), 365–382.

Tran, L. T. (2010). Embracing prior professional experience in meaning making: Views from international students and academics. *Educational Review, 62*(2), 157–173.

Uzuner, S. (2008). Multilingual scholars' participation in core/global academic communities: A literature review. *Journal of English for Academic Purposes, 7*(4), 250–263.

Vandermensbrugghe, J. (2004). The unbearable vagueness of critical thinking in the context of the Anglo-Saxonisation of education. *International Education Journal, 5*(3), 417–422.

Wang, L. (2010). Chinese postgraduate students in a British university: Their learning experiences and learning beliefs. (Doctoral dissertation). Durham University, UK. Retrieved from Durham E-Theses Online: http://etheses.dur.ac.uk/196/

Wette, R. (2010). Evaluating student learning in a university-level EAP unit on writing using sources. *Journal of Second Language Writing, 19*, 158–177.

Woodward-Kron, R. (2004). 'Discourse communities' and 'writing apprenticeship': An investigation of these concepts in undergraduate Education students' writing. *Journal of English for Academic Purposes, 3*, 139–161.

Zhou, A. A. (2009). What adult ESL learners say about improving grammar and vocabulary in their writing for academic purposes. *Language Awareness, 18*(1), 31–46.

Part One

Learning to Write for Academic Purposes

Chapter 2

Identifying and Addressing Challenges to International Publication Success for EFL Science Researchers: Implementing an Integrated Training Package in China

Margaret Cargill and Patrick O'Connor

1 Introduction

One group of EFL/ESL academic writers intimately involved in the challenges of learning to write effectively in English is science researchers. For them, successful submission to international journals of article manuscripts written in English forms an essential requirement for both establishing their career and progressing in it. This chapter is concerned in particular with the part of this group working in China; these scientists are increasingly represented in statistics for both submitted and accepted papers (pers. comm., Prof. I. Alexander, Chair, New Phytologist Trust, 21 November 2009; Li & Flowerdew, 2007), an increase driven in part by the requirement of many Chinese universities that candidates must publish a paper in a journal listed in the international Science Citation Index before they are eligible for the award of their PhD or Master-by-research degree (Li, 2006b). Training of novice authors for this publication task is not often available in any systematic form (Li & Flowerdew, 2007), and the work of ensuring that the manuscripts are ready for submission often falls to the researchers' academic supervisor or thesis advisor, adding to an already very heavy workload (Cho, 2009; Li, 2006a; Li & Flowerdew, 2007). This work, however, is most likely to concentrate on preparing a high-quality final product, and the amount of training the novice member of the author team actually receives during the process can be variable, to say the least. On one hand, little is known about the practices of senior authors of science papers in terms of training their junior colleagues or students in paper writing. On the other hand, calls are increasing for a more systematic approach to this training, both in China and other EFL contexts (Cho, 2009;

Li & Flowerdew, 2007), and an understanding of the issues and challenges faced is an important prerequisite. This chapter aims to contribute in all these areas.

Training for writing science articles for publication is often envisaged by English language professionals to focus mainly on language and discourse features (e.g. Cho, 2009), and by scientists to focus mainly on meeting the audience's expectations of the content – what to write, at the expense of how to do so (e.g. Day & Gastel, 2006). However, Li & Flowerdew (2007) suggest a need on the ground for 'systemized partnerships between language professionals and subject professionals' (p. 100), in order that EFL authors may have access to assistance with the full range of issues likely to affect the decision of the journal editor and referees regarding acceptance for publication. We represent such a partnership, being an applied linguist/research communication consultant (Margaret) and a research ecologist/environmental consultant/science educator (Patrick). Since 2000, we have been working together to develop a practical approach towards publication skill training for scientists that effectively integrates relevant concerns from the domains of language, science and pedagogy (Cargill, 2004; Cargill & O'Connor, 2006a, 2006b).

In pursuing this aim, we have built on the understandings of many others in the fields of English for Specific Purposes (ESP) and English for Academic Purposes (EAP) that collaborative work between language specialists and subject specialists can have very positive outcomes for learners in a range of educational contexts. Models for designing such interactions are usefully summarized for an Australian context by Jones, Bonanno and Scouller (2001), who explain the conceptual differences among several different models. Dudley-Evans (2001) in the UK has also usefully distinguished three levels of partnership between language specialists and subject specialists. The first involves language specialists running language courses which they design based on 'cooperation' from subject specialists who provide prior input about their students' specific language needs and target tasks. The next level is termed 'collaboration', and involves language and subject specialists working together outside the classroom to design classroom tasks for the language course, such that specifically-tailored and timely language support can be provided to students to help them in their subject course. The third level in this taxonomy is 'team teaching', where both specialists work together in the same classroom. We use elements of both 'collaboration' and 'team teaching' in our approach.

In the USA and elsewhere, approaches involving various degrees of shared work across discipline boundaries are named Writing Across the Curriculum (e.g. Bazerman et al., 2005) and Content-based Instruction (e.g. Brinton et al., 1989). In all cases and continents, the programs and models have been developed in response to local contextual constraints, and the levels of collaboration and integration of the language and subject components vary accordingly. In the Jones et al. (2001) model, the two approaches most connected to our approach are called *integrated* (taught by language specialists, but often with subject specialists present) and *embedded* (which describes 'the collaborative design of a curriculum in which the development of generic skills and academic literacy is the organising principle for the course and which is ultimately taught by subject staff' (Jones et al., 2001, p. 11)). Both these types of collaboration are relevant in the discussion that follows of the approach that we have developed for training novice article authors.

For all these approaches, the literature reports challenges with the initial establishment and also with the maintenance of teaching programs as staff change and training and commitment are lost through attrition. A notable issue is the need for a common set of vocabulary to communicate clearly between the disciplinary world views, with Jones et al. (2001, p. 8) citing a call by Threadgold et al. (1997) for 'translation and retraining on both sides'. This issue has also arisen for us in developing and using our collaborative approach. The titles of our early papers included terms such as 'collaborating-colleague' and 'genre-based' as we struggled to find a name that would carry the appropriate messages for scientists as well as language professionals. We have now settled on Collaborative Interdisciplinary Publication Skills Education (CIPSE: Cargill & O'Connor, 2010) as the name of the approach, taking advantage of the growing interest in interdisciplinary teaching and research in higher education (Davies et al., 2010). Explaining it to scientists has been made easier through the publication of a teaching text *Writing Scientific Research Articles: Strategy and Steps* (Cargill & O'Connor, 2009) and the establishment of a companion website at www.writeresearch. com.au, where information can be provided with both 'academic' and 'pragmatic' focuses (Cargill & O'Connor, 2010), including on the training programs we offer in both EL1 and EFL/ESL situations.

It is important here to be specific about the complementary contributions made by the different sets of expertise that we each bring to the task of teaching and researching publication skill development through CIPSE. In particular, how is a CIPSE training event different from a course designed and taught by an experienced EAP teacher alone? Without wishing to repeat previously published descriptions of the workshops (Cargill & O'Connor, 2006a, 2006b) in detail, we can highlight the following three features that represent contributions from Patrick to the pedagogical process we use. First, the organising 'frame' for the workshops is a collated set of criteria, representative of those used by referees of science articles in preparing their reports for journal editors about the acceptability of submitted manuscripts for publication. The synthesised set of referee criteria is further reinforced by examples of author-referee correspondence and invitation to participants to share their own experiences of the refereeing process used by journals. The interpretation of examples of referee comments occurs within the context of the research sub-discipline wherever possible. Workshop participants are also encouraged to look at their own manuscript drafts as a referee would, in search of the evidence needed to respond to the questions asked of them: e.g. Is the contribution new? Is it significant? Is it suitable for publication in this journal? (Cargill & O'Connor, 2009, p. 16). Referees are presented as real working scientists, overworked and reviewing papers late at night, with the baby crying in the next room. The need for manuscripts to present their main messages clearly and emphatically is thus reinforced through a peer-to-peer conversation between working scientists, and the structural and language features that help such a presentation then take on new relevance. The authority of a working/publishing scientist as teacher cannot be overestimated and may in part explain why interdisciplinary teaching of science writing has not become the norm – scientists tend not to recognise, until it is demonstrated to them, the extra value that can be added by a complementary language-based component.

The second scientist-driven difference relates to the order in which article sections are dealt with in the workshops. Unlike most teaching or advice books on the topic (e.g. Weissberg & Buker, 1990), we begin not with the introduction but with the results, and the need to identify a coherent 'story' told by the results package selected as the basis for the article. Tables and figures must be refined so that each presents clear evidence for one or more components of the paper's 'take-home message'. The construction of packages of results is a process which generates questions about the novelty, importance and limitations of the research. The questions generated are best understood from within the framework of scientific research, preferably from within the discipline or sub-discipline of the research field. Practised understanding of how scientists read and interpret the results of other researchers' work is an essential capability of the scientist as a CIPSE trainer, and underpins traditional approaches of mentoring early career research-ers. It is only after the packaging of results that we talk about language chal-lenges such as the use of English verb tenses in writing about results, or the construction of figure legends.

The third feature we will highlight here is the emphasis placed on early selection of the most appropriate target journal for submission of each manuscript – a step taken after the results story is clear and its significance for the relevant field of science thought through, but ideally before the full draft is written. Steps for analysing prospective target journals are pre-sented, with a range of possible criteria for consideration by each author: e.g. How important is the impact factor in your current situation? Who do you really want to read this paper once it is published? Which journals do you cite most in your reference list? Are your findings of more local/applied/incremental significance, or more theoretical/global in applica-tion? (Cargill & O'Connor, 2009, pp. 69–72). Once these questions are answered and a short-list of journals prepared, participants find it very straightforward to engage with language related questions of how to begin the introduction, or how to justify the research effectively (using the rele-vant 'stage' or 'move' identified by applied linguistics research). Thus the scientist team member provides the specific information needed to create the 'context of situation' (Halliday & Hasan, 1985) that surrounds the genre being analyzed and written in the workshops. (Participants bring a published research paper from a prospective target journal for analysis, as well as analysed data to form the basis of a manuscript they will write or revise during the workshop, section by section.) Furthermore, now that an effective pedagogical structure has been developed for the workshops (see the table of contents for Cargill & O'Connor (2009) at www.writeresearch.com.au), other scientists can (and do) substitute for Patrick in the teaching team, when workshop participants come from fields of science that match their expertise.

Presenting CIPSE workshops in various training contexts in China has provided valuable research opportunities, enabling insights into the issues and challenges faced by writers in these locations. The data collected high-light both what participants most wanted to achieve before the training, and what they most valued in the training after they had received it. These results are presented in the second part of this chapter for four contexts: three 4–5 day workshops, each for 30–40 participants from a different disci-pline background (plant science for the Beijing workshop, applied chemis-try for Changchun and fields within engineering physics for Mianyang); and an event focused on helping Chinese supervising academics develop their skills for training others (Table 2.1). This final event was a three-day workshop in Kunming sponsored by the highly-ranked plant science journal *New Phytologist* with the aim of enhancing the skills of experienced scientists to train and mentor their students and junior colleagues to write manuscripts suitable for submission to that journal.

Readers of this volume are also likely to have an interest in both the effectiveness and the practical applicability of any approach suggested for addressing the specific challenges encountered by writers in a particular context. For science researchers, we consider that the key context of application is the department or institute where they work. (We do not include here university-wide applications where trainees necessarily come from a wide range of home disciplines; these present another highly complex set of issues and will be the subject of a forthcoming report.) In the third part of the chapter, we consider the effectiveness of the CIPSE approach in enhancing participants' confidence to both write and publish science articles in English, by analyzing data collected during the training events. Section 4 concentrates on the Kunming workshop alone; this analysis provides insights into the types of strategies Chinese scientists use to address the issues they face in mentoring and training juniors, and their views of the applicability of the CIPSE book and website package in their own situations. The final part of the chapter draws preliminary conclusions about ways in which the CIPSE approach can be used in EFL/ESL contexts to help address the issues and challenges experienced by scientist authors.

Table 2.1   Details of four CIPSE training events presented in China 2007–2009

Sponsor/site	Date	No. of days	Trainers[i]	n	Matched pairs[ii]	% enrolled students	% submitted ms to SCI-listed[iii] journal
New Phytologist Kunming	Nov 2009	3	4	24	24	8	100
New Phytologist Beijing	Nov 2007	5	4	33	29	30	94
China Academy of Engineering Physics, Mianyang	Dec 2009	5	2	40	35	25	62
Changchun Inst. of Applied Chemistry	July 2009	4	2	32	22	80	76

[i] Trainers always included Margaret Cargill and Patrick O'Connor, and in the Kunming and Beijing workshops, also two senior scientists with extensive experience as journal editors

[ii] Number of participants who completed both pre- and post-workshop questionnaires

[iii] SCI (Science Citation Index) provides bibliographic and citation information on popular journals

2 Issues and Challenges Identified by Chinese Workshop Participants 2007–2009

2.1 Data collection and analysis

The qualitative data analyzed here were collected via questionnaires administered in the first and final sessions of the workshops described in Table 2.1. Data on participants' initial goals were in response to the question 'What are the most important things that you want to achieve from this workshop?'. We take these responses as reflecting the issues participants wanted addressed, and therefore issues that they had found challenging in their past writing experience or their anticipation of future writing activities. As a second data source, we analyzed responses to a post-workshop evaluation question: 'What were the three most useful things in the workshop for you?'. We take these as indicating issues of concern that participants recognised as having been addressed in the workshops, even if they had not been identified before the workshop took place. Taken together, these two datasets provide rich insights into scientist writers' views of the issues and challenges they face.

The data were first analyzed using thematic analysis, by grouping keywords and phrases under salient categories until all could be represented appropriately (Cargill, 2004). The categories that emerged in the final analysis are listed in Table 2.2, with representative keywords used to identify instances. Combined datasets for all four workshops, for both 'Goals' and 'Most Useful Features', were also analyzed using *Wordle* software (http://www.wordle.net/advanced) to produce visual representations ('word clouds') of the frequency with which terms appeared.

2.2 Issues and challenges highlighted in participants' pre-workshop goals

When asked what they wanted to achieve in these workshops, which were presented under titles such as 'Writing a scientific article for international submission', a large proportion of participants responded in very general terms, such as 'how to write a science article' or 'improve scientific writing skills in English'. For analysis purposes, this very general language was placed in a category of its own (General Article Writing, GAW) exactly because it was not possible to distinguish whether it primarily related to writing processes, structuring of the document, or aspects of language use (Table 2.2). The highest percentage of these unclear responses came from the most experienced group (Kunming, 26.3%), but the category scored

Table 2.2 Category names used in the analysis of the open-ended data and examples of keywords and phrases used to identify instances of each

Category name	Identifying keywords
English & logical flow	Grammar, tense, modal verbs, vocabulary, expression, native-like, express ideas clearly, speaking/listening, write sentences, AdTAT software, corpus, sentence templates, noun phrases, connection, old information before new, conjunctions, logic
Article/segment structure	AIMRAD, sand-clock, abstract, introduction, methods, results, discussion, stages, organisation, structure
General article writing	[used when wording does not allow distinction between AS, WP (Writing Process), SD (Strategic Decisions) and E&LF] how to write a scientific article, improve writing ability
Submission/review	Cover letter, respond to editors/referees, publishing process, review reports
Strategic decisions	Choosing journals, target audience in writing, organise data, highlight data story, identify novelty, nominate referees
Writing process	Where to start, starting with results, checklists, editing/revising own draft, how to develop own skills, efficient manuscript production
Other	Difference between Chinese and English papers, cooperate with overseas researchers, improve confidence, workshop conduct and interaction

above 18% for all workshops (Table 2.3). Article/segment Structure (AS) accounted for between 8 and 24% of responses, mostly in inverse proportion to the percentage of GAW responses received. It was clear overall that writing and structuring an article is an important issue for scientist writers, but the details required further analysis.

The percentages of goals related to English and Logical Flow (E&LF) ranged between 13 and 27 and were consistently higher for workshops with higher proportions of enrolled students participating; it was the most frequent category for both the Mianyang and Changchun workshops (Table 2.3). This may indicate that students are more likely to conceive of their problems in terms of language when they first focus on the article writing task. Representative responses include these: 'How to express my ideas clearly and efficiently' (Changchun); 'Using English language more native and concise' (Mianyang); 'How to avoid the most common English mistakes' (Kunming).

Issues beyond language also featured consistently, and the pattern of occurrence was instructive. Combined percentages allocated to the categories of Submission/review (S/R) and Strategic Decisions (SD) ranged

Table 2.3 Participant goals by category for four CIPSE training workshops in China, as percentages of responses received

Category	Workshop			
	Kunming*	Beijing	Mianyang	Changchun
English & logical flow	13.2	16.3	27.0	25.0
Article/segment structure	7.9	23.6	12.7	20.0
General article writing	26.3	23.6	17.5	18.3
Submission/review	10.5	7.2	14.3	10.0
Strategic decisions	23.7	23.6	14.3	15.0
Writing process	5.3	3.6	1.6	6.6
Other	13.2	1.8	12.7	5.0

* This workshop had an up-front aim of training supervisors to better mentor or train their students and colleagues.

between 25.0 and 34.2 (Table 2.3), and increased with level of participant experience (Table 2.1), rising in the order Changchun < Mianyang < Beijing < Kunming. This result suggests the increasing priority given to these issues once some experience of the publishing process had been obtained. Examples of responses from the S/R category include these: 'Learn how to address comments and critics from editor and reviewers' (Kunming); 'How to deal with manuscript rejections' (Mianyang); 'Some methods of cover letter' (Beijing).

The SD category covered higher proportions of responses (approx. 23%), as would be expected, for the two workshops sponsored by the international journal; participants were already focused on getting submissions accepted by this high-ranking publication. However, the category was not the lowest ranking among goals for the more student-heavy workshops and covered between 14 and 15% of responses, indicating that the concerns in this category were salient for groups with many less experienced writers as well. Example of responses include these: 'How to find the novel point about the results' (Beijing); 'How to emphasise my scientific opinion' (Changchun).

An overall picture of the issues Chinese scientists identified as important before they undertook training was obtained by analyzing the combined dataset of goal responses (Figure 2.1). The overarching importance ascribed to English issues is clear, as is the high frequency of general, rather than specifically targeted, terms. More nuanced information was revealed when these goal issues were compared to those identified in post-workshop evaluations.

FIGURE 2.1 Visual representation of a frequency analysis of terms appearing in **participant goals** for four CIPSE training workshops (n = 129), prepared using Wordle software following merging of singular and plural versions of nouns.

2.3 Issues and challenges highlighted in post-workshop evaluations

Article/segment Structure was the category mentioned most frequently by the participants after all four workshops, covering between 29.9 and 35.8% of the features given (Table 2.4). The GAW category covered much smaller percentages of the responses after the workshops (2–11%) than before (18–30%), suggesting that the workshops may also have given participants access to an improved metalanguage to describe their issues and challenges overall. This result may also indicate that many of the concerns labelled as GAW under 'goals' had been addressed by the material presented on the structure of articles and their segments. Representative responses falling in the AS category are quoted below:

> The class helped me to know the structure of an article clearly. (Changchun)
>
> Before came to the workshop it is ambiguous in my brain of each section of the paper, in other words I don't know the aim, and don't know how to write them. (Beijing)
>
> Many details were got about introduction and discussion. I always think these two parts are the most important parts. (Kunming)

Table 2.4 Most useful features by category for four CIPSE training workshops in China, as percentages of responses received

Category	Workshop			
	Kunming*	Beijing	Mianyang	Changchun
English & logical flow	19.6	21.8	24.1	26.8
Article/segment structure	32.1	35.8	35.7	29.9
General article writing	10.7	4.3	2.7	2.1
Submission/review	19.6	22.8	16.1	19.6
Strategic decisions	3.6	8.7	9.8	8.2
Writing process	7.2	3.3	10.7	7.2
Other	7.2	3.3	0.9	6.2

* This workshop had an up-front aim of training supervisors to better mentor or train their students and colleagues.

The next most frequently mentioned categories were E&LF (20–27%) and S/R (16–23%), with the former predominating in the workshops with higher student cohorts and the two having almost equal status in those with more experienced participants, where increases for E&LF were noted (Table 2.4) over the position in the 'goals' analysis (Table 2.3). This result indicates that the more experienced researchers had found the teaching involving E&LF more relevant and useful than they might have expected, suggesting that these aspects may play a greater part in the challenges they face than they were at first aware of. This is not surprising given that at least some of the specific issues taught may not have been part of their experience of English teaching previously, as indicated by these responses: 'Verb usage to claim author's opinion' (Kunming); 'The usage of AdTAT to helping English writing' (Mianyang)[1].

The percentage of responses fitting into the S/R category increased for all cohorts after the workshops (7–15% pre-workshop goals, 16–23% post-workshop useful features, Tables 2.3 and 2.4), indicating that the training provided had addressed issues of importance to participants in this regard, even if they had not been identified as high-priority concerns beforehand. Representative examples include these:

Dealing with editorial decisions and referee comments. (Changchun)
Know how to do communication with editor and referee. (Mianyang)

The workshop is really helpful especially the discussion of response to editors. It's far as I know there is no book or lesson dealing with this topic up to now. It is necessary training for successful publication of paper to Chinese authors. (Kunming)

It is the inclusion of an emphasis on the specific S/R and SD aspects for a particular science context, and their relevance to the process and product of manuscript writing, that most clearly characterises the CIPSE package. The appearance of these categories in participants' goals indicate that they form an important component of the issues and challenges Chinese scientists feel they face in writing manuscripts in English. The increasing frequency with which specific S/R and SD aspects feature as useful elements after the workshops reinforces the benefits of the interdisciplinary collaboration of the CIPSE approach as these aspects are dealt with as both issues for decision within the context of the scientific discipline and for action using the tools from applied linguistics.

This finding is reinforced by the analysis of the combined dataset for 'Most Useful Features' from all workshops (Figure 2.2). The terms 'referees' and 'editors', 'response' and 'comments' appear with much enhanced prominence compared to the goals analysis in Figure 2.1, as does 'structure'. 'English' is much diminished in relative frequency, and 'introduction' and 'discussion' feature strongly. Overall, frequent terms are more specific than before the training, suggesting that a clearer view of issues, challenges and solutions has been developed post training.

FIGURE 2.2 Visual representation of a frequency analysis of terms appearing in participant responses as **most useful features** of four CIPSE training workshops (n = 129), prepared using Wordle software following merging of singular and plural versions of nouns.

3 Effectiveness of CIPSE Workshops in Enhancing Confidence in Scientist Authors

Evaluating the effectiveness of training interventions such as the workshops discussed in this chapter is an exercise of considerable complexity. Although some researchers maintain that increase in publication output is the only valid measure (McGrail et al., 2006), our view is that the relationship between a training workshop and an accepted manuscript is confounded by several important factors, including the quality of the research being reported and the input of a range of co-authors and other contributors (Burrough-Boenisch, 2003). We have therefore preferred to evaluate effectiveness through self-assessed confidence to write an article in English for international submission and to deal with the publishing process in English. This domain-specific self-assessment reflects Bandura's concept of self-efficacy, which he supports as being a better predictor of intellectual performance than skills alone (Bandura, 1997). This has been measured using a 7-point Likert scale before and after attendance at the workshops (Cargill & O'Connor, 2006a). Questionnaires were administered anonymously but identified by participants' date of birth to enable matching of pre- and post-workshop responses.

Participants' mean level of confidence to write a scientific article in English increased significantly after all four workshops, with increases ranging from 0.9 to 1.5 points on the 7-point scale (Table 2.5). Participants' mean level of confidence to deal with the publishing process in English increased by between 0.6 and 1.8 points on the 7-point scale after the four workshops, with the differences being highly statistically significant for all but the Beijing workshop. Several participants in each workshop recorded a lower level of confidence to deal with the writing or publishing process in English after the workshop than before. It is likely that these individual decreases reflect a fuller understanding of the publishing process and the challenges it presents after participation in the workshop than before. This interpretation is borne out by some (optional) comments provided by participants when reporting their post-workshop confidence levels: 'Not very confident. Many times we fear about our language may offend the editor unconsciously. We are seldom taught in how to appropriately show your respect.' (Changchun); 'Can't effectively communicate with editor.' (Mianyang). This may represent justified conservatism on the part of novice scientists and students who have not yet encountered the complete set of challenges associated with writing and publishing in an international journal.

Table 2.5   Mean increases in self-assessed confidence to **write a manuscript in English for international submission**, and to **deal with the publishing process in English**, measured before and after four CIPSE workshops in China (repeated measures on the same individual using a 7-point Likert scale: 1 = not confident, 7 = very confident)

	Workshop			
	Kunming	**Beijing**	**Mianyang**	**Changchun**
Increase in confidence to write	0.9*	0.9*	1.1*	1.5*
Increase in confidence to deal with publishing	1.0*	0.6	1.8*	1.5*
n	24	36	35	22

* indicates a significant difference at p < 0.01 (2-tailed student's t-test on repeated measures).

Nevertheless, the strong overall increases observed in confidence indicate that the workshops were perceived as very successful by the scientist writers who participated, and these results are similar to those obtained in other international and Australian contexts (Cargill, 2004; Cargill & O'Connor, 2006a). It is clear that the CIPSE approach can enhance the confidence of EFL scientist authors to write research articles in English, and deal with the publishing process. Can it also help train mentors/supervisors to support their students and junior colleagues?

4 Senior Scientists Assisting Others: The Kunming Workshop

The 3-day Kunming workshop was specifically designed to support more senior Chinese scientists as they work with their junior colleagues and students to improve the likelihood that manuscripts will be suitable for publication in *New Phytologist*. This journal is a popular target for plant scientists as it had a 2008 impact factor of 5.178 and was ranked 9/155 journals in Plant Sciences (ISI Journal Citation Reports® http://www.newphytologist.com/view/0/index. html). Participants were recruited from research groups that had previously published in the journal, and ranged in experience level from late-candidature students to a senior researcher with a PhD completed 16 years previously. Twenty-five researchers attended most of the workshop, but respondent numbers vary slightly for the different sets of data presented due to restricted international email access in some regions pre-workshop, and absences from some sessions due to local work pressures.

Table 2.6 Confidence levels of participants before and after the Kunming workshop (1 = not at all confident; 7 = very confident; n=24)

	Doing				Teaching			
	Write an article		Deal with publishing		Teach others to write an article		Teach others to deal with publishing	
	Before	After	Before	After	Before	After	Before	After
Median	5	5	5	6	4	5	4	5
Mean	4.5	5.5	4.7	5.7	3.9	5.3	3.9	5.6
SD	1.1	0.8	1.0	1.0	1.1	0.9	1.1	0.9

In spite of the avowed purpose of the workshop, helping others to write better manuscripts was not the only, and not the primary, focus for the attendees. There were only six mentions (13.6%) of helping others among the goals listed pre-workshop by participants (n = 23), and only four mentions among the most useful things after the workshop (6.7% of total responses, n = 24). Thus participants clearly had an additional, and very strong, concern to improve their own manuscript writing ability. However, all but two participants had assisted others (up to seven per scientist) with manuscripts during the previous 12 months.

Interestingly, strong increases were seen in the mean confidence of these more senior participants to train/mentor students and junior colleagues to both write an article (1.33 points on the 7-point scale, repeated measures on a mean of 24 individuals) and deal with the publishing process in English (1.63 points). These figures are higher than the increases in their mean confidence to do these tasks themselves (Table 2.5). The greater increases recorded for training/mentoring confidence also reflects lower starting confidence than for doing the tasks themselves (Table 2.6).

4.1 Issues and challenges for senior scientists assisting others

To ensure that the workshop focused appropriately on participants' perceived issues in terms of training others, we included a structured brainstorm activity early in the workshop. Participants listed in small groups the training/mentoring issues they faced and selected the three most important. Collated responses are listed in Table 2.7, along with the relevant categories from the analysis of writer issues presented earlier (Table 2.2). The points listed cover all issues raised in the workshop session but with no indication of frequency of mention or priority ascribed.

Table 2.7 Major mentoring/training issues faced by 25 Chinese scientists in helping students and junior colleagues write manuscripts suitable for international publication

Mentoring/training issue	Relevant analysis categories
Students are not familiar with the structure of a scientific paper – organisation	Article/segment structure
Introductions using the literature	Article/segment structure
Difficulty moving from Results to Discussion	Article/segment structure Strategic decisions
Challenging to tell a story and to 'identify significance'	Strategic decisions
Controlling the data to tell the story	Strategic decisions
Putting their own work in the big picture	Strategic decisions Article/segment structure
Writing in their own words – author's voice	English and logical flow Strategic decisions
Difficulty constructing the logic of ideas	English and logical flow
Flow of language to advance the logic – sentence cohesion	English and logical flow
ENGLISH	English and logical flow
Masters students are time-pressured – educational structural constraints	Contextual issue*
Time constraints on research leaders/ supervisors	Contextual issue*

* Additional issue not mentioned by writers.

Contextual issues of workload and program structure are the focus of two of the twelve issues listed, and these ring true for parallel situations both within and beyond China in our experience of discussing, with workshop participants and managing academics, options for improving publication outputs. Of the remaining ten, Article/segment Structure is the focus of four, Strategic Decision issues cover five, and English and Logical Flow covers four (three issues were allocated to dual categories in this analysis). This outcome indicates a tight match between the concerns of mentor/trainers and those of writers (and with the coverage of the book/website package as represented in the training workshops – it was not necessary to adjust the planned content of the Kunming workshop to cover these issues effectively).

The explicit naming of issues related to logical flow is a key difference between the concerns of mentor/trainers in Table 2.7 and those of writers themselves, where language concerns are more likely to be named in general terms (English) or in terms of sentence-level grammar and vocabulary issues (Figures 2.1 and 2.2). This emphasis on the importance of logical flow and connectedness also reflects comments of mentor informants in the study of Li and Flowerdew (2007, p. 109). However, it should be noted that the Logical Flow component of the E&LF category was more of a focus post-workshop than beforehand in three of the four workshops studied (data not shown), including very noticeably so in this workshop

(Kunming). This suggests that, post-workshop, participants were more likely to recognise and articulate the importance of flow and connection to the creation of a 'story' and the meeting of editor or referee requirements in this regard.

For comparison purposes, we presented in the workshop a list of issues prepared by the presenting team, indicating the most important issues we see regularly in manuscripts we are asked to read in our various capacities (here followed by initials of the relevant analysis categories from Table 2.2):

- Consistency – all parts telling the same story (SD/AS).
- Conclusions drawn not all or not clearly related to the data presented (AS).
- Not clear why the study was done, or why/how it is important (SD/AS).
- Unclear what is from the literature and what is from the present study (E&LF).
- Careful preparation and editing not done (WP/ E&LF).

Issues of 'story' and structure were again prominent in this list. The third dot-point relates clearly to the points raised by the trainers/mentors regarding 'Introductions using the literature', 'Difficulty moving from the Results to Discussion', and 'Challenging to tell a story and identify significance', and fits into two of the earlier analysis categories: SD (in relation to story construction) and AS (in terms of how the Introduction and Discussion are written). The issue about uncertainty of the source of information, literature or the study itself has been categorised as E&LF because it most often relates to problems with English tense usage. Overall, there is a notable consistency among the issues identified by the presenting team and the EFL scientists as writers and as mentors/trainers.

The final point in this set, 'Careful preparation and editing not done', is one of the few overall that relates to the practice of article writing and preparation, and has been categorised as Writing Process (WP). This category covers only few of the responses received as 'goals' from writers (Table 2.3), and not many more of those received as 'useful features' from writers, except for the Mianyang workshop where it rated more highly at 10.7% of responses (Table 2.4). Examples of wordings of responses falling into this category are given below:

It's very useful to follow the order of drafting a whole manuscript you told us. (Changchun)

How to turn our results into knowledge (how to begin a draft with the results); The use of pre-review checklists that can help our paper more complete (Mianyang)

I think the suggestions for developing my publishing skills are also very useful. (Kunming)

I think the most useful things for me are to learn how to prepare a science manuscript ... (Beijing)

We now move from identifying issues to addressing them, and discuss our survey data on practices Chinese scientists use to train or mentor others in article writing and publishing.

4.2 Strategies and practices of scientists for assisting novice authors

The pre-workshop information provided by 23 Kunming participants showed that 'Track Changes' (within a word-processing program) was the most frequently used technique, followed by 'Meeting' (Table 2.8). Both 'Track Changes' and 'Meeting' were scored as 'always' by 5 senior researchers (10–16 years since PhD completion), 4 mid-career researchers (5–9 years), 4 early-career researchers (1–3 years) and 1 student. Running classes was the least frequently used technique (Table 2.8). There were no notable differences in strategy use between career stages, indicating that experience level did not seem to influence choice of strategy in the small number of respondents we surveyed.

As part of the final workshop session, participants were asked to provide an Action Plan for implementing in their own context the training they had received. All but one of the 24 action plans submitted[2] referred to some kind of teaching input in participants' home department or institute based on the workshop material. This result suggests some shift, in intention at least, from participants' positions before the workshop. The actions envisaged

Table 2.8   Strategies used by 23 Chinese scientists for assisting students/colleagues with manuscript writing, reported before attending the Kunming workshop (1 = never, 5 = always)

Strategy for assistance	Mean frequency of use
Track changes	4.5
Meeting	4.0
Annotations	3.0
Written Report	2.6
Run classes	2.4

ranged from initial single seminar presentations given as part of an existing series, to two or three half-day sessions, to regular annual programs of varying length. Two mid-career and one senior researcher indicated they would begin by training their own students and evaluate the improvement seen before making recommendations for more general adoption of a training program based on the workshop materials. Thirty percent of senior and 40% of mid-career researchers stated that they intended to use the workshop textbook (Cargill & O'Connor, 2009) as the basis for planned training. None, however, mentioned seeking input from local English teachers.

The most commonly mentioned content elements for inclusion in the proposed training were teaching on the structure of articles and their various component sections (mentioned by 56% of participants) and the use of the AdTAT software in conjunction with discipline-specific collections of journal articles (44%). Early-career researchers were more likely to identify specific article sections as a focus for teaching (e.g. Introductions, Abstracts), whereas senior researchers tended to give more detail and include both delivery methods and content to be taught. Elements of writing process that had been presented were mentioned in only three plans, and a suggestion was even made that it would have been better to follow the conventional order of article sections in our teaching, rather than starting with the results, a key feature of our approach (Cargill & O'Connor 2009, p. 21), as noted previously. This suggests that there may have been a limited willingness to move beyond conventional understandings and teaching methods, especially in the light of heavy workloads, and that it was the content rather than the methods of the approach that had resonated most strongly with these more senior researchers.

A notable change was recorded for one senior researcher, who had reported in the pre-workshop questionnaire that he did not help others; his only strategy was to write the manuscripts himself. His 'Action Plan' following the workshop included the following points:

- This training is very important for a Chinese scientist to write articles in English, usually this kind of training is very few. The training will improve the quality of the manuscripts of mine in the future.
- I am going to train the students in my group in writing each year.
- The book 'Writing scientific research articles' will be the basic textbook, plus what the lecturers directed.
- Introduction and Discussion are two sections difficult to write for students. I learnt a lot in this training program, and will teach the skills to my students and even my colleagues.

At the other end of the experience scale, one of the early-career researcher participants reported in her action plan that she would give a one and a half day workshop for colleagues and students at her home institute immediately following the Kunming workshop. She was assisted in this by a late-candidature student who had also attended. The first author, from the original presentation team, was also in attendance to support the presenters and contribute as requested. This workshop was entitled 'Be a more successful scientific author', and was presented largely in Chinese (except for input by Margaret) based on selected and adapted slides from the Kunming workshop. Thirty-four people attended the first half-day session, and twenty-nine evaluation questionnaires (from twenty-four research students and five staff) were collected after the third session. Participants were asked which parts of the workshop they found most useful. Eight indicated that all the parts were useful; others highlighted aspects that reflected those mentioned by participants in the full CIPSE workshops, including the structure of the article and its component sections, language issues, responding to editors and referees, and, interestingly, the writing process. Typical responses are quoted below:

> The organisation of the paper is helpful to me. Before listening this lecture, I never paid more attention on the analysis of the results in experiments. I didn't know the result is the core of the story.
>
> I think the order of which part of articles should be written first is very useful. I'm very interesting in the verb, including tense, it is also very helpful.
>
> Referee's comments are most useful for me; and the differences verbs, such as demonstrate, are also important. I want to learn more about it.

Participants were also asked for specific suggestions of the aspects on which they needed more input. The two most commonly mentioned aspects were the 'Discussion' section, and preparing and discussing tables and figures. This information is valuable for planning future training at the institute, as well as contributing to our understanding of priority issues facing novice scientist authors in China.

5 Conclusions

Chinese scientists writing manuscripts for international journals clearly face a wide range of issues and challenges, as reflected in their goals and learning outcomes from training using the integrated CIPSE approach. However, trainees reported strongly increased confidence after all CIPSE workshops, both to write articles and to deal with the publishing process in English, suggesting that the training had successfully addressed many issues of concern. When directed towards assisting more senior scientists to train and mentor others in paper writing and publishing, the training also had positive outcomes. Participants reported strongly increased confidence to provide such training in their home contexts, and identified both content for inclusion and delivery methods they planned to use.

The issues and challenges identified were found to cluster under five categories: Article/segment Structure, English and Logical Flow, Submission/review, Strategic Decisions and, to a lower degree, Writing Process. A less meaningful category of General Article Writing was strongly represented among the goals reported, but diminished in importance after the workshops, suggesting that the workshops had helped trainees to develop a more nuanced ability to name the issues they face. Organisation and structuring of the article and its sections was the most frequently mentioned issue after the training regardless of the experience level of the trainees, and seemed to be the category most likely to have been intended by the more general terms that featured in the pre-workshop goals.

Issues to do with English and Logical Flow featured more strongly among goals when participants had lower prior experience levels, suggesting that less experienced writers were more likely to perceive their difficulties in terms of language. However, more experienced researchers recorded a higher proportion of issues in this category after the training than before, perhaps because the language-related training they had received in the workshops had been extremely specific to their needs, including the use of concordancing software with corpora of discipline-specific articles. This combination was recognised as a valuable tool by all trainee groups and has a clear place in training for EFL/ESL research writers. Overall, the prominence of 'English' as a named issue decreased after the training, as more specific terms became more prominent.

The second important set of issues and challenges identified was those clustering under the categories of Submission/review and Strategic Decisions related to targeting the audience effectively in terms of both content and writing. Among goals, these were more strongly present for more experienced than less experienced researchers, but Submission/review issues increased in importance for all groups after the training. Clearly these issues need to feature strongly in approaches designed to assist scientist authors in manuscript writing, along with language- and structure-related issues. The CIPSE approach provides one model for integrating these areas, and one that has been effective in a range of contexts in China, as discussed in this chapter. A question then arises as to the future prospects of this approach being taken up more widely, both in China and other comparable contexts.

The data from the Kunming workshop suggest that the approach has strong possibilities for use by scientists in their own research institutes or groups. Training using the approach and the book can enhance scientists' confidence to move beyond a one-on-one track changes approach to something more systematic, time-effective and tailored to the needs and opportunities existing in particular institutes or departments. The wide range of scientific disciplines covered by the workshops analyzed in this chapter (plant science, applied chemistry and engineering physics) suggests broad applicability for the approach, and this potential is enhanced by the growing range of 'extra examples' on the companion website (currently featuring analyzed articles from gastroenterology, geology, remote sensing and applied chemistry). We now consider that the best and most cost-effective use of our time as presenters is to conduct training for senior scientists and research managers, or in a train-the-trainer mode, so that the CIPSE approach can be adapted for use in ways that suit prevailing contextual constraints. Once the CIPSE approach is experienced by people fully aware of the breadth of challenge presented by international publication of research in English, then local possibilities can be canvassed for partnerships between language and subject specialists. Some suggestions for guiding this process are presented in Cargill and O'Connor (2006b).

Thus, until the wider establishment in EFL science contexts of the systematised interdisciplinary partnerships advocated by Li and Flowerdew (2007), the CIPSE book/website package seems to represent a workable and effective entry point and resource bank for scientists wanting to address the full range of issues and challenges they face in writing articles in English for international submission. In addition, it may also represent an effective entry point or training manual for English professionals in China and other EFL/ESL contexts who are unfamiliar with science articles but nevertheless need to teach or support scientists writing in English for publication. In this situation it could be used by EAP teachers using any of the three levels of interaction described by Dudley-Evans (2001), depending on local conditions and possibilities. These are EAP teachers teaching alone using a 'cooperation' model, with the book providing resources and information; teaching by EAP teachers with local scientists providing specific input into planning and materials to supplement those in the book (a 'collaboration' model); or 'team teaching' by EAP teachers and local scientists along the lines suggested in Cargill and O'Connor (2006a) but adapted to suit local constraints and possibilities. We hope that this integrated book-website package may make a contribution to fostering collaboration between EAP professionals and scientists in EFL and ESL contexts, as the data analysed in this chapter indicate the added value provided by such collaboration in helping scientist authors meet the challenges they face in getting their research work published in English. It is also our hope that the analysis presented here may encourage the exploration of collaborative interdisciplinary approaches by teachers and curriculum designers in ESL/EFL contexts more broadly. The range of approaches summarised above offers options which can be adapted for contexts where different levels of cooperation or collaboration are possible, and which can be used to support the achievement of many of the academic purposes for which English is learned and taught.

Acknowledgements

We thank Professors Ian Alexander and F. Andrew Smith and Dr Airong Li for their support for and input to the workshops, the *New Phytologist*, the China Academy of Engineering Physics and BHP-Billiton for funding support, and all the workshop participants for their enthusiasm and insights.

Notes

[1] This comment refers to concordancing software introduced, which is freely available on the University of Adelaide website at http://www.adelaide.edu.au/red/adtat/

[2] One SR seemed to have misunderstood the task and provided requests for additional support he would find useful.

References

Bandura, A. (1997). *Self-efficacy: The exercise of control*. New York: Freeman.

Bazerman, C., Little, J., Bethel, L., Chavkin, T., Fouquette, D., & Garufis, J. (2005). *Reference guide to Writing Across the Curriculum*. Santa Barbara, CA: Parlor Press and the WAC Clearinghouse.

Brinton, D. M., Snow, M. A., & Wesche, M. B. (1989). *Content-based second language instruction*. New York: Newbury House.

Burrough-Boenisch, J. (2003). Shapers of published NNS research articles. *Journal of Second Language Writing, 12,* 223–243.

Cargill, M. (2004). Transferable skills within research degrees: A collaborative genre-based approach to developing publication skills and its implications for research education. *Teaching in Higher Education, 9*(1), 83–98.

Cargill, M., & O'Connor, P. (2006a). Developing Chinese scientists' skills for publishing in English: Evaluating collaborating-colleague workshops based on genre analysis. *Journal of English for Academic Purposes, 5*(3), 207–221.

Cargill, M., & O'Connor, P. (2006b). Getting research published in English: Towards a curriculum design model for developing skills and enhancing outcomes. *Revista Canaria de Estudios Ingleses, 53,* 79–94.

Cargill, M., & O'Connor, P. (2009). *Writing scientific research articles: Strategy and steps.* Oxford, UK: Wiley-Blackwell.

Cargill, M., & O'Connor, P. (2010). Structuring interdisciplinary collaboration to develop research students' skills for publishing research internationally: Lessons from implementation. In M. Davies, M. Devlin, & M. Tight (Eds.), *Interdisciplinary higher education* (pp. 279–292). Amsterdam: Emerald Group Publishing Ltd.

Cho, D. W. (2009). Science journal paper writing in an EFL context: The case of Korea. *English for Specific Purposes, 28,* 230–239.

Davies, M., Devlin, M., & Tight, M. (Eds.). (2010). *Interdisciplinary higher education: Perspectives and practicalities.* Amsterdam: Emerald Group Publishing Ltd.

Day, R. A., & Gastel, B. (2006). *How to write and publish a scientific paper* (6th ed.). Westwood, CN: Greenwood Press.

Dudley-Evans, T. (2001). Team-teaching in EAP: Changes and adaptations in the Birmingham approach. In J. Flowerdew & M. Peacock (Eds.), *Research perspectives on English for Academic Purposes* (pp. 225–239). Cambridge: Cambridge University Press.

Halliday, M. A. K., & Hasan, R. (1985). *Language, context and text.* Geelong, Australia: Deakin University Press.

Jones, J., Bonanno, H., & Scouller, K. (2001). Staff and student roles in central and faculty-based learning support: Changing partnerships. In B. James, A. Percy, J. Skillen & N. Trivett (Eds.), *Changing identities: Proceedings of the 2001 Australian Language and Academic Skills Conference.* Wollongong, Australia. Retrieved from http://learning.uow.edu.au/LAS2001/selected/jones_2.pdf

Li, Y. (2006a). A doctoral student of physics writing for publication: A sociopolitically-oriented case study. *English for Specific Purposes, 25*(4), 456–478.

Li, Y. (2006b). Writing for international publication: The case of Chinese doctoral science students. (Unpublished doctoral dissertation). City University of Hong Kong, Hong Kong.

Li, Y., & Flowerdew, J. (2007). Shaping Chinese novice scientists' manuscripts for publication. *Journal of Second Language Writing, 16*(2), 100–117.

McGrail, M. R., Rickard, C. M., & Jones, R. (2006). Publish or perish: A systematic review of interventions to increase academic publication rates. *Higher Education Research and Development, 25*(1), 19–35.

Weissberg, R., & Buker, S. (1990). *Writing up research.* Englewood Cliffs, NJ: Prentice Hall Regents.

Chapter 3

Text and Corpus Work, EAP Writing and Language Learners

Giuliana Diani

1 Introduction

Over the last twenty years, great interest has been shown in the application of corpus linguistics to language teaching.[1] In particular, the use of corpora has had a considerable impact on the teaching and learning of English for Academic Purposes (EAP) (e.g. Flowerdew, 2002; Hyland, 2006; Lee & Swales, 2006; Schlitz, 2010; Thompson, 2000, 2007; Thurstun & Candlin, 1998; Tribble, 2002). The increased familiarity of students with electronic tools for corpus analysis has contributed to the development of their language awareness (e.g. Bondi, 1999) and favoured learner autonomy (e.g. Lynch, 2001).

A significant development in the field of EAP pedagogy is the integration of corpus-based approaches with discourse analytical methods (e.g. Flowerdew, 2005; Weber, 2001), with important implications for teaching academic writing. In particular, Charles (2007) emphasizes the need to reconcile top-down and bottom-up approaches in the production of EAP teaching materials through a pedagogical approach which combines discourse analysis with corpus investigation.

The aim of this chapter is to contribute to the on-going debate on the relevance of the joint contribution of text and corpus work in the foreign language classroom, specifically undergraduate classes in Italy with students specializing in English as a foreign language. I illustrate the work of Italian final year undergraduate students performing discourse and corpus analysis in a module designed to teach them how to write research papers in English. The materials for undergraduate students described in detail below were designed not only to introduce corpora and concordancing, but also to develop EFL learners' recognition and understanding of the textual and discursive functions of the genre under investigation.

2 Background

The study described in this chapter was carried out at the University of Modena and Reggio Emilia (Italy) within a 20-hour English Linguistics module in the degree course in languages and European studies. The module, called *Writing in English for Academic Purposes,* had twenty five students who attended one 2-hour class per week for a total of ten weeks.

The purpose of this module was twofold: (i) to introduce corpus work, and (ii) to develop awareness and understanding of the pragmatic functions of a text-type that is one of the most important target genres in my Italian students' English syllabus in the degree course in languages and European studies at the University of Modena: the written assignment. Students attending this module were required to write an assignment of about 3,000 words by conducting a small-scale study on a topic of their choice. This mini research paper had to have an 'introduction' (including a literature review, the research aims and the questions to be addressed), a section on 'methods and materials' (setting out the methods for analysis of the corpus collected and principles upon which it was designed), the 'results and discussion' (i.e. a presentation of the results of the analysis according to the methodology adopted), and a 'conclusion'.

To achieve the goals described above, the module was divided into two parts: Part 1 was devoted to text work, in the context of genre analysis (weeks 1–3 of the ten-week term). Part 2 was dedicated to corpus work (weeks 4–6). In weeks 7–10 the students carried out investigations individually, searching the corpus for information to help with their own language problems.

A corpus of ten research papers in the field of linguistics, written by final-year undergraduate students who were native speakers of American English, was used in the class (approximately 45,000 words). The papers were taken from the *Michigan Corpus of Upper-level Student Papers* (MICUSP), available at http://micusp.elicorpora.info/. Only ten research papers were available in linguistics. All the papers are single-authored texts.

The corpus I used is a specialized corpus. It is not, however, only specialized insofar as it represents a specialized text-type, but also because it was created for a specific teaching interest. It is a corpus that is traditionally labelled as a 'small' corpus. The small size of the corpus was considered to be an advantage for the classroom. In particular, it meant that the students were faced with only a limited amount of data as they came to grips with the techniques of searching and interpreting concordance examples.

The advantages of using small specialized corpora for EAP pedagogy have been well documented (e.g. Flowerdew, 2004; Ghadessy et al., 2001; Tribble, 2001). For example, Flowerdew (2004) observes that specialized smaller corpora offer more advantages than general corpora from a methodological perspective because they provide more contextual information than larger corpora. This is especially true for genre-based EAP. As you will see throughout this chapter, my genre-based lessons clearly benefit from the use of the small specialized corpus I rely on, which helps students to grasp more accurately the function and use of language in the genre under investigation.

In Part 1 of the module, students were introduced to genre-based investigations of the MICUSP_research paper corpus. In pairs or small groups, they carried out genre-based tasks to develop their awareness of the moves of the genre under investigation and the ways in which those moves can be realized linguistically. Each genre part of the class ended with whole-class feedback and discussion to highlight the insights that the language learners had gained in their group work.

In Part 2 of the module, students moved on to corpus work with the aid of a computerized concordance programme, which enables easy electronic access to the texts stored in a corpus and provides a range of functions to analyze language phenomena and highlight interesting aspects about the language captured in the corpus. Three of the most commonly used software packages for corpus analysis are *WordSmith Tools* (Scott, 1996), *MonoConc Pro* (Barlow, 1999) and *AntConc* (Anthony, 2006). While the first two packages are commercial and require a license, *AntConc* is free, which is one of the reasons why I decided to use it with my students.[2] Without a concordance programme like *AntConc*, a corpus would be of no use other than being an electronic repository of texts that could then be read on screen (or on paper printouts) in the normal linear fashion. The concordancer, however, allows different (and faster) ways of accessing corpus texts. The software 'selects, sorts, matches, counts and calculates' (Hunston & Francis, 2000, p. 15), and in so doing, it provides different views on the data captured in the corpus, e.g. it may highlight what the most frequent 3-word combination is or which words tend to occur immediately to the left of a noun in a certain type of discourse.

Corpus concordances and other types of corpus queries were made available on a dedicated web page some days ahead of each lesson so that the students attending could print them out and take them to class. During the lessons, paper versions of concordances were also handed out, so that students could study them further at home, enabling those who did not complete the class tasks or who were absent to catch up in their own time. The provision of paper versions of the concordances was important in giving students a record of what they had done, which allowed them to return to it in future. It also supplied many other examples of language use, in addition to those that were the focus of the class. At the end of each corpus-based lesson, feedback and discussion with the whole class allowed each group or pair to contribute what they had noticed and to check their findings and interpretations against those of the others in the class.

3 Text and Corpus Work for Teaching EAP Writing in an EFL Context

In the following sections, I describe ways of applying text and corpus work to the teaching of EAP writing in an EFL context. To illustrate this, I will use examples from the genre- and corpus-based lessons I developed for teaching Italian undergraduate students of English how to write a research paper in English.

3.1 The genre-based lessons

The aim of the genre-based lessons was to offer EFL learners an explicit understanding of how a research paper is structured and why it is written in the way it is. To achieve this goal, I devoted the first genre-based lesson to an introduction to genre analysis, which proposes 'moves' as basic elements of a genre (Swales, 1990). Using the MICUSP_research paper corpus collected for the module, this lesson aimed to make students aware of the relationship between the communicative purpose of the genre, the context, and language chosen to achieve the purpose.

In each genre-based lesson, paper versions of five research papers taken from the corpus were provided and students were encouraged to work in pairs or small groups and search for the pragmatic moves constituting the generic structure of the paper. This included a hand-tagged moves-analysis. They were led to recognize the moves by being shown the move analysis exemplified by Swales (1990) in his seminal description of research article introductions and by Hopkins and Dudley-Evans (1988) in their model for research article discussions (see Table 3.1).

Table 3.1 The research paper IMRD move descriptions (Swales, 1990; Hopkins & Dudley-Evans, 1988)

MOVES

INTRODUCTION (Swales, 1990)

Move 1: Establishing a territory

> *Step 1: Claiming centrality*
> and/or
> *Step 2: Making topic generalization(s)*
> and/or
> *Step 3: Reviewing items of previous research*

Move 2: Establishing a niche

> *Step 1A: Counter-claiming*
> or
> *Step 1B: Indicating a gap*
> or
> *Step 1C: Question-raising*
> or
> *Step 1D: Continuing a tradition*

Move 3: Occupying the niche

> *Step 1A: Outlining purposes*
> or
> *Step 1B: Announcing present research*
> *Step 2: Announcing principal findings*
> *Step 3: Indicating RA structure*

METHOD (description of appropriate methodology)

RESULTS (analysis of results)

DISCUSSION (conclusions that can be drawn) (Hopkins & Dudley-Evans, 1988)

- Background information (recapitulating main points, highlighting theoretical information).
- Statement of results.
- (Un)expected outcome (commenting on whether result is unexpected or not).
- Reference to previous research (for comparison with present research or to support present research).
- Explanation (suggesting reasons for a surprising result).
- Exemplification (to support an explanation).
- Deduction and Hypothesis (to make a claim about the generalisability of some or all of the reported results).
- Recommendation (need for further research and/or suggestions about possible lines of further investigation).

With this description in mind, students proceeded to check whether these moves were also present in the MICUSP_research paper corpus. They were asked to:

1. identify textual segments with communicative functions corresponding to the moves and steps that characterize the genre;
2. identify linguistic clues which might signal the communicative function of the move.

A class discussion then followed this task. Sometimes there were disagreements about where one move ended and another began, or whether a certain move existed at all in a given text. These matters were discussed in class and students learnt that there were somewhat different interpretations of what was going on in a particular example text. Students then attempted to determine whether there was any pattern in the organization of the moves and whether some moves were optional. After studying the texts and performing their own move analysis on them, students were able to determine the order of the moves, and whether a move was likely to be obligatory or not.

In the final part of each lesson, the language of each move of the genre was examined in detail. Students worked in groups on language awareness exercises, analyzing examples according to a set of questions designed to focus their attention on relevant linguistic points. Students were asked, for instance, to underline the subjects and verbs of the main clauses which signalled the communicative function of particular generic moves, to classify the subjects and verbs according to different parameters given to them, and to study the particular behaviours of the most frequent verbs found in the corpus. (See the sample worksheet in the Appendix for more details.) These activities allow students to develop fundamental learning and analytical skills, which is important because an attitude of inquiry towards language constitutes the necessary basis for developing language awareness and for fostering autonomous language improvement.

3.2 The corpus-based lessons

In the corpus-based lessons, students were taught how to produce and read concordances with *AntConc.*[3] As Barnbrook (1996) has said, 'the concordance provides a simple way of placing each word back in its original context, so that the details of its use and behaviour can be properly examined' (p. 65). Thanks to the software's performance of advanced searches with context words, students were able to stipulate that a certain word or phrase occurred within a specified number of places to the right and/or left of the search item. The ability to specify the contextual environment of the search term in this way was particularly important for the investigation of the parts of a text in which a given communicative function may occur. Students were asked to decide upon the meaning and use of some words on the basis of context and also to make generalizations or draw conclusions about differences between sections/moves. Concordance lines remained the main tool of analysis, but wordlists, keyword lists and clusters were also used when necessary.[4]

Concordances were generated for words that signalled the communicative function of the moves found in the MICUSP_research paper corpus. For example, in the Introduction move that was systematically found in the corpus (outlining the students' purposes and announcing the research reported), concordances were produced for words related to the students' authorial presence, such as first person pronouns *I* and *we*. The reason for asking students to pay attention to these pronouns is because students writing in a foreign language may be unaware of the norms of disciplinary culture and how first person pronouns work to convey authorial stance. Even native English speaking students often fail to acquire and use the variety of lexical bundles appropriate to published academic writing (Cortes, 2004, p. 413). Therefore, students need guidance in noticing how and where stance appears in texts. Once students have noticed the expressions authors use to signal their presence, to interact with other authors and to express membership in their community, it should be easier for them to grasp that such interaction exists. My assumption is that if students can become more aware of some of the language used to express authorial stance in the texts they read, they will achieve two things: improve their mastery of that language in their own writing and take another step towards becoming members of a discourse community (as defined by Swales, 1990).

Research has shown that research article writers use the first person pronoun *I* for a number of discourse functions, mainly to state the goal or purpose of their paper, to outline procedures carried out and to make a knowledge claim (Harwood, 2005; Hyland, 2001; Kuo, 1999). However, undergraduate writers have been found to make much less use of the first person pronoun, and to use it for a narrower range of functions in discourse (Hyland, 2002a). Tang and John (1999) point out that the undergraduate students they studied use the first person pronoun in ways that do not establish a strong authorial presence. Hyland (2002a) shows that the disciplinary variation in self reference noted in published writing is blurred

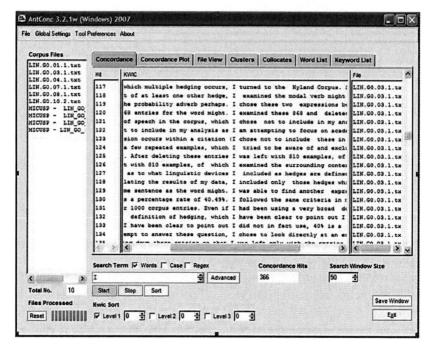

Figure 3.1   *AntConc* concordance of the word *I* in the MICUSP_research paper corpus.

in novice student writing and concludes that the undergraduate students studied have not been socialized into the epistemological practices of their individual disciplines.

To investigate this feature in the MICUSP_research paper corpus, students were asked to generate concordances for all instances of *I* and *we*. Since the aim was to identify the occurrences where *we* was an instance of the exclusive *we* signalling the 'authorial' *we* (Wales, 1996), a manual filtering process of all occurrences of *we* was necessary to make sure that only such occurrences were considered. Figures 3.1 and 3.2 show part of the *I* and *we* concordances generated by the students.

Students were first asked to compare the frequency of occurrences of *I* and exclusive *we* in the corpus in order to establish to what extent student writers intrude in their writing and to determine what pronouns are the favoured choice. Then they were instructed to compare the concordance lines of *I* and exclusive *we* and describe the use of each pronoun within the context of the moves identified in the MICUSP_research paper corpus. Since the size of the computer screen (and the *AntConc* window) is limited, only a certain amount of context can be displayed in each concordance

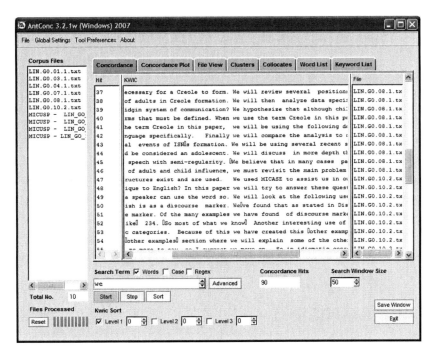

Figure 3.2 *AntConc* concordance of the word *we* in the MICUSP_research paper corpus.

line. The *AntConc* 'File View' tool makes it possible to view any of the loaded files at any time by clicking on the search word in the concordance line. Figure 3.3 presents the file view for the *I* concordance search (with *I* marked in black).

Students were then asked to look at the verbs that collocate with the first person pronouns identified and discuss whether those verbs referred to research processes (occurring in statements of findings, e.g. *observe, notice, show* or procedures e.g. *analyze, explore*), mental processes (e.g. *believe, think, predict*) or verbal processes (e.g. *argue, suggest, discuss*). Students had to note down their observations in a table such as Table 3.2, and compare the dominant verbal categories identified with those they typically use in their own writing.

Another topic of discussion in the module was the use of citation in student writing. In their assignments, students have to demonstrate the ability to locate and use relevant academic and supporting resources. That typically represents a problem for them as they often repeat what each author says rather than synthesize literature for their own purposes and apply their reading in writing the assignment. Second language learners may find it

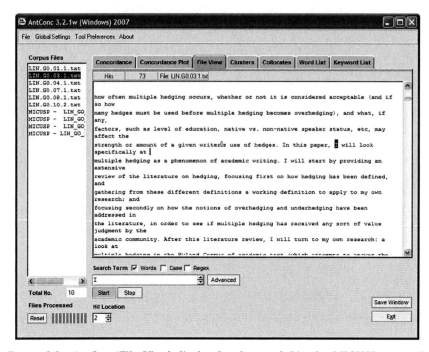

FIGURE 3.3   *AntConc* 'File View' display for the word *I* in the MICUSP_research paper corpus.

difficult to choose from among the wide variety of reporting verbs available as they may not understand the subtleties of language necessary for reporting claims (Flowerdew, 2001; Hyland, 2002b; McEnery & Kifle, 2002) or the importance of expressing their own opinions in their academic writing (Hyland, 2005). In fact, second language writers often have their own self-imposed criteria for choosing reporting verbs. For instance, students often seem concerned about varying their vocabulary choices, so they may freely substitute one reporting verb for another without regard for how such substitutions could affect their readers' perceptions of their attitudes towards the claims being expressed. Thus, helping students understand how to use reporting verbs to achieve their own rhetorical purposes should be an important component of a pedagogy for academic writing (e.g. Swales & Feak, 1994; Thompson & Tribble, 2001).

I worked with students on this problem, by focusing on citations which use a reporting verb with a *that*-clause complement. Students were asked to retrieve the concordance lines of the word *that* in the corpus so as to identify finite reporting clauses. They were instructed to select only instances where *that* was used to introduce a complement clause.

Table 3.2 An exercise table for students to note down the verbs associated with first person pronouns within the four-move structure identified in the MICUSP_ research paper corpus

I + verbs of research processes	*I* + verbs of mental processes	*I* + verbs of verbal processes
Introduction move	Introduction move	Introduction move
Method move	Method move	Method move
Results move	Results move	Results move
Discussion/Conclusion move	Discussion/ Conclusion move	Discussion/Conclusion move
we + verbs of research processes	*we* + verbs of mental processes	*we* + verbs of verbal processes
Introduction move	Introduction move	Introduction move
Method move	Method move	Method move
Results move	Results move	Results move
Discussion/Conclusion move	Discussion/ Conclusion move	Discussion/Conclusion move

In particular, they counted only cases where the subject of the projecting clause was an individual, where the lexical verb presented the type of projecting, and where the *that*-clause presented the projected idea or speech. Figure 3.4 displays part of the concordance of finite reporting clauses with a *that*-clause complement found in the MICUSP_research paper corpus.

Through the concordancer, the students identified the verbs most frequently used in citation as well as their different uses. This, in turn, led to a consideration of the wider context of the citation and the reasons for using a particular phraseology within that context. As Biber et al. (1998) put it, concordancing can help in the analysis of 'the extent to which a pattern is found' and 'the factors that influence variability' (p. 3), both of which are related to the problems non-native English students have with citing claims. Some of the more subtle distinctions, such as whether the attitude of the writer towards a claim is favourable or unfavourable, can only be understood in terms of the larger rhetorical context in which the claim is made. Therefore, as Hunston (2000) notes, the use of reporting verbs can require a great deal of specificity in order to establish the credibility of both the writer and the claims, so that there is a greater likelihood that the reader will accept the position the writer is taking. Non-native English students do not always have the linguistic resources for learning how to make these kinds of distinctions. Relying on simple dictionary definitions, for instance, is not always a useful strategy for learning how to express one's stance towards a claim. The reason, as de Beaugrande (2001) observes, is that

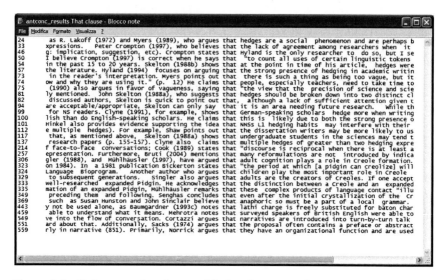

FIGURE 3.4   Finite reporting clauses with *that*-clause complement used in citation in the MICUSP_research paper corpus.

there is sometimes a disconnect between the meanings of words found in a dictionary and how they are commonly used in actual rhetorical contexts. Since it is rare for two words to mean the exact same thing and to hence be freely interchangeable, it is necessary for learners to look at how words are used in the specific contexts in which they are found (Partington, 1998; Tognini-Bonelli, 2001).

The finding about reporting verb choice in citation has important pedagogical implications. For example, my students learned that the majority of uses of the verb *argue* demonstrate an approach for creating negative evaluation of the reported claim either within the sentence or in the following sentences. Here are some examples from the MICUSP_research paper corpus:

(1)   *Cortazzi argues that* narratives are introduced into turn-by-turn talk using the following sequentially ordered elements [...] **While very insightful, Cortazzi's model seems somewhat narrow** in that he describes the narratives he analyzed as extended turns with no transition relevance points, indicating that he views narratives as being mostly personal rather than co-constructed.

(2)   *Singler also argues that* adults are the creators of Creoles. [...] Of course, this assumption is based on the idea that all Creoles do in fact have a substrate influence. **In the case of Nicaraguan Sign Language,**

however, it is somewhat more difficult to define what the substrate languages are, given that in most cases the home sign systems that the children used were no more complex than a Pidgin, certainly not complete languages themselves, although they would be the best equivalent of a person's native or ancestral language in terms of the elements of a 'normal' language contact scenario.

One of the advantages of using concordancing is that it facilitates the location of samples of sentences that extend or even contradict the students' own definition of a word or a rule they had been taught. One such example is the difference in how the reporting verbs *claim* and *argue* were used in the MICUSP_research paper corpus. Although their semantic meanings are fairly similar (these two verbs mainly indicate construction of argument and conflict), the students noticed that while there were a number of instances of *argue* being used to express disagreement with the reported, there were no instances where *claim* was used in this way in the corpus. For example, in (3), *claim* is used with no indication of any possible contradiction:

(3)   Clyne (1991), for example, shows that German-speaking scholars hedge more when writing in English than do English-speaking scholars. *He claims that* this is likely due to both the strong presence of hedging in German and a lack of comfort when writing in a foreign language. According to Clyne, the abundance of hedges in German authors' written English is not wrong, per se, but it can be problematic, for German-speaking author and English- speaking reader, because it does not meet the 'expectations of discourse' of academic written English.

This finding is of course not meant to imply that *claim* cannot be used to express disagreement with the reported. Hunston (1995), for instance, provides examples from academic articles where *claim* is associated with negative attributor judgement, construing disagreement between writer and attributor. Although working with a small corpus has many benefits (as earlier discussed), it is important to bear in mind that such a corpus may not contain all the possible or legitimate uses of a particular reporting verb. A class activity such as this, however, can provide opportunities for discussing with students how actual examples of language use may or may not match their preconceptions or what they were previously taught.

It should also be noted that the approach discussed here does not provide the student with either 'correct' or 'incorrect' examples. Rather, as

Johns (1997) has pointed out, concordancing allows students to become 'language detectives' who get the opportunity to see for themselves how real writers make meaning in real texts (p. 101).

Aston (2000) has noted that using corpora in teaching is valuable for providing opportunities for students to observe the communicative nature of texts, and although linguists researching in the areas described here may see several avenues for more in-depth and delicate corpus analysis that would lead to a deeper understanding of how language is used in research papers, I feel that the kinds of activities described here are adequate as a starting point for undergraduate students of English with very little experience writing up research papers, and satisfactorily meet the overall goals of the module.

4 Exploring Moves Through the Concordancer

Putting move analysis at the centre of the investigation leads to a different kind of corpus consultation. The purpose is still to look for repeated regularities, but these are patterns of discourse, rather than lexis or grammar. Such patterns, which show a high degree of variability, are likely to be signalled by combinations of linguistic features and are likely to be extended over longer stretches of text. Thus, it is necessary to expand the concordance lines in order to see the patterning and understand how it operates. Moreover, instead of reading down the concordance and looking at the words immediately to the right and left of the search term, users have to read the whole of each concordance entry carefully, sometimes working with lines that have been expanded to paragraph length, or even going back to the original text when the pattern or its function is unclear (see Figure 3.3 above). Individual concordance entries are therefore studied in much greater detail. In the type of corpus consultation advocated here, the search term is used as a probe to locate the parts of a text in which a given communicative function may occur and which may thus merit closer study. The ability to expand concordance lines and read extended context at will provides a prime example of how corpora can offer a resource that contributes to enriching the overall pedagogical environment (Aston, 1995, 1997).

5 Corpus-based Activities: Pedagogical Implications

In the classroom tasks described above, it is the teacher who controls the searches that the students carry out. This differs from much data-driven learning, in which teacher and student discover together answers to questions posed by the students themselves (Bernardini, 2002; Johns, 1991a). Due to the amount of teacher control exercised in the tasks that I designed, it may seem that many of the advantages usually associated with corpus work have been forfeited. For example, the student is clearly not on an equal footing with the teacher as regards knowledge of likely search outcomes. Nor is the student the initiator of the investigative process. The students are neither acting as 'researchers' in the fullest sense implied by Johns (1991a), nor are they truly allowed to inhabit the role of the 'traveller', freely exploring the data with minimal backup from the teacher (Bernardini, 2001).

I would suggest, however, that at the early stages of corpus work, there are good arguments in favour of exerting the amount of teacher control seen here, that the advantages of 'discovery learning' (Bernardini, 2002) are by no means lost, and that the value of controlled work outweighs any benefits that may be relinquished. Several writers have pointed out the many pitfalls associated with 'free' corpus searches (e.g. Chambers, 2005; Frankenberg-Garcia, 2005; Kennedy & Miceli, 2001). For example, students may have difficulty with search techniques – they may make typographical errors, or their searches may be too narrow to yield any results or too wide for them to identify the relevant data. Even with a well-formulated search, students may have difficulty at the next stage in interpreting the data – they may have problems with understanding and analyzing the concordance lines; they may make over-generalizations or may not notice crucial information. While it is true that training and practice in concordancing will lead to an improvement in these areas, it is often the case that there is insufficient class time for students to develop their skills under the guidance of an experienced corpus investigator. Thus, there are persuasive reasons for devoting the limited time in class to searches known to be of value for the matter under investigation.

As Gavioli (2005) points out, the issue is not so much whether the role of the teacher should be cut out in favour of allowing students direct access to the data, but rather of 'which type of filter they [teachers] should exercise and in what way' (p. 30). Providing a controlled introduction to concordancing with a limited number of concordance lines and a clearly defined set of questions can assist students, not only to gain specific answers to the questions posed, but also to develop their searching and interpreting techniques. By following a set of detailed instructions, for example, they learn how important it is to be accurate in entering a search and will soon find out, from other students or from the teacher, if they have gone wrong and in what way. By responding to questions that are given, students are encouraged to focus on the purpose of the search, to pay attention to specific linguistic features of the concordance lines and to notice similarities and differences between lines. This helps them gradually to develop an understanding of which aspects of the data are likely to be significant and how to make valid generalizations from the material.

However, it is also important to point out that, although the teacher can aim to exercise some control over the students' consultation of the corpus, in practice it is neither possible nor desirable to attempt to enforce conformity. In the module I taught, some students who became familiar with the procedures opted to carry out their own searches or, seduced by the richness of the data, became involved in answering their own questions rather than those of the task. Such freedom to pursue their own interests is inherent in the corpus as a tool for exploration, and the benefits of the 'serendipitous' learning that may ensue have rightly been emphasized, particularly by Bernardini (2000). Thus, while offering a framework for controlled discovery, the teacher should also be prepared to stand back and allow students to go in a direction that better suits their immediate needs. Even when a high degree of control is ostensibly exercised, corpus work always leaves scope for student input, and indeed, takeover. It is worth emphasizing that this freedom is not present to the same extent with paper-based materials, as the scope for students' own explorations is necessarily limited by the examples that are given in the handout or textbook.

Finally, of course, controlled tasks can give way to more flexible ones. Corpus searches have a tendency to lead to new questions, which in turn can lead on to new searches not originally envisaged by the teacher. Thus, the controlled tasks can be seen both as a temporary measure to ensure a fruitful (if somewhat limited) outcome for the class work and as a basis for the further development of the students' searching and interpreting skills. In this sense, they provide a 'jumping off' point, from which the more motivated and skilled students can pursue their own enquiries.

6 Concluding Remarks

In this chapter, I have described a pedagogical approach for teaching EAP writing to EFL learners which combines a genre methodology with a corpus methodology. I have shown how such an integration can provide enriched input for EFL learners, thus enabling them to make the connection between the communicative/pragmatic purpose of the genre under investigation and specific lexico-grammatical choices.

As several studies have pointed out (e.g. Aston, 2001; Gavioli, 2005; Johns, 1991b), the process of searching a corpus for a given pattern is of great value in itself, since it promotes active engagement by students in their own learning. In particular, with a context-sensitive search, the student is faced with a problem that immediately excites his/her interest: What, if anything, do these concordance examples have in common? It is this drive to distinguish underlying patterns that promotes detailed attention to the context of the search terms and leads students to notice and think about linguistic features that might otherwise be overlooked. Because students perform the searches themselves, they also have a greater investment in finding out about the concordance examples they have retrieved. Although the materials used in the module give instructions as to which searches are to be performed, it is still the students who carry them out and manipulate the lines, sorting, deleting and grouping them in any way they choose. In this way, then, the corpus lessons actively promote 'discovery learning'.

I would suggest, however, that it is the combination of text and corpus work that is particularly valuable in the materials I used. The use of genre-based tasks allows the teacher to present several ways in which a single pragmatic function may be performed. Not all of these will necessarily be suitable for corpus investigation, but students can gain some awareness of the variability that characterizes the realization of these functions. With corpus-based tasks, on the other hand, multiple instances of a single pattern are easily retrieved, which allows students to see more examples than could be presented in the extract form. In this way, students can gain further insight into the grammatical and lexical features of each individual pattern. This focus on patterning helps students to understand the extent of the regularity of language, even at the discourse level. The genre-based lesson, then, lays the foundation for the work on corpora by providing a wider range and greater variety of patterns, while the corpus investigations deepen and enrich the text work by revealing the frequency and detail of a limited number of those patterns. It is important to emphasize, however, that both the genre and corpus lessons involve different types of work and are designed to achieve different, and complementary, outcomes. In the genre lesson, students focus predominantly on pragmatic functions. They are encouraged to notice the occurrence of the rhetorical feature and to discuss its effect. By contrast, in the corpus lesson, the focus is on form. Students are asked to examine specific linguistic patterns in detail. Thus, in moving from genre to corpus, the class moves from studying what texts do, to investigating how they do it. It is this combination of lesson types that provides the student with a richer experience of the rhetorical pattern than would be achievable through work of either type alone.

Appendix

Sample teaching material

Worksheet

1) Study the corpus of student assignments and underline the subjects and verbs of the main clauses which signal the communicative function of the moves constituting the generic structure of the assignment.
2) Work in groups. Different groups will work on (i) and (ii). Then appoint someone to report to the whole class.
   i) Study the subjects you have underlined above and discuss in your group whether they refer to:
      a) discourse participants (*I, we, the authors,* etc.)
      b) discourse units (*this paper, many studies, this assumption,* etc.)
   ii) Study the verbs you have underlined and discuss in your group whether they refer to:
      a) research processes
      b) mental processes
      c) verbal processes
3) Study the most frequent verbs found in the corpus. What types of verbs are dominant according to the categories listed above?
   i) Extract the concordances of the most frequent verbs and underline the subjects of the main clauses. Which of the categories listed above do you think is dominant?
   ii) Check on the concordances of the verb you have selected to see if the verb can be freely used with subjects that refer to both discourse participants and discourse units. Underline the specific subjects and compare.

Notes

[1] For an overview of this topic, see Aijmer, 2009; Aston, 2001; Aston et al., 2004; Burnard & McEnery, 2000; Campoy-Cubillo et al., 2010; Frankenberg-Garcia et al., 2011; Gavioli, 2005; Ghadessy et al., 2001; Johns, 1991a, 1991b; Johns & King, 1991; Kettemann & Marko, 2002; Lewandowska-Tomaszczyk & Melia, 1997, 2000; Partington, 1998; Sinclair, 2004; Tan, 2002; Tribble & Jones, 1990; Wichmann et al., 1997.

[2] *AntConc* was developed by Laurence Anthony of Waseda University, Tokyo, Japan (see Anthony, 2006). The software is free for download from the author's homepage at http://www.antlab.sci.waseda.ac.jp/.

[3] A concordance is a list of occurrences (all or a selected number) of a word or a phrase in a corpus. The concordancer generally lays these occurrences out on the page (or on the computer screen) by the search word or phrase in the middle and 40–50 characters of context on both sides of it. This layout is called KWIC (key word in context).

[4] A wordlist gives information on the frequency of the words in a corpus. A keyword list compares lists from different corpora and calculates those words which are significantly more or less frequent in one set. A cluster consists of all recurrent word combinations from a concordance that match a certain predefined cluster span.

References

Aijmer, K. (Ed.). (2009). *Corpora and language teaching*. Amsterdam: John Benjamins.

Anthony, L. (2006). Developing a freeware, multiplatform corpus analysis toolkit for the technical writing classroom. *IEEE Transactions on Professional Communication, 49*(3), 275–286.

Aston, G. (1995). Corpora in language pedagogy: Matching theory and practice. In G. Cook & B. Seidlhofer (Eds.), *Principle and practice in applied linguistics* (pp. 257–270). Oxford: Oxford University Press.

Aston, G. (1997). Enriching the learning environment: Corpora in ELT. In A. Wichman, S. Fligelstone, T. McEnery & G. Knowles (Eds.), *Teaching and language corpora* (pp. 51–64). Harlow: Longman.

Aston, G. (2000). Corpora and language teaching. In L. Burnard & T. McEnery (Eds.), *Rethinking language pedagogy from a corpus perspective* (pp. 7–17). Hamburg: Peter Lang.

Aston, G. (2001). Learning with corpora: An overview. In G. Aston (Ed.), *Learning with corpora* (pp. 7–45). Bologna: CLUEB.

Aston, G., Bernardini, S., & Stewart, D. (Eds.). (2004). *Corpora and language learners*. Amsterdam: John Benjamins.

Barlow, M. (1999). *Monoconc Pro* [computer software]. Houston: Athelstan.

Barnbrook, G. (1996). *Language and computers*. Edinburgh: Edinburgh University Press.

de Beaugrande, R. (2001). Large corpora, small corpora, and the learning of 'language'. In M. Ghadessy, A. Henry & R. L. Roseberry (Eds.), *Small corpus studies and ELT* (pp. 3–28). Amsterdam: John Benjamins.

Bernardini, S. (2000). Systematising serendipity: Proposals for concordancing large corpora with language learners. In L. Burnard & T. McEnery (Eds.), *Rethinking language pedagogy from a corpus perspective* (pp. 225–234). Hamburg: Peter Lang.

Bernardini, S. (2001). 'Spoilt for choice': A learner explores general language corpora. In G. Aston (Ed.), *Learning with corpora* (pp. 220–249). Bologna: CLUEB.

Bernardini, S. (2002). Exploring new directions for discovery learning. In B. Kettemann & G. Marko (Eds.), *Teaching and learning by doing corpus analysis* (pp. 165–182). Amsterdam: Rodopi.

Biber, D., Conrad, S., & Reppen, R. (1998). *Corpus linguistics: Investigating language structure and use*. Cambridge: Cambridge University Press.

Bondi, M. (1999). Language awareness and EFL teacher education. In P. Faber, W. Gewehr, M. Jiménez Raya & A. J. Peck (Eds.), *English teacher education in Europe* (pp. 91–107). Frankfurt: Peter Lang.

Burnard, L., & McEnery, T. (Eds.). (2000). *Rethinking language pedagogy from a corpus perspective.* Hamburg: Peter Lang.

Campoy-Cubillo, M. C., Bellés-Fortuño, B., & Gea-Valor, M. L. (Eds.). (2010). *Corpus-based approaches to English language teaching.* London: Continuum.

Chambers, A. (2005). Integrating corpus consultation in language studies. *Language Learning and Technology, 9*(2), 111–125.

Charles, M. (2007). Reconciling top-down and bottom-up approaches to graduate writing: Using a corpus to teach rhetorical functions. *Journal of English for Academic Purposes, 6*(4), 289–302.

Cortes, V. (2004). Lexical bundles in published and student disciplinary writing: Examples from history and biology. *English for Specific Purposes, 23*(4), 397–423.

Flowerdew, J. (2001). Attitude of journal editors to nonnative speaker contributions. *TESOL Quarterly, 35*(1), 121–150.

Flowerdew, L. (2002). Corpus-based analyses in EAP. In J. Flowerdew (Ed.), *Academic discourse* (pp. 95–114). Harlow: Longman.

Flowerdew, L. (2004). The argument for using English specialized corpora to understand academic and professional language. In U. Connor & T. Upton (Eds.), *Discourse in the professions: Perspectives from corpus linguistics* (pp. 11–33). Amsterdam: John Benjamins.

Flowerdew, L. (2005). An integration of corpus-based and genre-based approaches to text analysis in EAP/ESP: Counting criticisms against corpus-based methodologies. *English for Specific Purposes, 24*(3), 321–332.

Frankenberg-Garcia, A. (2005). A peek into what today's language learners as researchers actually do. *International Journal of Lexicography, 18*(3), 335–355.

Frankenberg-Garcia, A., Flowerdew, L., & Aston, G. (Eds.). (2011). *New trends in corpora and language learning.* London: Continuum.

Gavioli, L. (2005). *Exploring corpora for ESP learning.* Amsterdam: John Benjamins.

Ghadessy, M., Henry, A., & Roseberry, R. L. (Eds.). (2001). *Small corpus studies and ELT.* Amsterdam: John Benjamins.

Harwood, N. (2005). 'We do not have a theory. The theory I present here attempts to fill this gap': Inclusive and exclusive pronouns in academic writing. *Applied Linguistics, 26*(3), 343–375.

Hopkins, A., & Dudley-Evans, T. (1988). A genre-based investigation of the discussion sections in articles and dissertations. *English for Specific Purposes, 7*(2), 113–122.

Hunston, S. (1995). A corpus study of some English verbs of attribution. *Functions of Language, 2*(2), 133–158.

Hunston, S. (2000). Evaluation and the planes of discourse: Status and value in persuasive texts. In S. Hunston & G. Thompson (Eds.), *Evaluation in text* (pp. 176–207). Oxford: Oxford University Press.

Hunston, S., & Francis, G. (2000). *Pattern grammar.* Amsterdam: John Benjamins.

Hyland, K. (2001). Humble servants of the discipline? Self-mention in research articles. *English for Specific Purposes, 20*(3), 207–226.

Hyland, K. (2002a). Authority and invisibility: Authorial identity in academic writing. *Journal of Pragmatics, 34*(8), 1091–1112.

Hyland, K. (2002b). Activity and evaluation: Reporting practices in academic writing. In J. Flowerdew (Ed.), *Academic discourse* (pp. 115–130). Harlow: Longman.

Hyland, K. (2005). Stance and engagement: A model of interaction in academic discourse. *Discourse Studies*, 7(2), 173–292.

Hyland, K. (2006). *English for academic purposes: An advanced resource book.* London: Routledge.

Johns, T. (1991a). Should you be persuaded: Two samples of data-driven learning materials. In T. Johns & P. King (Eds.), *Classrooom concordancing* (pp. 1–16). Birmingham: ELR University of Birmingham.

Johns, T. (1991b). From printout to handout: Grammar and vocabulary teaching in the context of data-driven learning. In T. Johns & P. King (Eds.), *Classrooom concordancing* (pp. 27–37). Birmingham: ELR University of Birmingham.

Johns, T. (1997). Contexts: The background, development and trialling of a concordance-based CALL program. In A. Wichmann, S. Fligelstone, T. McEnery & G. Knowles (Eds.), *Teaching and language corpora* (pp. 100–115). Harlow: Longman.

Johns, T., & King, P. (Eds.). (1991). *Classrooom concordancing.* Birmingham: ELR, University of Birmingham.

Kennedy, C., & Miceli, T. (2001). An evaluation of intermediate students' approaches to corpus investigation. *Language Learning and Technology*, 5(3), 77–90.

Kettemann, B., & Marko, G. (Eds.). (2002). *Teaching and learning by doing corpus analysis.* Amsterdam: Rodopi.

Kuo, C.-H. (1999). The use of personal pronouns: Role relationships in scientific journal articles. *English for Specific Purposes*, 18(2), 121–138.

Lee, D., & Swales, J. (2006). A corpus-based EAP course for NNS doctoral students: Moving from available specialized corpora to self-compiled corpora. *English for Specific Purposes*, 25(1), 56–75.

Lewandowska-Tomaszczyk, B., & Melia, P. J. (Eds.). (1997). *PALC'97: Practical applications in language corpora.* Łódź: Łódź University Press.

Lewandowska-Tomaszczyk, B., & Melia, P. J. (Eds.). (2000). *PALC'99: Practical applications in language corpora: Papers from the international conference at the University of Łódź, 15-18 April 1999.* Frankfurt am Main: Peter Lang.

Lynch, T. (2001). Promoting EAP learner autonomy in a second language university context. In J. Flowerdew & M. Peacock (Eds.), *Research perspectives on English for academic purposes* (pp. 390–403). Cambridge: Cambridge University Press.

McEnery, T., & Kifle, N. A. (2002). Epistemic modality in argumentative essays of second-language writers. In J. Flowerdew (Ed.), *Academic discourse* (pp. 182–195). Harlow: Longman.

Partington, A. (1998). *Patterns and meanings.* Amsterdam: John Benjamins.

Schlitz, S. A. (2010). Introduction to special issue: Exploring corpus-informed approaches to writing research. *Journal of Writing Research*, 2(2), 91–98.

Scott, M. (1996). *WordSmith tools.* Oxford: Oxford University Press.

Sinclair, J. (Ed.). (2004). *How to use corpora in language teaching.* Amsterdam: John Benjamins.

Swales, J. M. (1990). *Genre analysis.* Cambridge: Cambridge University Press.

Swales, J. M., & Feak, C. B. (1994). *Academic writing for graduate students.* Ann Arbor: University of Michigan Press.

Tan, M. (Ed.). (2002). *Corpus studies in language education.* Bangkok: IELE Press.

Tang, R., & John, S. (1999). The 'I' in identity: Exploring writer identity in student academic writing through the first person pronoun. *English for Specific Purposes, 18*, S23–S39.

Thompson, P. (Ed.). (2000). *Patterns and perspectives: Insights into EAP writing practice.* Reading: The University of Reading, Centre for Applied Language Studies.

Thompson, P. (Ed.). (2007). Corpus-based EAP pedagogy. Special issue of *Journal of English for Academic Purposes, 6*(4).

Thompson, P., & Tribble, C. (2001). Looking at citations: Using corpora in English for academic purposes. *Language Learning and Technology, 5*(3), 91–105.

Thurstun, J., & Candlin, C. (1998). Concordancing and the teaching of the vocabulary of academic English. *English for Specific Purposes, 17*(3), 267–280.

Tognini-Bonelli, E. (2001). *Corpus linguistics at work.* Amsterdam: John Benjamins.

Tribble, C. (2001). Small corpora and teaching writing. In M. Ghadessy, A. Henry & R. L. Roseberry (Eds.), *Small corpus studies and ELT* (pp. 381–408). Amsterdam: John Benjamins.

Tribble, C. (2002). Corpora and corpus analysis: New windows on academic writing. In J. Flowerdew (Ed.), *Academic discourse* (pp. 131–149). Harlow: Longman.

Tribble, C., & Jones, G. (1990). *Concordances in the classroom.* Harlow: Longman.

Wales, K. (1996). *Personal pronouns in present-day English.* Cambridge: Cambridge University Press.

Weber, J. J. (2001). A concordance- and genre-informed approach to ESP essay writing. *English Language Teaching Journal, 55*(1), 14–20.

Wichmann, A., Fligelstone, S., McEnery, T., & Knowles, G. (Eds.). (1997). *Teaching and language corpora.* Harlow: Longman.

Chapter 4

The Impact of Experience and Beliefs on Chinese EFL Student Writers' Feedback Preferences

Guangwei Hu and Hongwei Ren

1 Introduction

The past four decades have seen increasing research attention being paid to peer review as an important pedagogical activity in first (L1) and second language (L2) writing instruction and peer feedback as a useful source of information for improving student writing (DiPardo & Freedman, 1988; Ferris, 2003; Gere, 1987; Hyland & Hyland, 2006a). Peer review is a collaborative instructional activity that involves students in 'reading, critiquing, and providing feedback on each other's writing' (Hu, 2005a, p. 321). Meshing well with the process approach to writing instruction and the social constructive perspective on learning, peer review has the potential to afford 'a number of metacognitive, cognitive, socio-affective and linguistic benefits' (Hu, 2005a, p. 323). Apart from strong theoretical support (Elbow, 2000; Ferris, 2003), there has been considerable empirical evidence from L1 and L2 writing research that peer review can facilitate learner development, improve the quality of student writing, and enhance the acquisition of writing competence (Berg, 1999; DiPardo & Freedman, 1988; Hu & Lam, 2010; Min, 2006; Paulus, 1999; Stanley, 1992; Villamil & de Guerrero, 1998). At the same time, however, research has also identified potential problems with peer review in L2 writing instruction (e.g. Ferris, 2003; Leki, 1990; Mangelsdorf, 1992; Zhang, 1995), which has given rise to studies of how peer review can be effectively used (e.g. Hu, 2005a; Min, 2005; Stanley, 1992) and a growing awareness of the importance of judicious use of feedback sources (Hyland, 2006; Jacobs et al., 1998).

While the substantial body of research has contributed much to our understanding of various issues related to peer review and peer feedback, it is important to note that an overwhelming majority of the published studies have been conducted in L1 writing classrooms (see DiPardo & Freedman, 1988; Gere, 1987) and ESL contexts, especially North American ones (see Ferris, 2003; Hyland & Hyland, 2006b), as opposed to foreign language contexts. This raises a question about the extent to which findings obtained in these educational settings can be extrapolated to student writers who learn to write in a foreign language in other contexts. The question becomes doubly poignant when research (e.g. ESL studies conducted in North American universities) studies Asian students out of their native sociocultural contexts but interprets the obtained empirical results in terms of influences from these socio-cultural contexts. Arguably, because of their exposure to different socio-cultural and educational practices, such ESL students are not ideal for exploring the influences of their native sociocultural contexts on their beliefs and behavior with respect to peer review. Thus, there is a clear need for further research on peer review as a pedagogical activity in a variety of learning contexts involving learners of different sociocultural backgrounds.

This chapter reports on a survey-based study on Chinese EFL student writers in mainland China. The study was designed to investigate the impact of Chinese EFL student writers' experience and beliefs on their preferences for different sources of feedback on their English writing. Specifically, the following research questions were formulated for this study:

1. What kinds of experience do Chinese EFL student writers have with teacher feedback and peer feedback?
2. Which sources of feedback do they prefer?
3. How is their previous experience related to their feedback preferences?
4. What beliefs undergird their feedback preferences?

We hope that our study can contribute to an understanding of EFL learners' feedback preferences in their local contexts and inform the use of peer review in L2 writing pedagogy in sociocultural and educa-tional milieus different from those found in what Kachru (1986) refers to as the Inner Circle countries (i.e. Australia, Canada, UK and USA, among others).

2 Research on Peer Review and Students' Feedback Preferences

A number of potential benefits of peer review have been identified in the literature. One major benefit is the facilitating role of peer review in students' writing and revision. Students are found to be able to provide useful feedback on different aspects of each other's writing (Tsui & Ng, 2000; Villamil & de Guerrero, 1998). For example, peers can offer many interesting ideas (Hu & Lam, 2010; Jacobs et al., 1998) and spot problems that student writers have missed (Jacobs et al., 1998), including incongruities between the intended and understood meaning of their texts (Berg, 1999). Negotiation with peers also helps student writers understand different points of view (Mangelsdorf, 1992) and discover 'viable text alternatives' (Berg, 1999, p. 217). Compared with teacher feedback, peer feedback is usually higher in 'density', quicker in 'turnover' time (Rollinson, 2005) and easier to understand (Hu & Lam, 2010).

Another benefit of peer review is the positive effect it can have on students' longitudinal L2 writing development. Research suggests that peer review can encourage students to approach writing as a negotiated sociocognitive process (de Guerrero & Villamil, 1994; Hu, 2005a) and facilitate their move from writer-based writing to reader-based writing (Stanley, 1992) by helping them develop an awareness of audience (Mangelsdorf, 1992; Mendonca & Johnson, 1994; Tsui & Ng, 2000). As student writers are free to accept or reject peer comments, peer review also helps students gain a sense of text ownership (O'Brien, 2004; Rollinson, 2005; Tsui & Ng, 2000) and gives them opportunities to hone evaluative skills which can contribute to their long-term development as effective L2 writers (Berg, 1999; Nelson & Carson, 1998; Yang et al., 2006). Furthermore, peer review can increase students' repertoire of effective revision strategies, which they can apply to their future real-world writing tasks (Hu & Lam, 2010).

Research has also pointed to some beneficial effects of peer review on language acquisition and learner development in general. There are indications that the peer review process not only encourages collaborative learning (Cotterall & Cohen, 2003; Jacobs et al., 1998) but also pushes learners to develop self-regulatory behaviors (Villamil & de Guerrero, 1998) and gain learner autonomy (Hyland, 2000; Tsui & Ng, 2000; Yang et al., 2006). As peer review requires an evaluation of peer writing and peer feedback, it can promote the development of critical thinking (Berg, 1999; Yang et al., 2006). In addition, collaboration and negotiation between peers can enhance their communicative competence (Mendonca & Johnson, 1994) and prepare them for future social and professional relationships (Villamil & de Guerrero, 1996).

However, peer review and peer feedback are not always perceived in such a positive light. Researchers and student writers themselves have also identified potential problems with peer review as a pedagogical activity. Some of these problems arise from students' limited competence in the target language. As students are still learning the language and its rhetorical conventions, they may have difficulty in detecting problems in peers' writing and providing valid suggestions, and in discriminating between valid and invalid advice given by others (Hu, 2005a; Hu & Lam, 2010; Sengupta, 1998; Stanley, 1992; Tsui & Ng, 2000). Besides, perceptions of peers' linguistic limitations may lead student writers to mistrust peer opinions (Hu & Lam, 2010; Mendonca & Johnson, 1994; Nelson & Carson, 1998; Sengupta, 1998). There are also problems which could be caused by students' inadequate ability to critique. With little idea of what to look for in peers' writing, many students tend to focus on surface errors rather than textual or content issues when they respond to peers' drafts (Leki, 1990; Nelson & Carson, 1998). When they do try to comment on global or content issues, their comments tend to be too vague or general to be useful (Leki, 1990; Liu & Sadler, 2003).

Students may also have difficulty in collaborating with peers in peer review. Research shows that students may display behaviors and attitudes which are detrimental to peer collaboration (Mangelsdorf & Schlumberger, 1992). In a study on students' interaction in a peer review task, for example, Lockhart and Ng (1995) found that more than half of the students took authoritative or prescriptive stances towards each other's writing. Such stances restrict collaboration, ignore 'the dynamic aspect of writing' (Lockhart & Ng, 1995, p. 646), and therefore 'defeat the intended purposes of peer review' (Hu, 2005a, p. 326). In other studies, students were found to be over-critical (Nelson & Murphy, 1992) or to lack respect as reviewers (Villamil & de Guerrero, 1996), and to be over-defensive or worried as writers (Amores, 1997; Nelson & Carson 1998; Villamil & de Guerrero, 1996). Such behaviors and attitudes work against productive collaboration and detract from the effectiveness of peer review.

Some researchers (e.g. Carson & Nelson, 1994, 1996; Mangelsdorf, 1992; Nelson & Carson, 1998; Sengupta, 1998) have also suggested that peer review may be problematic for students with certain cultural norms antithetical to the pedagogical principles underlying peer review. For example, Paulus (1999) points out that students from teacher-centered cultures tend to see peers as unqualified to criticize their drafts. Carson and Nelson (1994) argue that prevalent beliefs in group cohesion and harmony may inhibit students in collectivist societies from criticizing peers' drafts and showing disagreement. Such discussions would suggest the inappropriateness of peer review as a pedagogical activity for students in China because it is deemed a prototypical collectivist society (Triandis, 1995) and there has been a long tradition of teacher-centeredness in Chinese society (Hu, 2002). However, the jury is still out on whether peer review is indeed unwelcome and unproductive for Chinese EFL students because studies involving Chinese students have not only yielded mixed findings (cf. Carson & Nelson, 1996; Hu & Lam, 2010) but have also been conducted mostly outside mainland China (e.g. Connor & Asenavage, 1994; Zhang, 1995).

A further gap we have identified in the literature is that apart from some speculative discussions (Connor & Asenavage, 1994; Tsui & Ng, 2000), student perceptions of and stances toward peer review have hardly been investigated in relation to previous experience with different kinds of feedback (Hu & Lam, 2010). However, it makes intuitive sense to hypothesize that student writers' previous experience with feedback from different sources would influence their perceptions of the usefulness of such feedback and, consequently, their feedback preferences. It is to address this and the other gaps identified above that we conducted the present study.

3 Method

3.1 Participants

The participants in this study were 116 junior English language majors at a major university in the People's Republic of China. They were aged between 19 and 23 years, with a mean age of 20.78 years. The female students ($n = 97$) accounted for 83.6% of the sample. Like most college students in China, the participants had studied English for at least six years before they went to college. As English majors, they would have completed an introductory English writing course during their second year at college. At the time of the data collection for this study, they had been taking an advanced English writing course for 16 weeks, with 90 minutes of instruction every week. In the writing course, they had been encouraged to review one another's written work and revise their own writing based on feedback from peers, in addition to receiving feedback from the teacher, as is traditionally the case in China. However, no training on peer review had been provided in the course, except for a brief explanation by the teacher about what they could do in peer review tasks.

3.2 Instrument

The data were collected through a written questionnaire comprising both closed- and open-ended items developed to elicit: (a) information about the participants' previous experience with peer and teacher feedback, (b) their evaluation of the usefulness of the feedback they had previously received from the different sources, (c) information about their feedback preferences (i.e. peer feedback alone, teacher feedback alone, both peer and teacher feedback, or no feedback), and (d) their reasons for the indicated feedback preferences. Only peer feedback and teacher feedback were focused on in the study because they are the major sources of other-directed feedback available to students in most Chinese EFL contexts. The four options for feedback preference were provided so as not to put students in a position where they were forced to select one type of preferred feedback – either peer feedback or teacher feedback. The questionnaire was administered to 124 junior English majors of the 2006 intake near the end of the fall semester of 2008. To encourage the participants to provide candid responses to the questions, the participants were asked to complete the questionnaire anonymously. Both the questionnaire and students' responses were in Chinese so as to ensure that students could fully understand the questions and express their opinions without any language problems. Of the responses returned, eight did not complete most of the questions and were excluded from data analyses. The remaining 116 responses were valid and were included in the analyses reported below.

3.3 Data analyses

To address the first two research questions and obtain a general picture of the participants' previous experience with teacher and peer feedback as well as their feedback preferences, responses to the relevant questions were tallied by source of feedback and response options. To answer the third research question, two Chi-square tests of independence were conducted respectively to determine if the participants' feedback preferences were independent of their perceived usefulness of the teacher and peer feedback they had received before. To complement the quantitative analyses, comments given by the students in relation to their previous experience were also examined qualitatively. To investigate the relationship between beliefs and feedback preferences, reasons given by the students for their feedback preferences were coded, classified, and analyzed qualitatively to identify underlying assumptions and beliefs. Frequency counts by reason and feedback preference were also made, and student responses that are quoted in this paper were translated from Chinese into English by the second author.

4 Findings

4.1 The students' previous experience and feedback preferences

Table 4.1 summarizes the statistical information that describes the participants' previous experience with teacher and peer feedback, their perceptions about the usefulness of the different sources of feedback they had received, as well as their feedback preferences. As is clear from the table, all the participants had received teacher feedback on their English writing before, and an overwhelming majority (88.79%) also reported receiving peer feedback previously. Most of the participants had had quite positive experience with both teacher and peer feedback. Over 78% of them perceived previously-received teacher feedback as 'very useful' or 'useful', and more than 53% said the same about the peer feedback they had received before. The difference between the two percentage figures, together with the 35.34% who perceived peer feedback as only 'somewhat useful' or 'not useful' suggests that, as a group, the participants had a more favorable attitude toward teacher feedback than peer feedback.

With regard to feedback preference, the majority of the students (60.35%) preferred to receive both teacher and peer feedback on their

Table 4.1 Profile of previous feedback experience and feedback preferences

Question	Response option	n	%
Previous experience with teacher feedback	Very useful	24	20.69
	Useful	67	57.76
	Somewhat useful	25	21.55
	Not useful	0	0
	No experience	0	0
Previous experience with peer feedback	Very useful	21	18.10
	Useful	41	35.35
	Somewhat useful	37	31.90
	Not useful	4	3.44
	No experience	13	11.21
Feedback preference	Teacher feedback only	44	37.93
	Peer feedback only	0	0
	Both teacher and peer feedback	70	60.35
	No feedback	2	1.72

written work. While no one indicated a preference for only peer feedback, nearly 38% of the students indicated that they would like to receive teacher feedback alone. Only two students showed little interest in feedback from others and would rather revise their writing on their own. As was the case with perceptions of the usefulness of previously-received teacher and peer feedback, the pattern of feedback preferences reported by the students is also indicative of a more positive attitude toward teacher feedback. In other words, while both teacher and peer feedback were seen as desirable sources of information in the English writing class, teacher feedback was valued more highly.

4.2 The relationship between previous experience and feedback preferences

Two Chi-square tests of independence were run to determine the relationship between previous experience and feedback preference. Because this study focuses on only teacher and peer feedback, the two students who reported a preference for no feedback were not included in the Chi-square tests. The first two-way (2 × 3) Chi-square test found no statistically significant relationship between feedback preference and perception of the usefulness of previously-received teacher feedback, χ^2 (2, $N = 114$) = .824, $p = .662$ (2-tailed). The effect size (Cramér's $V = .085$) is smaller than the criterion of .10 that Cohen (1988) recommends for a small effect. Table 4.2 presents the cross-tabulation of feedback preference and previous experience with teacher feedback. These results suggest that the source of feedback the participants preferred was independent of their perceptions of the usefulness of the teacher feedback they had received before. In other words, whether they preferred teacher feedback alone or both teacher and peer feedback was totally unrelated to whether they had received 'very useful', 'useful' or 'somewhat useful' teacher feedback.

Table 4.2 Cross-tabulation of previous experience with teacher feedback and feedback preference

Previous experience with teacher feedback	Feedback preference		
	Teacher feedback	Teacher + peer feedback	Total
Very useful	10	14	24
Useful	27	40	67
Somewhat useful	7	16	23
Total	44	70	114

This lack of relationship between previous experience with teacher feedback and feedback preference is most obvious in the seven students who reported receiving only 'somewhat useful' teacher feedback before but still indicated a preference for teacher feedback alone. Notably, these students accounted for 15.91% of those who preferred only teacher feedback. Speaking of his past experience with teacher feedback, one student commented: 'The teachers did not give enough feedback. As the teachers had to comment on many papers and were very busy, teacher feedback was usually too little to be of much use.' Another student observed that 'the teacher feedback was often limited to grammatical errors.' A third student complained that 'there was not much new in teacher feedback. I could even guess what the feedback would be. I did not feel I could learn much from it.' In contrast to such complaints about previously-received teacher feedback, several of the students actually reported receiving 'useful' or even 'very useful' peer feedback in the past. Given such experiences with teacher and peer feedback, what could have influenced these students' feedback preferences?

An examination of the reasons the seven students gave for their feedback preferences revealed a strong faith in the authority and expertise of teachers. For example, one student said, 'Teachers are authoritative. They teach students how to write and they know what is bad and what is good. Their expertise can help students write better.' In a similar vein, another student explained that 'Teachers are more experienced and more knowledgeable. They can give better feedback.' Such a conception of the teacher as 'expert' may have led to a corresponding perception of peers as less capable reviewers and therefore inadequate sources of feedback. Indeed, two students explicitly expressed their distrust of their peers' ability to provide useful feedback, with one of them saying, 'the teacher is authoritative and can give effective advice on writing. But students are at a similar level and cannot improve each other's writing.' Since their previous experience with teacher feedback did not have an impact on their feedback preferences, it would seem that their strong faith in the authority and usefulness of teacher feedback had cultural roots. In other words, although the students were not happy with some individual teachers' feedback on their writing, the popular conception of the teacher as an authoritative source of knowledge and expertise could have inclined them to have a deep-seated trust in teacher feedback in general.

In contrast to the results of the Chi-square test presented above, statistically significant results were yielded by the second two-way (2×4) Chi-square test of independence between feedback preference and previous experience with peer feedback. To run the test, the categories of 'not useful' and 'no experience' for the variable of previous experience with peer feedback were collapsed due to the small expected cell frequencies for the 'not useful' category. Without the combination, over 20% of the expected cell frequencies would have fallen below 5; consequently, an important assumption underlying the statistical test would have been violated (Field, 2005; Norušis, 2006). There was a statistically significant relationship between previous experience with peer feedback and feedback preference, χ^2 (3, $N = 114$) = 12.827, $p = .005$ (2-tailed). The effect size (Cramér's $V = .335$) was greater than the criterial level of .30 that Cohen (1988) sets for a medium effect.

The results indicated that the students' feedback preferences were reasonably strongly related to the perceived usefulness of their previously-received peer feedback. Table 4.3 cross-tabulates feedback preference with previous experience with peer feedback. A close examination of the data revealed that 66.67% and 75.61% of the students who reported receiving 'very useful' and 'useful' peer feedback respectively preferred to have both teacher and peer feedback on their writing. In contrast, 75% of the students who reported receiving 'not useful' peer feedback or having no previous experience with peer feedback preferred to have teacher feedback alone. Thus, students who had positive prior experience with peer feedback were more likely to choose both teacher and peer feedback, and students who had no or negative experience with peer feedback were more likely to choose teacher feedback alone. It should be noted, however, that 27.42% ($n = 17$) of the students who reported receiving 'useful' or 'very useful' peer feedback before indicated a preference for teacher feedback alone, accounting for 38.64% of the 44 students who made such a choice. Like those students who, despite less-than-happy previous experiences with teacher feedback, still preferred such feedback, these students had a strong belief in the superiority of teacher feedback that would seem to be culturally rooted.

Table 4.3 Cross-tabulation of previous experience with peer feedback and feedback preference

	Feedback preference		
Previous experience with peer feedback	Teacher feedback	Teacher + peer feedback	Total
Very useful	7	14	21
Useful	10	31	41
Somewhat useful	15	21	36
Not useful + no experience	12	4	16
Total	44	70	114

4.3 The relationship between beliefs and feedback preferences

The qualitative analysis of the reasons given by the students for their feedback preferences revealed that different beliefs and assumptions underlay the indicated feedback preferences. One important theme that emerged from the analysis is the widespread belief in the authority and utility of teacher feedback. An overwhelming majority of the students described teachers or teacher feedback with such words as 'authoritative', 'effective', 'valid', 'experienced' or 'expertise', and attributed their favorable attitude toward teacher feedback to such qualities. This is not only manifest in the students' explanations for their feedback preferences quoted in the previous section but is also further illustrated by the following quotations:

1. *Teachers are more competent and more experienced. They can give more comprehensive feedback of a better quality.*
2. *Teachers have been exposed to English much longer than peers, and they know much more about writing in English. Their feedback is more authoritative and more effective.*
3. *Teacher feedback is more authoritative and accurate, but peers' opinions cannot be trusted.*

Whereas students' belief in the authority of teacher feedback was a major influence on their preference for such feedback, their inclusion or exclusion of peer feedback in their feedback preference seems to also have been influenced by a number of other beliefs and assumptions. For the 44 students who preferred to have teacher feedback only, the strengths of teachers and their feedback were pitted against the weaknesses of peers and their feedback, as illustrated in the following quotations:

4. *Teacher feedback is more valid and effective. But peers are still learning to write themselves. They cannot see many of the problems in each other's writing, except for some grammatical mistakes.*
5. *Teachers are more knowledgeable and experienced, and can give better feedback. But peers are still learning, and what they know is quite limited. They can only point out some simple mistakes in grammar.*
6. *Teachers are experts. They can point out the problems in students' writing. However, most peers even have problems with their English. They may still make mistakes in their own writing. Their advice might be wrong.*
7. *Teachers are more authoritative and experienced. They can give me good advice to improve my writing. But my peers are at a similar level or are even not as good as I am. Their opinion may not be right.*

While over 93% of the students in this group perceived teachers as more knowledgeable, experienced, and capable of giving better and more comprehensive feedback, 77% thought peer feedback was not as effective as teacher feedback due to peers' limited ability, and over 50% mentioned that the usefulness of peer feedback was largely restricted to the identification of surface errors. Nearly 16% of the students also expressed their distrust of peer feedback explicitly. A few other problems with peer feedback were mentioned as well. Three students voiced the concern that peers might avoid being critical of each other's writing. One of them claimed that 'teachers can point out both the good and bad things in students' writing, but peers always try to praise others' work with some positive cliché, which does not help much.' Another student explained how letting peers read her written work would generate a feeling of discomfort because she was not as good in English as her peers. One student also believed that teacher feedback would motivate students to write but peer feedback would not encourage students to do their best. This would make a good example of what Hattie and Timperley (2007) describe as 'commitment ... induced by authority figures' (p. 89). Cutting across the various beliefs held by the 44 students who preferred only teacher feedback was the implicit assumption that teacher feedback alone was a sufficient source of information for addressing problems in one's writing.

By contrast, the 70 students who preferred both teacher and peer feedback held different beliefs and assumptions. Although they also shared a strong belief in teachers' authority and expertise, they showed more positive attitudes toward peer feedback and tended to regard teacher and peer feedback as complementary rather than competing sources of information. According to the students, peer feedback could complement teacher feedback in several different ways. For example, peer feedback and teacher feedback could address different aspects of students' writing, with the former focusing on lower-level issues such as grammatical and mechanical problems and the latter on higher-level issues such as organization and coherence. This belief is clearly reflected in the following quotations from the students:

8. *Teacher feedback and peer feedback are complementary. Teacher feedback is more authoritative and can improve students' writing at higher levels, while peer feedback is more meticulous and can identify grammatical and spelling mistakes.*
9. *Teachers can point out students' weaknesses in organization, coherence and other writing skills; peers can help correct each other's grammatical mistakes.*

10. *Teachers are more knowledgeable and experienced. They can deal with the more difficult issues in students' writing, such as logic and organization. Peers are more meticulous and can spot minor mistakes in each other's writing.*
11. *Teacher feedback can tell if students' writing reaches the standard, and peer feedback can help correct some grammatical mistakes.*

Many students also pointed out that compared with teacher feedback, peer feedback was more readily available and easier to understand:

12. *Teacher feedback is more authoritative and effective, but peer feedback is easier to understand.*
13. *Teachers are more knowledgeable and can give more effective feedback, but it is more convenient to communicate with peers, and we can understand each other better.*
14. *Teacher feedback is authoritative and valuable; peer feedback is easier to understand and closer to us.*
15. *Peers can tell me what they think about my writing from the perspective of someone who is at the same age as I am.*

It is worth noting the inherent paradox contained in Comment 13: Even though the student in question could understand peer feedback better than teacher feedback, he/she still regarded the latter as more effective. This comment is indicative of a deep-seated, unquestioned assumption about teacher feedback as an authoritative source of information.

A sizeable number of the students found peer feedback desirable because it could expand the amount of useful information that could help them improve their writing:

16. *We need to have as much feedback as possible to improve our writing.*
17. *The more feedback we have, the more chances there are to improve.*
18. *It's good to know how other people think of my writing.*
19. *Peer feedback can help us improve the quality of our writing before we turn it in for teacher feedback.*

In addition, peer feedback was also seen as beneficial in the following respects:

20. *Teachers are too busy to read students' writing carefully. Peers have more time to read each other's writing more carefully and can give more feedback.*

21. *By giving feedback to peers, we can also read others' work and see how they deal with the topic and learn from them.*
22. *Reading peers' work can help us realize the problems in our own writing.*

It is clear from the comments above that the students are cognizant of the many benefits of peer review as a pedagogical activity that have been discussed in the literature.

5 Discussion

A majority of the participants in this study made a rather positive evaluation of their previous experience with peer feedback. This result echoes Yang et al.'s (2006) finding in their comparative study of peer and teacher feedback in a Chinese EFL context. If the 13 students in our study who had no previous experience with peer feedback are excluded, 60% of the remaining students found their previously-received peer feedback 'useful' or 'very useful', a percentage that is highly comparable to that obtained for the peer feedback class in Yang et al.'s study. The majority of the students (60.35%) in our study also preferred to receive both teacher and peer feedback. In other words, these students welcomed peer feedback as a desirable source of information that could help them with their revision. This is consistent with the findings of studies such as Hu and Lam (2010), Jacobs et al. (1998) and Yang et al. (2006). This receptiveness toward peer feedback notwithstanding, it should be pointed out that most of the students tended to perceive peer feedback as being useful only in dealing with surface errors in students' writing or treat peer feedback as a supplementary source of information. These attitudes are indicative of the students' sense of insecurity about peers, and themselves, dealing with higher-level issues in writing. They also reflect the popular belief among our participants that peer feedback is secondary in importance and usefulness to teacher feedback. Indeed, several students explicitly stated that 'teacher feedback should be looked at as the standard' and that 'when there's a conflict between teacher and peer feedback, teacher feedback should be followed.' However, such perceptions of the limited value of peer feedback may prevent students from fully exploring and enjoying the various metacognitive, cognitive and socio-affective benefits that peer review as a pedagogical activity has the potential to offer (Hu, 2005a; Hu & Lam, 2010). Some of these potential benefits include the valuable opportunities that peer review can afford for student writers to 'create an authentic social context for interaction and learning' (Hyland, 2006, p. 105; de Guerrero & Villamil, 2000; Liu & Sadler, 2003; Tuzi, 2004), to 'gain confidence, perspective, and critical thinking skills' (Ferris, 2003, p. 70; Lockhart & Ng, 1995; Paulus, 1999), to cultivate learner autonomy and self-regulation (Hu & Lam, 2010; Villamil & de Guerrero, 1998; Yang et al., 2006), to develop an awareness of audience and a sense of text ownership (O'Brien, 2004; Rollinson, 2005; Tsui & Ng, 2000), and to enjoy the 'informal peer support mechanisms of camaraderie, empathy and concern' (Hyland, 2006, p. 105; Cotterall & Cohen, 2003; Jacobs et al., 1998).

The Chi-square tests of independence between the students' previous experience and their feedback preferences have produced interesting and revealing results. Which source of feedback the students preferred was found to be unrelated to their perceptions of the usefulness of their previously-received teacher feedback. Notably, although some students reported receiving only 'somewhat useful' teacher feedback, they still held a firm belief in the authority of teachers and preferred to have teacher feedback alone. Conversely, a sizeable number of participants reported receiving 'useful' or 'very useful' peer feedback before but indicated a preference for teacher feedback alone in spite of such positive experience. These results corroborate Tsui and Ng's (2000) finding that Chinese students' opinions of the value of teacher feedback was independent of their experience with it. At first blush, these results seem rather surprising. We might reasonably expect students to value and seek out processes that help them improve, but a fair number of students in our study rejected the opportunity to do this. However, the results are less surprising if we consider the various time-honored expectations about teachers, their knowledge, and their role in the learning process that have been associated with Chinese and other Eastern societies (see Carson & Nelson, 1994, 1996; Hu, 2002, 2005b; Jacobs, 1987; Nelson & Murphy, 1992, 1993; Zhang, 1995). With their historical roots in the Confucian tradition, contemporary sociocultural and educational practices in mainland China set great store by a hierarchical but harmonious relationship between teacher and student, celebrate the ideal of the teacher 'as a virtuoso performer' (Paine, 1990, p. 54), and value the respectful acquisition of received knowledge (Hu, 2002). Teachers are expected to play a directive role in the learning process, to be 'highly authoritative sources of knowledge' (Tweed & Lehman, 2002, p. 96), and to hold the prerogative of evaluating students' work and progress. A good teacher is commonly held to be one 'who knows what is useful and important to the students, has an intimate knowledge of the students' level... [and] has all the correct answers' (Hu, 2002, p. 99). Students, on the other hand, are expected to respect their teachers and to be receptive to the authoritative knowledge imparted by their teachers. These prevalent practices, beliefs and assumptions can not only account for why some of our participants preferred to have only teacher feedback despite their less-than-happy previous experiences with teacher feedback; they also shed light on why other participants preferred to receive teacher feedback alone in spite of their positive experiences with peer feedback.

Unlike previous experience with teacher feedback, the students' previous experience with peer feedback was found to be related to their feedback preferences. Students without peer feedback experience or with negative experience were much more likely to choose teacher feedback alone, whereas students who had received useful peer feedback in the past were much more likely to prefer both teacher and peer feedback. These results suggest the effects of factors other than sociocultural influences or culturally-based ideas about teachers. The impact of students' experience with peer feedback on their receptivity to the pedagogical activity has been discussed elsewhere. For example, based on their observation that students with process-oriented collaborative writing experience were more receptive to peer suggestions, Connor and Asenavage (1994) suggested that 'students' previous experience with collaborative activities may be a good indicator' (p. 26) of their receptivity to peer feedback. Yang et al. (2006) also commented that students' peer feedback experience can have positive impacts on their perception of this pedagogical activity. However, Hu and Lam (2010) did not find any impact of previous peer feedback experience on students' peer review performance in their study. They interpreted this result as indicating that Chinese students having no previous experience with peer feedback could be as receptive to peer feedback as those with such experience. Notably, the researchers also sounded a note of caution. As they acknowledged, the methodological limitation of using only a gross measure of previous experience (i.e. having vs. not having participated in peer review before) left the observed lack of a statistically significant relationship inconclusive. Furthermore, there might have been a complicating factor in that study in that the participants were students from China who were pursuing their master's degree in Singapore. There is good reason to believe that they were highly motivated and eager to get the most out of any pedagogical activity that would improve their L2 writing competence, including peer review.

Consistent with the results of the statistical analyses, the qualitative analysis of the reasons given for the indicated feedback preferences also revealed the impact of the students' beliefs on their preferred sources of feedback.

The great popularity of teacher feedback for the students was clearly related to a strong faith in teachers' competence and the authority of their knowledge, a relationship that has been uncovered in other studies as well (e.g. Hu & Lam, 2010; Tsui & Ng, 2000; Yang et al., 2006). Paralleling this strong faith in teachers and their feedback was another popular belief, the belief that peers would be much limited in their ability to use English and to give sophisticated feedback on each other's writing. Our analysis further revealed that when students pitted teacher and peer feedback against each other and perceived them as being in a competing relationship, they tended to prefer the former over the latter. However, when students perceived teacher and peer feedback as sources of information that could complement each other in multiple respects, they were inclined to see the latter as a desirable source of information as well.

To conclude our discussion, our study has come up with a more complex picture of Chinese students' preferences for feedback on their L2 writing and factors shaping their feedback preferences than what some previous research has suggested. On the one hand, some of our findings have corroborated results obtained in previous studies. For example, like students in other studies (e.g. Hu & Lam, 2010; Tsui & Ng, 2000; Zhang, 1995), many of our participants had a deep-seated trust in and a strong preference for teacher feedback in spite of their previous unfavorable experience with teacher feedback and/or their favorable experience with peer feedback. On the other hand, our study has also yielded new or different results from those reported elsewhere. For instance, we have found that previous experience can relate to feedback preferences differently depending on the source of feedback in question. In contrast to earlier findings about Chinese students' unwillingness to criticize others' work so as to maintain interpersonal harmony (Carson & Nelson, 1994; Nelson & Carson, 1998), avoidance of criticism does not seem to be a big issue in our study. Although a few students in this study voiced concerns about peers trying to be uncritical and complimentary, the number was too small to be significant. Furthermore, the very desire for critical comments is evidence of these students' understanding of the value of critical behavior in peer review. To sum up, our students did not form a monolithic group that was antithetical to peer review. Nor did they embrace peer feedback without an experiential grounding or cognizance of the potential benefits offered by such feedback. Rather, our study has uncovered a diversity of experience, perceptions and beliefs that may interact with different sources of feedback in complex ways to shape individual students' feedback preferences.

6 Conclusion

That the majority of the participants evaluated their previous experience with peer feedback positively and welcomed such feedback as a useful source of information constitutes good support for the use of peer review with Chinese EFL learners in China. Several implications can be derived from our findings for an effective use of peer review as an instructional activity. First, good experience with peer feedback can help students perceive peer review more positively. Thus, providing opportunities for students to engage in well prepared and carefully implemented peer review tasks can be a useful avenue to pursue in developing a favorable attitude toward this pedagogical activity. Second, in view of the prevalent belief in the superiority of teacher feedback over peer feedback, there is a great need to raise students' awareness of the various benefits that peer review can offer and the many ways in which peer feedback can usefully complement teacher feedback (Berg, 1999; Hu, 2005a; Stanley, 1992). To this end, explicit teacher explanation and guided student discussion about its benefits have been found to be effective (e.g. Berg, 1999; Ferris, 2003; Hu, 2005a). Finally, given the widespread student perception about the usefulness of peer feedback being largely restricted to lower-level problems, it is imperative to build up students' confidence in and capability of dealing with higher-level issues in their writing (also see Arndt, 1993; Lockhart & Ng, 1995). Training students to make 'productive response and revision' (Rollinson, 2005, p. 27) through demonstration and modeling with peer review samples or teachers' thinking-aloud protocols (e.g. Berg, 1999; Ferris, 2003; Hu, 2005a; Min, 2006) can promote their ability to both review peers' work and revise their own.

In spite of the insights gained in this study, we are aware of its limitations. One limitation lies in the lack of in-depth interview data to further explore some of the interesting issues arising in the questionnaire data. The questionnaire was administered anonymously to assure the students that their candid responses to the questions would not result in adverse repercussions for them. This was especially important because the survey was conducted near the end of the semester, when teachers were about to give final grades. However, this anonymity made it impossible for us to follow up on individual students' survey responses. A second limitation is that we have not been able to investigate the impact of previous experience with peer feedback training on feedback preference because none of our participants had received such training before. We suggest that these limitations can be addressed in future studies which are carried out at a less sensitive time and which involve students with previous peer review training. We also suggest that another useful path for teacher-researchers to explore would be to carry out action research with Chinese students of different profiles to determine the most effective ways of training different students to engage in peer review.

References

Amores, M. J. (1997). A new perspective on peer-editing. *Foreign Language Annals, 30*, 513–522.

Arndt, V. (1993). Response to writing: Using feedback to inform the writing process. In M. N. Brock & L. Walters (Eds.), *Teaching composition around the Pacific Rim* (pp. 90–116). Clevedon: Multilingual Matters.

Berg, E. C. (1999). The effects of trained peer response on ESL students' revision types and writing quality. *Journal of Second Language Writing, 8*, 215–241.

Carson, J. G., & Nelson, G. L. (1994). Writing groups: Cross-cultural issues. *Journal of Second Language Writing, 3*, 17–30.

Carson, J. G., & Nelson, G. L. (1996). Chinese students' perceptions of ESL peer response group interaction. *Journal of Second Language Writing, 5*, 1–19.

Cohen, J. (1988). *Statistical power analysis for the behavioral sciences* (2nd ed.). Hillsdale, NJ: Lawrence Erlbaum.

Connor, U., & Asenavage, K. (1994). Peer response groups in ESL writing classes: How much impact on revision? *Journal of Second Language Writing, 3*, 257–276.

Cotterall, S., & Cohen, R. (2003). Scaffolding for second language writers: Producing an academic essay. *ELT Journal, 57*, 158–166.

DiPardo, A., & Freedman, S. W. (1988). Peer response groups in the writing classroom. *Review of Educational Research, 58,* 119–149.

Elbow, P. (2000). *Everyone can write.* New York: Oxford University Press.

Ferris, D. (2003). *Response to student writing.* Mahwah, NJ: Lawrence Erlbaum.

Field, A. (2005). *Discovering statistics using SPSS* (2nd ed.). London: Sage.

Gere, A. R. (1987). *Writing groups: History, theory, and implications.* Carbondale, IL: Southern Illinois University Press.

de Guerrero, M. C. M., & Villamil, O. S. (1994). Social-cognitive dimensions of interaction in L2 peer revision. *The Modern Language Journal, 78*, 484–496.

de Guerrero, M. C. M., & Villamil, O. S. (2000). Activating the ZPD: Mutual scaffolding in L2 peer revision. *The Modern Language Journal, 84*, 51–68.

Hattie, J., & Timperley, H. (2007). The power of feedback. *Review of Educational Research, 77*, 81–112.

Hu, G. (2002). Potential cultural resistance to pedagogical imports: The case of communicative language teaching in China. *Language, Culture and Curriculum, 15*, 93–105.

Hu, G. (2005a). Using peer review with Chinese ESL student writers. *Language Teaching Research, 9*, 321–342.

Hu, G. (2005b). Professional development of secondary EFL teachers: Lessons from China. *Teachers College Record, 107*, 654–705.

Hu, G., & Lam, S. T. E. (2010). Issues of cultural appropriateness and pedagogical efficacy: Exploring peer review in a second language writing class. *Instructional Science, 38,* 371–394.

Hyland, F. (2000). ESL writers and feedback: Giving more autonomy to students. *Language Teaching Research, 4,* 33–54.

Hyland, K. (2006). *English for Academic Purposes.* London: Routledge.

Hyland, K., & Hyland, F. (2006a). Feedback on second language students' writing. *Language Teaching, 39,* 83–101.

Hyland, K., & Hyland, F. (Eds). (2006b). *Feedback in second language writing.* New York: Cambridge University Press.

Jacobs, G. M. (1987). First experiences with peer feedback on compositions: Student and teacher reactions. *System, 15,* 325–333.

Jacobs, G. M., Curtis, A., Braine, G., & Huang, S.-Y. (1998). Feedback on student writing: Taking the middle path. *Journal of Second Language Writing, 7,* 307–317.

Kachru, B. B. (1986). *The alchemy of English.* Oxford: Pergamon Press.

Leki, I. (1990). Potential problems with peer responding in ESL writing classes. *CATESOL Journal, 3,* 5–19.

Liu, J., & Sadler, R. W. (2003). The effect and affect of peer review in electronic versus traditional modes on L2 writing. *Journal of English for Academic Purposes, 2,* 193–227.

Lockhart, C., & Ng, P. (1995). Analyzing talk in ESL peer response groups: Stances, functions, and content. *Language Learning, 45,* 605–651.

Mangelsdorf, K. (1992). Peer reviews in the ESL composition classroom: What do the students think? *ELT Journal, 46,* 274–284.

Mangelsdorf, K., & Schlumberger, A. (1992). ESL student response stances in a peer-review task. *Journal of Second Language Writing, 1,* 235–254.

Mendonca, C. O., & Johnson, K. E. (1994). Peer review negotiations: Revision activities in ESL writing instruction. *TESOL Quarterly, 28,* 745–769.

Min, H.-T. (2005). Training students to become successful peer reviewers. *System, 33,* 293–308.

Min, H.-T. (2006). The effects of trained peer review on EFL students' revision types and writing quality. *Journal of Second Language Writing, 15,* 118–141.

Nelson, G. L., & Carson, J. G. (1998). ESL students' perceptions of effectiveness in peer response groups. *Journal of Second Language Writing, 7,* 113–131.

Nelson, G. L., & Murphy, J. M. (1992). An L2 writing group: Task and social dimensions. *Journal of Second Language Writing, 1,* 171–193.

Norušis, M. J. (2006). *SPSS 14.0 guide to data analysis.* Upper Saddle River, NJ: Prentice Hall.

O'Brien, T. (2004). Writing in a foreign language: Teaching and learning. *Language Teaching, 37,* 1–28.

Paine, L. (1990). The teacher as virtuoso: A Chinese model for teaching. *Teachers College Record, 92,* 49–81.

Paulus, T. M. (1999). The effect of peer and teacher feedback on student writing. *Journal of Second Language Writing, 8,* 265–289.

Rollinson, P. (2005). Using peer feedback in the ESL writing class. *ELT Journal, 59,* 23–30.

Sengupta, S. (1998). Peer evaluation: 'I am not the teacher.' *ELT Journal, 52,* 19–28.

Stanley, J. (1992). Coaching student writers to be effective peer evaluators. *Journal of Second Language Writing, 1,* 217–233.

Triandis, H. C. (1995). *Individualism and collectivism.* Boulder, CO: Westview.

Tsui, A. B. M., & Ng, M. (2000). Do secondary L2 writers benefit from peer comments? *Journal of Second Language Writing, 9,* 147–170.

Tuzi, F. (2004). The impact of e-feedback on the revisions of L2 writers in an academic writing course. *Computers and Composition, 21,* 217–235.

Tweed, R. G., & Lehman, D. R. (2002). Learning considered within a cultural context: Confucian and Socratic approaches. *American Psychologist, 57,* 89–99.

Villamil, O. S., & de Guerrero, M. C. M. (1996). Peer revision in the L2 classroom: Social-cognitive activities, mediating strategies, and aspects of social behavior. *Journal of Second Language Writing, 5,* 51–75.

Villamil, O. S., & de Guerrero, M. C. M. (1998). Assessing the impact of peer revision on L2 writing. *Applied Linguistics, 19,* 491–514.

Yang, M., Badger, R., & Yu, Z. (2006). A comparative study of peer and teacher feedback in a Chinese EFL writing class. *Journal of Second Language Writing, 15,* 179–200.

Zhang, S. (1995). Reexamining the affective advantage of peer feedback in the ESL writing class. *Journal of Second Language Writing, 4,* 209–222.

Chapter 5

Thesis and Dissertation Writing: Moving Beyond the Text

Brian Paltridge and Lindy Woodrow

1 Introduction

There are a number of discussions in the literature about the issues that second and foreign language students face when writing a thesis or dissertation in English. These include books that are aimed at supervisors such as Paltridge and Starfield's (2007) *Thesis and Dissertation Writing in a Second Language* and Ryan and Zuber-Skerritt's (1999) *Supervising Post-graduates from Non-English Speaking Backgrounds,* as well as books which reflect on students' writing experiences such as Casanave's (2002) *Writing Games,* Prior's (1998) *Writing/Disciplinarity,* and Casanave and Li's (2008) *Learning the Literacy Practices of Graduate School.* Researchers such as Belcher (1994), Belcher and Hirvela (2005), Braine (2002), Cadman (1997), Dong (1998), Gosden (1996), Hirvela and Belcher (2001), Paltridge (2012) and Starfield (2003, 2010) discuss these issues further. Few of these studies, however, discuss these issues within a setting where students are attending an instructed course on thesis and dissertation writing, although authors such as Allison et al. (1998), Paltridge (2003) and Starfield (2003) do touch on this in their discussions about the courses they have taught on this topic.

This chapter discusses the experiences of a group of students who were undertaking a course on thesis and dissertation writing at a university in Australia. The group comprised both local and international students, native and non-native English speaking students. As part of the course, the students were asked to write reflections on their experience of writing a thesis or dissertation in English. The students wrote these reflections in online journals that were posted on a blog for comment and feedback from the teacher of the course. The students were doing Master's or Doctoral degrees in areas such as business, economics, education, social work and veterinary science. This chapter discusses the experiences of the non-native English speaking students who were taking the course.

2 Background to the Study

One of the aims of teaching English for Academic Purposes (EAP) is the acquisition of what Bhatia (2004) terms 'generic competence'; that is, the ability to participate in and respond to new and recurring genres. This includes the ability to construct, use, and exploit generic conventions to achieve particular communicative ends. Bhatia defines generic competence as being different from, yet including, linguistic competence. That is, it includes both mastery of the language code and the ability to use textual, contextual, and pragmatic knowledge to both interpret and create contextually appropriate texts as instances of a particular genre. Generic competence is not simply about the ability to reproduce discourse forms (Berkenkotter & Huckin, 1995). It is the ability to understand what happens in real world interactions and to use this understanding to participate in real world communicative practices (Bhatia, 1999).

Clearly, then, EAP teaching needs to focus on more than just the development of students' linguistic competence. While a certain level of linguistic competence is clearly necessary, it is not, however, sufficient for students to be able to succeed in academic settings. To effectively use an academic genre, students also need knowledge of the culture, circumstances, purposes, and motives that prevail in particular academic settings (Johns, 1997). Writing an academic text, then, requires much more than having an appropriate level of language proficiency. It also requires an understanding of the social and cultural context in which the text occurs as well as how this impacts on what the students write, and under what conditions they write it.

Previous research into academic literacies has shown that students are not always aware of the university's or their department's expectations of them (Lea, 1995; Lea & Street, 1998; Lillis & Scott, 2008). While this is true of both native and non-native English speaking students, understanding the culture of the university is arguably more difficult for the latter because they may come from a context where the conditions and expectations of academic study may be quite different from the situation they now find themselves in (Ballard & Clanchy, 1997; Johns, 1997; Myles & Cheng, 2003; Paltridge & Starfield, 2007; Starfield, 2010). In Australia, studying for a research degree is very different from doing a research degree in countries such as the US where students undertake courses as part of their degree. In Australian research degrees, students typically fulfil the requirements of the degree purely by undertaking research and writing this up in a dissertation. Students are allocated a supervisor and are expected to work independently. They need to conceptualise their research project, write and defend a research proposal, and carry out their research. Study at this level is also very different from study at the postgraduate coursework level. Ballard and Clanchy (1997) make the distinction between an analytical teaching and learning style in taught coursework degrees and a more speculative style in research degrees. In research degrees, the role of the supervisor is seen as collegial rather than authoritarian, and skills of hypothesising and speculating are highly valued, in addition to the critical skills valued in coursework degrees. Research degrees typically demand independent work rather than group- and teacher-focused tasks as is the case with coursework degrees. A further difficulty for some non-native English speaking students is that their prior academic experience may have been characterised by reproductive teaching and learning practices, with the teacher being the most important source of information and assessment. High value may have been placed on the reproduction and memorisation of information (Ballard & Clanchy, 1997). To switch from one academic climate to another can be difficult for all students. However, the challenge is particularly difficult for international non-native English speaking students who, in addition to a lack of understanding of the new and different academic culture, are also working in a second language (Braine, 2002; Casanave & Li, 2008).

This chapter considers this issue by examining the comments made by non-native English speaking students in a dissertation writing class, and the questions that they ask about the social and cultural context in which their dissertation is being produced and, in turn, assessed. In particular, it looks at issues 'outside of the text' (Freedman, 1999) that students raise and that they need to understand in order to succeed in their particular academic setting.

2.1 Context of the study: The writing course

The writing course described in this chapter was run as a credit-bearing course for students who needed to write a dissertation in their degree. This course was introduced to support students in their dissertation writing in a way that often does not occur when the only other reader of their text is their supervisor and, at a later stage, their examiners. Prior to the introduction of this course, the conveying of information concerning dissertation writing had been left to the students' supervisors. However, the amount of support provided by individual supervisors varied. By grouping students and centralising this, instruction was thought to be more efficient. A language expert, who was also an academic with a PhD, taught the course. The course was informed by theories of genre and writing (e.g. Bhatia, 2004; Devitt, 2004), academic literacies (Blommaert et al., 2007; Lea, 2004; Lea & Street, 1998; Lillis & Scott, 2008; Street, 2010) and the notion of students researching their own writing (Johns, 1997).

The course comprised thirteen two-hour seminars run over a thirteen-week semester. The course was supported by an e-learning site to facilitate access to materials, communication between students, and for students to receive feedback from the instructor. The course had a particular emphasis on the social construction of writing in which students were encouraged to think about the academic discourse community they are a member of and how the values and expectations of this community influenced the texts they needed to write. The sessions were broadly organised according to the sections found in a 'simple traditional' dissertation (introduction, literature review, methodology, results, discussion and conclusion) (Paltridge, 2002). Whilst it is acknowledged that there are many different types of dissertation (Dong, 1998; Thompson, 1999; Paltridge, 2002; Paltridge & Starfield, 2007), these sections seem to exist in most theses and dissertations, in some way or other, regardless of the orientation of the student's project.

The sessions typically included presentation and analysis of extracts from previous students' dissertations, and discussion of how these sample texts could be drawn on to inform the students' writing. The lecturer synthesised common practice in the area concerned, supporting this with university policy documents where relevant. The students examined a range of theses and dissertations and carried out focused genre analysis tasks on the texts. They then discussed practice in relation to their own dissertation and area of study. As follow up, readings from research into dissertation writing and sections from dissertation writing manuals were made available and the students were able to discuss issues that concerned them through the online journals that they kept for the course.

3 The Students' Reflections

The cohort of students in this particular course comprised 27 students ($M = 7$; $F = 20$). Two students dropped out because of work commitments and another three students audited but did not contribute to the journals. Fourteen of the students were studying for doctoral degrees (PhD, Doctor of Education, Doctor of Social Work); two were studying for a Master of Philosophy with the view to upgrading to a doctoral degree, and eleven were writing a dissertation as part of their master's degree. The non-native English speaking students came from different backgrounds (Germany, China, Taiwan, Hong Kong, Singapore, Malaysia, Indonesia, Korea, Vietnam, Japan and Bangladesh). The students were at different stages of their dissertation writing, with some nearing completion and some in the early stages of drafting a formal proposal for their dissertation.

As part of the course, students were expected to reflect on issues in their dissertation writing by keeping individual online journals. Most students contributed to the online discussions. In the first instance, the postings were private between the instructor and the student. At the request of the students, the postings were made available to other students so that all of the students enrolled in the course could communicate with each other. The opportunity to communicate privately with the instructor was retained but this was rarely used.

The data were collected through the course webpage with the participants' permission. The topics that were suggested for the postings dealt with expectations of a dissertation, supervisor relationships, academic writing, writing about the research literature, research methodology, results and conclusions of the study, and plans after submission. These topics reflected the main topics in the dissertation writing course and served as an initial area for analysis. However, students were not limited by the designated topics. They could reflect on any issue that concerned them. Self-initiated entries occurred usually in reaction to a situation arising in that week and reflected an urgency a student had, for example, a supervisor issue. This meant that sometimes the categories overlapped.

While some of the reflections discussed the issue of the actual writing of their dissertation, many of the comments addressed much broader issues, showing that it is often difficult to separate the role of being a writing teacher from that of being an advisor on broader issues that are related to the research and writing experience. The students also discussed more personal issues such as dealing with their insecurities, managing student-supervisor relations, what students can expect their supervisor will (and will not) do for them, as well as what they might do in their future careers. Indeed, many of the topics the students discussed reflected the complex nature of genre knowledge including aspects of social and cultural (and indeed interpersonal) knowledge rather than just linguistic knowledge, showing the importance of moving beyond the text (Freedman, 1999) in academic writing instruction to help these (and indeed all) students achieve their goal of becoming members of their desired academic and disciplinary communities.

3.1 Issues emerging from the data

The participants' entries were analysed for recurring themes. The first journal focused on the students' motivation for studying. This served as an initial point for collegial contact as it provided personal information to the group. Subsequently, students reflected on their supervisory experience, reasons for choosing their study, dealing with insecurities, time management, motivation and student-supervisor expectations.

3.1.1 Reasons for choosing their study

Students were first of all asked to reflect on the reasons for choosing the topic of their research. This was chosen as an initial focus of the online discussion not only to familiarise the students with each other but also to raise issues of supervisor input. In some cultures supervisors are more dominant in the research process, including the selection of the research topic. The data did not, in every case, support this supposition. Of the eight students who reflected on this topic, the majority of the postings indicated very personal reasons for choosing a research topic. For example:

> I feel so strongly about the subject because it is what I have believed since my youth. (Tom) (All names in this chapter are pseudonyms)
>
> Before doing this topic, I haven't any theoretical frame, but I have some living experiences about that. For example, in most situations, those ordinary people experiencing high risks are always associated with negative outcomes. However, there are always some people who also experience high risks but develop very well. Thus these examples force me to think about the reasons. Sometimes, I also reflect on my past experience: when I face difficulty, what factors are important for me to deal with it? (Lily)

For one participant in the area of science, however, the topic for her research had been assigned by her supervisor:

> The background for my study is based on research that has been conducted by my supervisor and her colleagues and collaborators. (Serena)

Thus, something as seemingly simple as choosing a research topic is situated within the broader context of the research setting. In some cases, the topic and the theoretical framework are assigned by the student's supervisor, perhaps because the student's project is part of larger funded project and a continuation of the supervisor's previous work. In others, however, it is the student's responsibility to find a suitable topic. In one case, in a course one of us once taught, a student said he had waited all year for his supervisor to give him his topic. Then he realised this wasn't going to happen; he had to do this himself. So what for some students in the class was simply part of their knowledge of what is involved in doing doctoral research was for him a completely unfamiliar concept. Genre knowledge, then, is not only situated, it is often very local (Pennycook, 2010). This is something that many students are not aware of and needs to be discussed with them.

3.1.2 Reasons for choice of methodology

The participants reported using a range of methodologies and methods for their study. Table 5.1 lists some of these.

The students' reflections described their reasons for their choice of methodology. They recognised the influence of their disciplinary context and the values held in their discipline when reflecting on their methodology:

> Heuristic enquiry demands, necessitates, intimate and personal engagement of the researcher with not only the research, but the participant as well. There is shared commonality in the lived experience of that which brings researcher and co-researcher, that is, the participant, together. (Jane)
>
> I chose to use multiple case study method to gain in-depth data and comprehensive analysis from the stories of several participants with different backgrounds. Furthermore, multiple case studies help to improve the quality of theory building. (Lee)
>
> In pure science, methodology is a very laborious and detailed chapter outlining the step-by-step procedure of research. Every single thing about

Table 5.1 Method/methodology and disciplines of participants

Method/methodology	Discipline
Heuristic enquiry	Social Work, Social Policy
Action research	Education
In-depth interviews	Education, TESOL, Economics and Business
Phenomenology	Psychology
Discourse analysis	Economics and Business
Grounded theory	Education
Econometric methods	Economics and Business
Scientific experiment	Veterinary Science
Mixed methods	TESOL, Education
Quantitative questionnaires	TESOL
Qualitative questionnaires	TESOL
Case study	Social Work

the samples, methods and the materials used must be explained specifically to enable replication of research or lab work by anyone reading the journal/dissertation. (Serena)

The students found that the sharing of their reflections about methodology was helpful as it raised awareness of a range of methodological options and thus it required them to think more deeply about their own methodological choices.

I have learnt a lot since taking this course. I guess because the methodology and thinking is set in my discipline, taking a class with students with mainly qualitative backgrounds has made me more aware and question the philosophy behind the economics and econometrics way of thinking. (Fiona)

This sharing of information raised student awareness that there is not one 'right' way to engage in research. Any 'right' way, they found, was highly influenced by the research context in which the study was located. Notwithstanding this, they still needed to be able to account for their methodological choices. By explicitly focusing on such issues with students working across diverse areas of research, it was possible to help the students gain a broader perspective on the nature of their research and, in turn, their dissertation.

3.1.3 Dealing with insecurities

Being engaged in a research degree can cause insecurities to surface. Students undertaking a PhD degree, for instance, are often mature, experienced professionals who have high status in their own professional contexts. On crossing over into academia, such students may experience insecurities with their new identity as a researcher and as an academic. It was this group of students who reported experiencing the 'imposter syndrome' (Brems et al., 1994; Clance & Imes, 1978). This refers to the feelings of self-doubt that some students experience in relation to their perceived competence as a researcher. It can also reflect perfectionism whereby the dissertation never reaches the student's expectations. Paltridge and Starfield (2007) suggest that the imposter syndrome affects second language students more acutely as they may perceive English proficiency and intellectual ability as being related. The students in our class talked about their fears of being 'found out' as not being competent researchers. For example, one student said:

My heart was pounding and I felt as though my head was going to burst. I looked at everyone and thought to myself that I was in the company of experienced researchers; was my work good enough, would I 'cut it' as a researcher? I realise now, although I didn't know it at the time that I was suffering an acute attack of the dreaded Imposter Syndrome. (Jane)

3.1.4 Time management

The data from the journals also yielded issues relating to time management. Managing time in a research degree can be challenging because there can be so many unpredictable elements to research. For example, it may be necessary for a student to delve into an area of the literature that he/she is unfamiliar with, or it may take a long time to get approval from an ethics committee. Combining study, work and family requires careful negotiation to avoid one of these areas suffering because of the others (Rudestam & Newton, 2007). Indeed, some students reported finding it a challenge to strike a balance among their various commitments.

> The reason causes my progress moving like a snail is the duty to take care of my baby. When he's healthy I got only maximum 4 hours but when he's unwell I can barely have time to study. (Linda)
>   I can relate to those people who are writing about time management. The more I read, the more I seem to discover to read.... where does it stop?! I am not sure how I would go trying to meet self-imposed deadlines. (Rachel)

As High and Montague (2006) point out, planning and time management are key to a student's success. Many students underestimate the time it will take them to complete their degree. This is especially the case when factors beyond the research itself intervene, and draw students' time away from the carrying out of their research.

3.1.5 Issues with supervision

Issues with supervision were also raised. One of the issues relates to a mismatch between the student's expectations and the supervisor's idea of what the role of a supervisor entails, for example, in relation to the amount and type of input that would be provided by the supervisor. Another issue that emerged in our data concerns disagreements concerning the direction of the student's research. The students who referred to these problems experienced a great deal of worry and frustration and were greatly affected by them. The quotes that follow illustrate this.

> Unfortunately, my supervisor was also advised that I was on the wrong track and now I need to convince her that we need to stick to the original plan as first intended. Do you have any advice of the best way of going about this as I realise that I do not have the status or kudos of a visiting professor! (Susan)
>
> But for a moment, it really made me feel totally helpless. I'm still scarred over the situation and do not feel extremely confident over the outcome. It feels like a very risky move to change supervisors at this late stage but then again, change is definitely better than no change given the current circumstance and the stagnant state the dissertation was in last year. (Mary)

The expectations of supervision varied, however, greatly across the group. Some students reflected on previous experiences in their own countries and felt that they would like their supervisors to direct their project more.

> When in China the relationship between supervisor and student is more like the one between a mother and young daughter: the supervisor makes the decisions she suggests what to read, how to read, proofreading our drafts one sentence by one sentence, setting the goals to achieve tell us everything. (Rose)
>
> Initially I was wondering why not tell me directly what I should do next so that I can simply follow the suggestion and start doing the task. Later on I realised the supervisor was trying to make me a totally independent researcher.... However, I think, as a novice researcher it would be time-saving and straightforward if I can get a little bit of hints of what and how to do it. (Jin)
>
> In my country, generally speaking, a supervisor should select a research topic for a student and a student should obey his/her decisions and follow his/her directions without any violating opinions....... Therefore, I keep the same expectation from my supervisor and I would like to finish the study step-by-step by following her directions. I thought my supervisor should plan a clear map for me to follow and check the planned schedule regularly in order to ensure the project I am doing is on the right tract. Especially, as an international student, I have a language barrier to present my deep thoughts and sometimes have no ideas about what my

supervisor said. Then, a supervisor should have the patience to assist a student to finish the project, to check the writing of the dissertation and to ensure the grammatical structures and the whole passage are correct. After that, a supervisor should provide feedback as well; then a student can develop and improve the research competence. (Louise)

As Eley and Murray (2009) point out, the relationship between students and their supervisors is all-important. This can, and often does, vary cross-culturally (Owens, 2007). Because of the potential cultural differences in expectations, supervising research students from a different cultural and linguistic background is, for supervisors, often more complex than supervising students who have been schooled within the supervisor's own educational context. No two dissertation supervisions, further, are the same. We cannot always know what these differences will be, but supervisors and writing advisors do need to expect that there will be differences, and that it is often not just a case of expectations being 'the same but different', but rather a case of them being 'very very different'. Supervisors need to keep their minds open as to how they respond to such differences.

A number of books discuss the role of the supervisor and ways in which supervisors can support their students in the higher degree research process (e.g. Delamont et al., 1997; Eley & Murray, 2009; Wisker, 2005). Advice is given to supervisors on managing students and to students on managing their supervisor (e.g. Cryer, 2000; Phillips & Pugh, 2005; Sharp et al., 2002; Wisker, 2007). However, an area not typically covered in this literature is how non-native English speaking students can negotiate the relationship with their supervisor and how common understandings can be reached in these kinds of settings. Sometimes finding the 'right' supervisor can be a matter of chance (Deem & Brehony, 2000; Kuwahara, 2008; Starfield, 2010). This might arise for pragmatic reasons such as supervisors being allocated to students based on workload allocations rather than their subject expertise. This creates a real problem for students as the person they are studying with may not always be the best person for them in terms of subject-matter knowledge (and indeed supervisory experience).

3.1.6 Motivation

Motivation in dissertation writing may be difficult for students to maintain because of the scale and complexity of the project and the limited number of extrinsic motivators, such as exams or due dates. Most of the motivation needs to come from intrinsic sources, from within the student. Students need persistence and they need to maintain interest if they hope to complete their dissertation. Negative emotions such as self-doubt and flagging interest are common complaints in dissertation writing (Cryer, 2000). Throughout the journals that our students kept, reference was made to having to deal with negative emotions that threatened to sap their motivation:

> Recently I always have the feeling that there is a huge pressure on me, sometimes this feeling is overwhelming, especially when I was pretty tired of the reading and writing, or the part-time job at Subway. At that time I even began to doubt my ability. (Lee)
>
> There is nothing so terrible as spending many years on something and not being able to deliver your arguments soundly in a presentation. Then there is the fear that you may just look like a complete fool in front of your examiners. (Fiona)
>
> I find myself very motivated every time we have our weekly [dissertation writing] classes, as that is the only time I can fully think about writing and not my lab work. But when I reach home (about 2 hours later) I am always too tired to actually follow up on my 'brilliant' and exciting ideas for writing I had in class, and end up going to work the next day with my lab work as my priority again. This goes on every week, and I am finding this frustrating! (Serena)

4 Writing as Social Practice

So far, the examples we have given of the comments that the students made are all text external in that they were not, by and large, related to the actual writing of the students' texts. This does not mean, however, that writing is not influenced by social and cultural factors in the same way as other aspects of a student's research. Our students were, in general, aware of this, and they knew that the way they were required to write was very much influenced by these sorts of factors. As one student said:

> The norms of academic writing style in marketing and consumer research varies depending on one's research paradigm. The mainstream positivist paradigm would use a more formal and scientific discourse in its language constructions. On the other hand, the interpretive paradigm embraces a more diverse writing style which is but a reflection of their diverse research topics and methodologies incorporating the types found

in humanities and social sciences. Personal language is acceptable, and the writing style is much more reflective and interpretive. (Jeaney)

This reflects an understanding that writing is a social practice that varies with context, culture and genre (Street, 2010). Writing in the academy, for all students, involves the acquisition of a repertoire of linguistic practices which are based on complex sets of discourses, identities and values (Lea & Street, 1998). Students learn the preferred practices of particular settings, learning to understand, as they write, why they are writing as they are, and what the position they have taken implies. As another student commented:

> academic writing concerns more than acknowledging other peoples' ideas or avoiding plagiarisms, there are other norms, which are as important, to be considered. Such norms cover the clarity; conciseness; the use of personal pronouns; use of formal vocabulary; passive and active voice; expressing caution; and the use of complex and simple sentences. (Yenny)

Each of these is clearly related to the context, culture and genre of the doctoral dissertation and, importantly, issues of epistemology and identity, rather than just the acquisition of academic skills of their own (Street, 2010). So what, on first sight, may seem like a textual issue often is as much a social and cultural issue and really needs to be understood and explained to students in these terms as well.

5 Discussion and Conclusions

The reflections the students wrote, then, by and large, were about the social and cultural knowledge of what is involved in writing a thesis or dissertation. That is, they focused mainly on the 'complexities involved in academic communication' (Lillis & Scott, 2008, p. 6) and the contexts in which they were writing.

Concerns with supervisor relations, in particular, emerged as an issue of importance for the students. The issues that emerged often seemed to reflect a mismatch in student and supervisor perceptions of what their respective roles are. International students may come from a context where they would receive a lot more guidance from their supervisor. It is important, then, to discuss these sorts of issues in dissertation writing courses so that students are clear on what is expected of them by the institution and by their supervisor. As James and Baldwin (1999, p. 130) argue:

> The most rewarding supervisory relationships are those in which the lines of communication between student and supervisor are established early and clearly. The most frustrating are those in which supervisor and student are working at cross-purposes.

All of the students struggled with time management and motivational issues. The time management issues concerned making adequate progress as measured by milestones, such as the dissertation proposal defence required at the end of the first year of enrolment. Balancing family, work and study was a challenge in all of this. Motivational issues also reflected the students' perceptions of their ability to achieve their goals. This highlights the importance of supporting non-native English speaking students as they work towards membership of their desired academic community.

In Australian universities, support for non-native English speaking students comes in various forms and is available to varying degrees. The most common forms are through support provided by the supervisor and by EAP teachers working in learning centres. In either scenario, however, there can be problems. From the supervisor's perspective, while they will certainly be familiar with the expectations of a dissertation from their personal experience, they probably do not know a lot about writing or what this entails, especially from a second language perspective. On the other hand, EAP teachers know about writing but in many cases may be unfamiliar with what is involved in writing an extended research dissertation in a specialised field.

Johns (1988, 1997) recognises this difficulty by suggesting we train ESL students to 'act as researchers' as a way of helping them uncover the knowledge and skills that are necessary for membership of their particular academic community. As Johns (1997) argues, we cannot hope to predict all of our students' possible literacy requirements. We can, however, help them to ask questions of the texts they are required to produce, and the contexts in which these texts occur. In this way, we can help our students negotiate academic literacies (Zamel & Spack, 1998), learn the conversations of their disciplines (Bazerman, 1980; Flowerdew, 2000), as well as find out what counts in their area of study.

Clearly more than knowledge about language is needed for students to succeed in academic settings. Language *is*, however, important. The aim of our chapter is not to argue against helping students with language issues and helping them to structure their dissertations in appropriate ways. Both of these are essential. This, however, is not enough. Students also need to be helped to deal with social and cultural issues that surround their writing so that they can understand how they can go about achieving what it is that they want to do. The use of online journals, as we have described in this chapter, can give us important insights into students' writing experiences as well as help us 'see learners as they see themselves'. They can also help us to focus on 'not just what learners want to be able to **do** in a language but also who they want to **become** through language' (Belcher & Lukkarila, 2011, p. 89).

References

Allison, D., Cooley, L., Lewkowicz, J., & Nunan, D. (1998). Dissertation writing in action: The development of a dissertation writing support program for ESL graduate research students. *English for Specific Purposes, 17*, 199–217.

Ballard, B., & Clanchy, J. (1997). *Teaching international students: A brief guide for lecturers and supervisors.* Deakin, ACT: Education Australia.

Bazerman, C. (1980). A relationship between reading and writing: The conversational model. *College English, 41*, 656–661.

Belcher, D. (1994). The apprenticeship approach to advanced academic literacy: Graduate students and their mentors. *English for Specific Purposes, 13*, 23–34.

Belcher, D., & Hirvela, A. (2005). Writing the qualitative dissertation: What motivates and sustains commitment to a fuzzy genre? *Journal of English for Academic Purposes, 4*, 187–205.

Belcher, D., & Lukkarila, L. (2011). Identity in the ESP context: Putting the learner front and center in needs analysis. In D. Belcher, A. M. Johns & B. Paltridge (Eds.), *New directions in English for specific purposes research* (pp. 73–93). Ann Arbor: University of Michigan Press.

Berkenkotter, C., & Huckin, T. N. (1995). *Genre knowledge in disciplinary communication: Cognition/culture/power.* Hillsdale, NJ: Lawrence Erlbaum.

Bhatia, V. K. (1999, August). *Analysing genre: An applied linguistic perspective.* Keynote address given at the 12th World Congress of Applied Linguistics, Tokyo.

Bhatia, V. K. (2004). *Worlds of written discourse.* London: Continuum.

Blommaert, J., Street, B., & Turner, J. (2007). Academic literacies: What have we achieved and where to from here? *Journal of Applied Linguistics, 4*, 137–148.

Braine, G. (2002). Academic literacy and the non-native speaker graduate student. *Journal of English for Academic Purposes, 1*, 59–68.

Brems, C., Baldwin, M. R., Davis, L., & Namynuik, L. (1994). The imposter syndrome as related to teaching evaluations and advising relationships of university faculty members. *Journal of Higher Education, 65*, 183–193.

Cadman, K. (1997). Thesis writing for international students: A question of identity? *English for Specific Purposes, 16*, 3–14.

Casanave, C. P. (2002). *Writing games.* Mahwah: NJ: Lawrence Erlbaum.

Casanave, C. P., & Li, X. (Eds.). (2008). *Learning the literacy practices of graduate school.* Ann Arbor: University of Michigan Press.

Clance, P. R., & Imes, S. A. (1978). The imposter phenomenon in high achieving women: Dynamics and therapeutic interventions. *Psychotherapy: Theory, Research and Practice, 15*, 241–247.

Cryer, P. (2000). *The research student's guide to success* (2nd ed.). Buckingham, UK: Open University Press.

Deem, R., & Brehony, K. J. (2000). Doctoral students' access to research cultures – are some more unequal than others? *Studies in Higher Education, 25*, 149–165.

Delamont, S., Atkinson, P., & Parry, O. (1997). *Supervising the PhD.* Buckingham, UK: Open University Press.

Devitt, A. J. (2004). *Writing genres.* Carbondale, IL: Southern Illinois University Press.

Dong, Y. R. (1998). Non-native graduate students' thesis/dissertation writing in science: Self-reports by students and their advisors from two U.S. institutions. *English for Specific Purposes, 17*, 369–390.

Eley, A., & Murray, R. (2009). *How to be an effective supervisor.* Maidenhead, UK: Open University Press.

Flowerdew, J. (2000). Discourse community, legitimate peripheral participation, and the nonnative-English-speaker scholar. *TESOL Quarterly, 34*, 127–150.

Freedman, A. (1999). Beyond the text: Towards understanding the teaching and learning of genres. *TESOL Quarterly, 33*, 764–767.

Gosden, H. (1996). Verbal reports of Japanese novices' research writing practices in English. *Journal of Second Language Writing, 5*, 109–128.

High, C., & Montague, J. (2006). Planning and organizing your research. In S. Potter (Ed.), *Doing postgraduate research* (2nd ed.) (pp. 92–113). Milton Keynes, UK: Sage.

Hirvela, A., & Belcher, D. (2001). Coming back to voice: The multiple voices and identities of mature multilingual writers. *Journal of Second Language Writing, 10*, 83–106.

James, R., & Baldwin, G. (1999). *Eleven practices of effective postgraduate supervisors.* Melbourne: Centre for the Study of Higher Education and The School of Graduate Studies, The University of Melbourne.

Johns, A. M. (1988). The discourse communities dilemma: Identifying transferable skills for the academic milieu. *English for Specific Purposes, 7*, 55–59.

Johns, A. M. (1997). *Text, role and context: Developing academic literacies.* Cambridge: Cambridge University Press.

Kuwahara, N. (2008). It's not in the orientation manual: How a first-year doctoral student learned to survive in graduate school. In C. P. Casanave & X. Li (Eds.), *Learning the literacy practices of graduate school* (pp. 186–200). Ann Arbor: University of Michigan Press.

Lea, M. R. (1995). 'I thought I could write until I came here': Student writing in higher education. In D. Graddol & S. Thomas (Eds.), *Language in a changing Europe* (pp. 64–72). Clevedon, UK: Multilingual Matters.

Lea, M. R. (2004). Academic literacies: A pedagogy for course design. *Studies in Higher Education, 29*, 739–756.

Lea, M. R., & Street, B. (1998). Student writing in higher education: An academic literacies approach. *Studies in Higher Education, 23*, 157–172.

Lillis, T., & Scott, M. (2008). Defining academic literacies research: Issues of epistemology, ideology and strategy. *Journal of Applied Linguistics, 4*, 5–32.

Myles. J., & Cheng, L. (2003). The social and cultural life of non-native English speaking international graduate students at a Canadian university. *Journal of English for Academic Purposes, 2*, 247–263.

Owens, R. (2007). Valuing international research candidates. In C. Denholm & T. Evans (Eds.), *Supervising doctorates downunder: Keys to effective supervision in Australia and New Zealand* (pp. 146–154). Camberwell, VIC: ACER Press.

Paltridge, B. (2002). Thesis and dissertation writing: An examination of published advice and actual practice. *English for Specific Purposes, 21*, 125–143.

Paltridge, B. (2003). Teaching thesis and dissertation writing. *Hong Kong Journal of Applied Linguistics, 8*, 78–96.

Paltridge, B. (2012). Theses and dissertations in English for specific purposes. In C. Chapelle (Ed.), *The encyclopaedia of applied linguistics*. Hoboken, NJ: Wiley-Blackwell.

Paltridge, B., & Starfield, S. (2007). *Thesis and dissertation writing in a second language: A handbook for supervisors*. London: Routledge.

Pennycook, A. (2010). *Language as a local practice*. London: Routledge.

Phillips, E. M., & Pugh, D. S. (2005). *How to get a PhD* (4th ed.). Maidenhead: Open University Press

Prior, P. (1998). *Writing/disciplinarity*. Mahwah, NJ: Lawrence Erlbaum.

Rudestam, K. E., & Newton, R. R. (2007). *Surviving your dissertation* (3rd ed.). London: Sage Publications.

Ryan, Y., & Zuber-Skerritt, O. (Eds.). (1999). *Supervising postgraduates from non-English speaking backgrounds*. Buckingham: The Society for Research into Higher Education and the Open University Press.

Sharp, J. A., Peters, J., & Howard, K. (2002). *The management of a student research project* (3rd ed.). Aldershot, UK: Gower.

Starfield, S. (2003). The evolution of a thesis-writing course for arts and social sciences students: What can applied linguistics offer? *Hong Kong Journal of Applied Linguistics, 8*, 137–154.

Starfield, S. (2010). Fortunate travellers: Learning from the multiliterate lives of doctoral students. In P. Thompson & M. Walker (Eds.), *The Routledge doctoral supervisor's companion* (pp. 138–146). London: Routledge.

Street, B. (2010). Academic literacies: New directions in theory and practice. In J. Maybin & J. Swann (Eds.), *The Routledge companion to English language studies* (pp. 232–242). London: Routledge.

Thompson, P. (1999). Exploring the contexts of writing: Interviews with PhD supervisors. In P. Thompson (Ed.), *Issues in EAP writing research and instruction* (pp. 37–54). Reading: Centre for Applied Language Studies, University of Reading.

Wisker, G. (2005). *The good supervisor: Supervising postgraduate and undergraduate research for doctoral theses and dissertations*. Basingstoke, UK: Palgrave.

Wisker, G. (2007). *The postgraduate research handbook*. (2nd ed.). Basingstoke, UK: Palgrave.

Zamel, V., & Spack, R. (1998). Preface. In V. Zamel & R. Spack (Eds.), *Negotiating academic literacies* (pp. ix–xviii). Mahwah, NJ: Lawrence Erlbaum.

Part Two

Features of ESL/EFL Learner Discourses

Chapter 6

The Challenges of Writing a Successful Thesis Conclusion

Jo Lewkowicz

1 Introduction

The number of students undertaking higher degrees in and through the medium of English is rising, and this seems to be a worldwide phenomenon. The UK alone, which was reported in 2004 to have the second highest global market share of the Higher Education Industry after the US (Böhm et al., 2004), saw a staggering 80% rise in the number of overseas postgraduate students between 1996/1997 and 2002/2003 (*Overseas Students in the UK*, 2004), and a rise of 9.5% in the number of overseas postgraduates from the period 2007/2008 to 2008/2009 (Higher Education Statistics Agency, 2010). Böhm et al. in 2004 suggested that, given 'an optimistic scenario' (p. 6), by 2020, there would be in the UK over 850,000 international students (with more than 50% of these being postgraduates). Although this 'target' is now unlikely to be reached given the UK's introduction of new immigration rules in 2011 affecting non-EU citizens and the rising cost of higher education affecting all students (other than those wishing to study in Scotland), it must be remembered that not only students studying in English-medium countries such as the UK are using the English language to complete their postgraduate studies. Increasingly, for example, European Union countries are offering degree programmes in languages other than their official language *(Higher Education Admissions and Student Mobility within the EU, 2001)*.

Numerous factors have come together which may account for this promulgation of English in higher learning. Invariably, the globalization of English has played its part. The widespread use of English in academic publications, for example, has put pressure on those wishing to establish themselves in academia to be able to communicate in English (e.g. Cargill & O'Connor, this volume; Ferguson et al., 2011; Hyland, 2009; Lillis & Curry, 2010). Although the original estimates that 80% of scientific publications appear in English (e.g. Garfield, 1983, cited in Swales, 1990) are now recognized as exaggerated (Swales, 1990), there is no doubt that 'the anglo-phone grip on published research communication is both strong and tightening' (Swales, 1990, p. 97). Recognizing that so much scientific knowledge that students have to familiarize themselves with is in English, some countries such as the Netherlands are offering higher degree courses in English (Crystal, 2003).

Within the European Union, there are also numerous scientific organisations that use English as their working language. Among these are the European Academy of Anaesthesiology, the European Academy of Facial Surgery and the European Association of Cancer Research to mention just a few (Crystal, 2003). In addition, benchmarking practices evaluating research output in many universities throughout Europe rely on citation indices such as the Philadelphia List that privilege publications in English. This, for example, is the list adopted by the National Research Commission in Poland (Duszak & Lewkowicz, 2008). Thus, undertaking studies conducted in English may be seen as a move towards achieving long term academic objectives.

Much has been written in recent years about the greater commercialisation of higher education (see, for example, De Vita & Case, 2003; and for a discussion of some of its consequences, Devos, 2003, and Marginson, 2006, among others). Such commercialisation has also had its role in the promulgation of higher degrees taught in English. British universities, for example, 'make £2bn by selling degrees abroad' (Sudgen, 2009) through satellite campuses outside the UK. In addition, to attract foreign students, universities outside the core English-speaking countries have started offering higher degree programmes in English (Crystal, 2003) as well as jointly-run degrees with core country universities such as those from Great Britain, Australia and the United States.

The required outcome of such degrees is frequently a final dissertation or thesis written in English[1]. Many students are thus faced with the challenge of writing this extensive document in an additional or foreign language, often with limited guidance as to what the thesis should look like or contain. Students are supervised in their field of study by experts who may have limited knowledge or understanding of the language conventions that need to be employed in writing a thesis and who will likely not see their role as language consultants. Writing a thesis has thus, at least until comparatively recently, been considered a skill that one acquires through osmosis, as if absorbing the knowledge from those who have written a thesis before them. The situation has improved somewhat since the 1990s, and we are now seeing an increase in the number of systematic studies examining various aspects of thesis-writing in English (e.g. Bunton, 1998, 2002, 2005; Paltridge, 2002; Peters, 2011; Soler-Monreal et al., 2011; Thompson, 2001, 2005).

This chapter reviews some of the relevant literature in this area and then considers how the research carried out to date relates to those writing a thesis in English but outside a dominant English-medium culture. It reports on a study of 12 PhD conclusions written in English by postgraduate students in Poland as part fulfilment of their doctoral studies. The chapter then goes on to consider some of the differences between the findings reported in earlier studies and those obtained in the present study, as well as the pedagogical implications that arise from these differences.

2 Literature Review

As a number of researchers (e.g. Bunton, 2005; Starfield, 2003) have pointed out, whereas the research article (RA) genre has been extensively investigated in terms of its component parts (e.g. Samraj (2002) and Swales & Najjar (1987) looked at RA introductions; Yang & Allison (2003) looked at discussions and conclusions), the academic thesis has drawn much less attention. A reason that is commonly given for this is its length. Because the shorter research article is considered to mirror many of the same characteristics as the thesis, this has in the past resulted in using our knowledge of the way research articles are written as the basis for designing thesis writing coursebooks in English for second and foreign language learners (e.g. Cooley & Lewkowicz, 2003; Swales & Feak, 2004).

In recent years, however, the need to develop appropriate EAP materials based on authentic sources which postgraduate students can readily relate to has motivated studies of the thesis itself at Master's and PhD levels (Samraj, 2008). Some of these studies have focused on the overall organisation of the thesis. Paltridge (2002), for example, carried out an investigation of both Master's and PhD theses completed at an Australian university across a range of disciplines. He differentiated between four types of thesis which varied in terms of the body of the text. All types, however, had in common an introduction to the thesis as well as a conclusion.

Other studies of the thesis genre have focused on specific sections of the Master's and PhD thesis, the more substantive sections such as the introduction (e.g. Arulandu, 2006; Bunton, 2002; Samraj, 2008) and the discussion (e.g. Dudley-Evans, 1986; Rasmeenin, 2006), as well as those of less importance, at least in terms of judging the quality of the research, such as the acknowl-edgements (Hyland, 2004; Zhao & Jiang, 2010). The section that has come under greatest scrutiny is the introduction. This is perhaps not surprising as it is at the start of their thesis that writers have most in common—they have yet to establish themselves and their research. The conclusion, on the other hand, has drawn much less attention. This can be partially explained by the fact that the early studies of the thesis genre such as that carried out by Dudley-Evans (1986) on seven MSc theses did not distinguish between the discussion and the conclusion. However, more recent research (Bunton, 2005; Paltridge, 2002; Thompson, 2005) suggests that those writing a thesis include a separate 'Conclusion' in their work and that this needs to be analysed in its own right.

Bunton (2005) was able to show that the conclusion of the thesis, being part of a longer piece of writing, differs from the discussion section of the shorter research article. He based his analysis on 45 PhD conclusions which he subjected to a two-level 'Move and Step' analysis, describing the distinc-tion between the two in the following way: 'Move captures the function and purpose of the segment of text at the more general level, while the Step spells out more specifically the rhetorical means of realizing the function of the Move' (Bunton, 2005, p. 215, citing Yang & Allison, 2003, p. 370). He found that thesis conclusions may be of two types: the majority are 'thesis-oriented' in that they focus on the thesis itself, setting out to consolidate the research space following four moves: IR^C^P^FR, where IR stands for 'introductory restatement', C for 'consolidation of research space', P for 'practical implica-tions of the research' and FR for 'recommendations for future research'. All the conclusions in his sample included the consolidation of research space move, most had an introductory restatement, while the other two moves appeared optional. The other type of conclusion Bunton identified was 'field-oriented' in that they 'focussed mainly on the field and only mentioned the thesis and its findings or contributions in the context of the whole field' (Bunton, 2005, p. 215). This less frequently identified 'Conclusion' type tended to follow either a problem-solution or argument structure.

The studies reported so far have emerged predominantly from English-medium universities in core countries including Australia, Great Britain, and the USA, or in Hong Kong where, as Bunton (2005) notes in relation to his study, 'about 40% of the supervisors and 60% of the external examin-ers at the time were non-Chinese from other countries, indicating a strong influence of *international academic conventions* on the thesis writing process' (p. 210, my emphasis). To date, our understanding of thesis writing expec-tations and practices in non-core countries seems very limited. Swales

(2004), citing a study by Stalhammer (1998) of PhDs written in English at a Swedish university, suggests: 'From an overall reading of the available literature, a reasonable working assumption would be that the doctoral thesis or dissertation is lightly or only obscurely influenced by national traditions' (Swales, 2004, p. 103). However, as Lewkowicz (2009) has shown in a preliminary study of Master's theses 'Conclusions' written in English at a Polish university, the expectations of what to include in a thesis or how to structure and present information may be somewhat different to those discussed in the literature as a result of local expectations and traditions of academic writing. In order to determine whether such differences also occur in the writing at PhD level, this study takes a careful look at the conclusions of twelve theses completed at Polish universities. Of specific interest is whether these 'Conclusions' follow the generic structure proposed by Bunton (2005) and if not, what factors impact on the information presented in the conclusion and the structure of that information.

3 The Study

Twelve PhD theses from the field of English studies (i.e. linguistics, applied linguistics, literature and translation) were made available for analysis by the authors of the works (on the proviso that the writers' anonymity be maintained when reporting the results of this study). This field was chosen to ensure that all the writers had an excellent command of the English language and that difficulties with language did not impact on the writing outcomes. The theses had been successfully completed and defended at Polish universities between 2004 and 2008, where the vast majority of supervisors and examiners would have also been Polish. This is an important fact to note as it is likely that their expectations of the students' theses and writing would be partially, if not totally, determined by conventions internal to Poland.

Of interest for the study were the conclusions/concluding sections of the theses. These were selected for a number of reasons. In many cases, students are under intense pressure to complete their work and as Swales (2004) has pointed out, conclusions are often seen as the weakest part of the PhD document and therefore one with which students may need more guidance. Furthermore, by this stage of the writing process, the student researcher should have established his/her position in the field and it was of interest to ascertain whether this was evident in the students' writing and if so, how this was manifested. Finally, it was believed that the conclusion would allow for greater variability among writers than, for example, the introduction, where writers appear to have a common goal of acquainting readers with the topic at hand and the purpose of their study. By the conclusion, it is likely that the writers, having followed different trajectories through their theses, would have differing aims in bringing their work to a close, as has been suggested in Bunton's (2005) analysis.

Once the conclusions were identified, the procedure adopted by Bunton (2005) in his study of thesis conclusions was replicated. The conclusions were analysed according to their length, structure and the 'Moves and Steps' the writers had taken in achieving their writing goals, with a 'Move' being more general and reflecting the purpose of a segment of text, and a 'Step' being the specific means through which the Move is realized (Swales, 1990). The initial analysis revealed that not all the conclusions fitted the framework suggested by Bunton (2005). Therefore the conclusions were read and reread to determine what different moves or strategies were taken by the writers and what factors seemed to have an impact on the conclusions. The findings from the analysis of the PhD conclusions were then compared with the analysis of Master's thesis conclusions conducted earlier (Lewkowicz, 2009) and with the advice available to Polish PhD candidates in guidebooks on thesis writing.

4 Findings and Discussion

The findings from the analysis of the conclusions identified for this study are presented and discussed, first in terms of their overall structure, their length, and the approach adopted by individual writers. Then, the different types of conclusions that emerged from the analysis are presented and their characteristics described.

4.1 Identifying the conclusions

In the 12 theses analysed for this study, it was not difficult to identify the conclusion. All had a chapter or section so titled. A distinctive feature of nine of the conclusions was that, like the introduction to the thesis, the conclusion was presented as if separate from the body of the text. The conclusion was neither a numbered chapter nor part of the final chapter, and this feature was confirmed by scrutinizing the Table of Contents. The titles of these sections appeared indicative of the writers' intent and ranged from 'conclusion' (3 instances), 'conclusions' (4 instances), 'coda' (1 instance), to 'final remarks' (1 instance). The remaining three conclusions were numbered chapters titled 'Summary and conclusions', 'Conclusions and recommendations for further development of [the subject of investigation][2] and 'The way forward'. It will be noted that only one of these titles included the word 'summary'. Yet, as will be seen later, summarizing emerged as the primary aim of many of the concluding sections/chapters.

In academic books, it is not uncommon for the introduction and sometimes the conclusion to be set off from the rest of the text. It may be that the thesis is perceived as a text of similar nature, and this might explain the practice among Polish thesis writers of presenting the conclusion as an entity separate from the body of the text. This was a common feature in the Master's theses analysed as well (see Lewkowicz, 2009) and it appears to be in line with much of the advice available for writing a thesis in Polish (see, for example, Apanowicz, 2005; Mendel, 2009). Apanowicz (2005) specifies, 'The introduction as well as the conclusion also appear in the Table of Contents, but are not numbered or subdivided into sections' (p. 89, author's translation). Such advice could suggest that the conclusion is seen as being a less substantive part of the thesis - something that the reader could omit as one may do when using an academic textbook. However, Zenderowski (2009), admittedly addressing primarily students writing at the Master's level, has suggested that the conclusion, like the introduction, *is* important, though both these sections differ from the remaining chapters in that they are more focused, devoid of digressions, examples and other extraneous information. He further suggests that there should be a one-to-one correspondence between the introduction and the conclusion, with the latter showing the degree to which the questions/hypotheses presented at the outset have been addressed through the study undertaken.

4.2 Length of the conclusions

The conclusions varied in length from 2 pages to 14.5 pages. The average length was 5.75 pages, which is considerably shorter than the average of 17.2 for humanities and social science texts in Bunton's (2005) study, but longer than the two-page average length of the Master's thesis conclusions analysed in Lewkowicz (2009). The brevity of some of the conclusions, in comparison to the overall length of the theses (which varied from 155 pages to 576 pages, excluding references and appendices, with an average length of 275 pages), seems to confirm the notion that these sections are not seen by their authors as substantive. It would appear that these writers have not taken on board the guidelines offered in some Polish guidebooks regarding the importance of the conclusion section. The advice given in Mendel (2009), for example, is that '*important parts of the thesis are the introduction and conclusion*' (p. 52, my translation, original emphasis).

4.3 The use of headings

One of the main ways of indicating writer intent is through the use of headings and subheadings. As Bunton (2005) points out, section headings 'are helpful in showing what the writer is hoping to accomplish in different parts of the chapter' (p. 213). Yet, such headings were totally absent in seven of the thesis conclusions. In the remaining five conclusions, the number of subheadings varied from two to seven. Again, the average number of subheadings found in the conclusions in this study, 1.4, is considerably lower than the figure of 5.2 reported by Bunton (2005) for the humanities and social studies theses he looked at, which may be partly explained by the shorter average length of the conclusions in this study.

The majority of the subheadings were generic, indicating the purpose of the subsection, with such keywords as 'summary' or 'summative findings' appearing as an initial subheading and 'future research' occurring several times as the final subheading, but also appearing as a medial subheading (see Table 6.1). None of the headings were topic specific. The subheadings of one of the conclusions is of interest, since three of its seven subheadings related to specific chapters by number, indicating that the focus of the text to follow was on summarizing the main content of the chapter (a point that will be developed further).

4.4 Types of conclusions

Bunton (2005) differentiated between two types of conclusions: thesis-oriented and field-oriented. In this data set also, there were both types of conclusions. The majority, that is 11 of the 12, were thesis-oriented, while the remaining one, within the field of literary studies, was classified as field-

Table 6.1   Headings within the concluding section/chapter

Initial subheadings	Medial subheadings	Final subheadings
Introduction (2)	Problematic areas (1)	Directions for future research (1)
Summative findings (1)	Postulated conclusions (1)	Suggestions for future research (1)
Summary of findings (1)	Reflection (1)	The way forward (1)
	Summary of findings (1)	Towards future research avenues (1)
	Implications of findings (1)	Closing remarks (1)
	Suggestions for further research (1)	Coda (1)
	Chapter 1, 2, 3 etc. (1)	
	A few remarks on methodology (1)	

oriented. The thesis-oriented conclusions will be discussed first. Then the field-oriented conclusion will be presented.

4.4.1 Thesis-oriented conclusions

The thesis-oriented conclusions could be further subdivided according to the approach their writers adopted. While 9 of the writers adopted a more discursive style of writing, two of the conclusions were presented more or less entirely as bullet-pointed lists. The writers of these latter two conclusions seem to have adopted what could be termed a 'telegraphic style' of writing, aiming to summarize as briefly and as directly as possible the main points raised in the preceding chapters. One of these conclusions was made up of 3 bullet-pointed lists, with the first two summarizing different aspects of the research findings and the final one, illustrated in Example 1, offering a succinct list of potential follow-up studies.

Example 1

As a result of the above conclusions, the following areas of further research were identified:

- The influence of the content of the tasks, especially the context of the knowledge of other subjects on X [X = the materials under investigation].
- The influence of the response format of tasks on X.
- The influence of skill integration on X.
- Analysis of the individual tasks that make up X on the basis of the approach adopted in this dissertation.
- The influence of teaching methods adopted [in place A] on X.

The other thesis conclusion of this type first summarized in point form the main conclusions arising from the review of literature, that is the 'theoretical conclusions', then listed the assumptions adopted in the study and finally proceeded to two lists relating to different aspects of the findings, with some of the points in each of the lists being briefly elaborated.

Conclusions as summaries

The practice of summarizing the thesis as a whole was evident not only in one of the bullet-pointed conclusions, but also in four of the more discursive thesis-oriented conclusions. In one case, as indicated above, the intention of the author to summarize individual chapters was indicted by using chapter numbers as headings. In the other 3 instances, mention of the chapter was made within the text, as can be seen from the following examples:

Example 2

The work has been divided into several chapters. After a brief introduction, I proceed to the main tenants of Theory X paying particular attention to Y [Y = a way of implementing X theory to analysing text] ... Chapter two, which deals with failures in Theory X approaches is divided into two parts, the first of which presents various accounts of these failures whereas the second part is devoted entirely to Z's [Z = reference to the literature] classification of these failures ... In chapter three, I have given a short account of the problems of W [W = a form of analysing Theory X failures]...

Example 3

Chapter Three, has intended to describe the process of developing X [X = a teaching module]. ... Chapter Four has reported on the first classroom implementation of X in Y [Y = a place] ... Chapter Five has dealt with the classroom implementation of the final version of X ...

Example 4

The first three chapters addressed Objective 1 of the thesis. In Chapter 1 a detailed review of the literature was provided. ... Chapter 2 presented the theoretical point of departure from perspective X [X being a theory]. Chapter 3 was an attempt to fill the gap between the theory and scarcity of empirical findings ...

In both Examples 3 and 4, each chapter warranted at least one paragraph of text.

In over one-third of the theses studied, it would appear that a major focus of the conclusion was to summarize and highlight the main points of each successive chapter, giving more or less equal prominence to the literature discussed in the early part of the thesis and to the actual study undertaken and its findings. Even so, the literature is often discussed in very general terms as can be seen from Example 2.

Rather surprisingly, the average number of 11 cited references in these summary conclusions is lower than the average of 18 for all the thesis-oriented conclusions. This seems to confirm the notion that the writer's aim is to paint a general picture of each chapter and to use the cited references as background rather than to tie the thesis together through relating the study findings to previously cited research or to show where the study has confirmed or refuted earlier work carried out in the field under investigation.

Focusing on successive chapters of the thesis would appear to be at odds with Bunton's (2005) findings, where the move of consolidating one's research space was indeed accomplished by summarizing the methods, results/findings and/or claims but this was achieved through reference to previous research, and not simply by summarizing in turn each section including the literature. The focus on providing a summary discerned in the theses in the current study is also contrary to the advice given by Swales and Feak (2004) for writing the discussion section of a paper (which they see as including the conclusion), since they suggest that '[d]iscussions, then, should be *more than* summaries' (p. 269, my emphasis). However, the approach adopted by the thesis authors in this study seems more in line with some of the guidelines available for writing such a text in Polish. Apanowicz (2005), for instance, proposes that '[t]he final conclusion is a *recapitulation of the entire work* in the form of a synthesis of the findings arising from *individual chapters*' (p. 89, my translation and emphasis). Interestingly, even among Polish guidebook authors, there is a lack of consensus about the summarizing function of conclusions, with Zenderowski (2009), for instance, differing from Apanowicz and warning against using the conclusion simply to summarize what has been written earlier in the thesis.

The phenomenon of Polish students viewing the conclusion as a summary was also evident in the Master's thesis conclusions reported on by Lewkowicz (2009). There it was suggested that the conclusions were being used as a backward signpost, reminding the reader of the important points in the text rather than moving the text forward in terms of consolidating the research space by relating the study to the previously discussed research. However, emphasis in the PhD theses on what is included in each chapter may at least partially be influenced by another factor: reviewers in Poland who examine theses are required to write a summary of each chapter before briefly commenting on it. Candidates and their supervisors may consider that providing reviewers with such a chapter by chapter summary will facilitate the reviewers' task. Whatever the reason for this approach to the conclusion, the summary seems to be a separate move accomplished through summarizing individual chapters and the overall effect seems to be to consolidate the thesis as a whole, rather than to consolidate the research space or gap that was identified at the outset and addressed by the research undertaken.

The extent to which the theses in this category go beyond providing readers with a chapter by chapter summary varies. In 3 of the 4 discursive conclusions that provided a chapter by chapter summary there was an initial move restating the aims or purposes of the undertaken study, as illustrated in the following extracts:

Example 5

This work was entirely devoted on one problem: X. The work has been based on failures of X and how these can be recognized. The work has been based on Theory Y which has provided the theoretical background for my dissertation.

Example 6

This thesis attempted to accomplish three objectives. The first has been to...

Such an introductory restatement was also present in one of the bullet-pointed conclusions. However, in no instance did this move go beyond a statement of fact to justifying or explaining the need for the research undertaken, which Bunton (2005) suggests was evident in the theses conclusions he studied.

The chapter by chapter summary was also followed by an additional move or moves in 3 of these 4 discursive conclusions. In one case, following the chapter summaries, a list of practical recommendations was put forward. In three instances, suggestions for future research were presented as separate sections (though not always preceded by a subheading), and in one instance, following the chapter summary and before the suggestions for future research, there was an evaluation of the methodology employed in the study as well as of its findings. This move should be recognized as one of consolidating the research space. It is, however, about half the length of the chapter by chapter summary, which is why the conclusion has been classified as focusing on summarizing the individual chapters.

Extending beyond the summary was also evident in the two 'telegraphic' (bullet-pointed) conclusions discussed above, with both of the authors suggesting potential follow-up research, and one additionally evaluating the study undertaken and suggesting its limitations which could again be considered as an attempt to consolidate the research space. Thus, in comparison with the conclusions in the Master's theses (Lewkowicz, 2009), these are longer and they generally attempt to accomplish more than a straightforward summary of what was presented earlier in the thesis.

Conclusions to consolidate the research space

Four of the remaining 5 thesis-oriented conclusions may be regarded as following more closely the thesis-oriented conclusions described by Bunton (2005) in that they include a substantial move of consolidating the research space through situating the findings of the undertaken study in relation to the research gap identified at the outset. In three of these cases, this move is preceded by an introductory restatement of the research problem or issues, while in the remaining case the consolidation move is preceded by a recapitulation of the literature and its relationship to the current study. One further conclusion includes a summary of the literature towards the beginning of the chapter, just after the initial restatement. The importance accorded to the literature reviewed here seems to be in line with the summary theses described above. However, where this conclusion differs from those classified as 'summary conclusions' is that it does not then proceed to summarizing the next chapter; it progresses to consolidate the research space through reiterating the research findings and highlighting their significance.

The final thesis-oriented conclusion was distinctive in that it did not summarize each chapter, nor did it consolidate the research space. It focused almost entirely on the limitations of the study in terms of the methodology used, the sampling adopted and the conditions under which the study was conducted. It then ends by suggesting that the findings presented are the best that could be achieved under the circumstances, despite maximum effort having been put into the project.

Move and step analysis of the thesis-oriented conclusions

A distinction has been made above between those conclusions that focus on summarizing successive chapters and those that attempt to draw on different parts of the thesis to consolidate the research space. While these moves are not mutually exclusive (indeed in some cases, writers move from a chapter summary to consolidation), in most instances writers opted for one approach or the other. Thus, they progressed in all but one case according to either of the following patterns: $(IR)^\wedge S^\wedge (P)^\wedge (FR)$ or $(IR)^\wedge (S)^\wedge C^\wedge (P)^\wedge (FR)$, where the brackets indicate the optional nature of the move and the moves are:

IR = introductory restatement
S = summary chapter by chapter
P = practical implications/recommendations
FR = suggestions for further research
C = consolidation of research space.

Where the writers opted for a chapter by chapter summary, the steps taken to achieve this move were determined largely by the content of the chapter. Thus, for example, the section summarizing the findings chapter would present each of the main findings in turn. In one respect these chapter by chapter summaries could be viewed as more discursive forms of the telegraphic approach adopted in the conclusions that were presented in bullet-point form.

In three of the four discursive conclusions where the chapter summary approach was adopted, additional steps were embedded within one or more of the chapter summaries. In one instance, embedded in the chapter summary on methodology was an evaluation of the methodology employed, while in another instance practical implications for teaching were embedded in the chapter summary reporting findings. Limitations were also embedded in one instance and claims arising from the findings were evident in all four instances. However, progression tended to be linear, both from one chapter to another as well as within the chapter summary, with the summary being followed by an evaluation, limitation(s), recommendation(s) or relevant claims.

In contrast to the conclusions that progressed along the lines of each chapter, the other thesis-oriented conclusions tended to be more cyclical in nature as described by Bunton (2005), with the consolidation move showing the most iterative steps. In the four conclusions that were classified as including the consolidation move, there were, within this move, a total of 33 Findings reported, 20 Claims made about the research or its findings, and 19 References to the literature. On average, therefore, within the consolidation move, there were 8 Findings, 5 Claims and 5 references to the literature per thesis. Embedded within this move in all cases but one was at least one reference to the methodology employed in the study, thus confirming Bunton's (2005) claim of the prominence given in the conclusion to this aspect of the study. (It must be noted that in the 'summary conclusions', a summary of the methodology was included in each case.) Limitations were also embedded in two of the consolidation moves as were the following steps: restatement of research questions or hypotheses (2 instances), suggestion for future research (1 instance), assumptions underpinning the study (1 instance) and recommendations (1 instance).

In three of the four instances, the consolidation move was preceded by an introductory restatement highlighting the aims or goals of the study, in one case justifying the approach adopted in the study, and in another, explaining how and why the goals were addressed in the way that they were in the thesis. All four conclusions made recommendations for future research, with two of them doing so by drawing attention to some of the limitations of the study undertaken and how these could be addressed in future work. Only one of the three considered implications of the study and did so from both a practical and theoretical perspective.

Finally, it is worth noting that one of these conclusions included some concluding remarks in which the writer highlighted the importance of the study and his contribution to the field. Concluding remarks are not a feature of any of the other conclusions discussed so far, though the contribution made by the researcher is embedded in a further three conclusions.

4.4.2 Field-oriented conclusion

Only one field-oriented conclusion, in literature in English, was identified in this corpus. The main focus of this conclusion was to further interpret the analysis presented in the earlier part of the thesis and so to a large extent it followed an argument structure of Claim-Counterclaim-Justification (e.g. Jordan, 1984) and therefore did not lend itself to a 'Move and Step' analysis. In this respect, it mirrored the English literature conclusion described by Bunton (2005). However, the conclusion in question briefly started with a thesis-focus orientation in that it drew readers' attention to the aims of the study and what had been discussed earlier as well as the conclusions drawn at the end of specific earlier chapters. It therefore seemed to combine the two approaches by first orienting itself on the thesis and providing a restatement move, but then moving forward to reflect on the field as a whole by presenting new arguments, claims and counterclaims and only referring to the thesis in the context of the whole field.

5 Conclusions and Implications for Teaching

Even within this rather limited, field-specific corpus of PhD conclusions, there appears to be great variability in the ways in which the conclusions have been drawn up. Some of the variability mirrors that reported by Bunton (2005). However, over 50% of the conclusions studied displayed one or more features that can be attributed to local expectations for writing the concluding section/chapter of a thesis in that the conclusion was presented as a compilation of chapter summaries, sometimes in point-form, and it was often not integrated in the body of the text, but presented as if an afterword. All the theses, however, included a readily identifiable conclusion.

The fact that the average length of the conclusions in my study was very short – considerably shorter than either the humanities and social science or the science and technology thesis conclusions studied by Bunton (2005), suggests that this section in the Polish thesis, though a requirement, is not seen to carry much weight. Even though some of the guidebooks written in

Polish emphasize the importance of the conclusion and suggest that it should relate back to the questions or hypotheses presented in the introduction and show the extent to which these have been successfully addressed (e.g. Mendel, 2009; Wojcik, 2005), the doctoral candidates in this study appear to perceive the preceding chapters as more substantive. Indeed, one of the authors, when asked about her conclusion, indicated that for her, the conclusion was made up of the chapter on implications together with some final concluding words. It is also possible that these PhD candidates consider the oral presentation they are required to give during their public defence as a better opportunity to consolidate their research space and to highlight their contribution to the field.

The adoption of a very direct and easily accessible organization for the conclusion along the lines of successive chapter summaries or even in point form appears to impact on the overall effect the conclusion has on the reader. Rather than consolidate the research and highlight its significance, the chapter summaries appear to act as backward looking signposts, simply reminding the reader of what came before.

The use of bullet-pointed lists in the conclusion does not seem to be specifically advocated in the literature. Yet it is not an uncommon feature of current academic papers written in Polish. A lot has been written about the change in Polish academic style and how it has been influenced by the more direct non-Teutonic style used in English (see, for example, Duszak & Lewkowicz, 2008). Numerous guidebooks also stress the need to use succinct and clear language (e.g. Mendel, 2009; Wojcik, 2005). It is possible that the belief that written English has to be clear, concise and to the point is being translated into the telegraphic style used by some of the authors in this study.

There appears to be little doubt that local influences are evident in the presentation of these thesis conclusions. The question that remains is whether these differences warrant attention. I would argue that they do on two counts. First, if such influences are perceived within the conclusion, it is likely that they may exist within other parts of the text as well. It is also likely that in other cultural contexts, different local demands will be placed on writers. The differences may not be as insignificant and obscure as Swales (2004) suggests, and only with an understanding of such differences will advisors be able to help students meet local and international expectations.

Secondly and perhaps more importantly, given the fact that many PhD programmes now include a module on academic writing to help candidates complete their thesis and also to get published in the field, the differences noted here can be used to inform the design and content of academic writing modules. If comparative studies of thesis writing practices can be undertaken across languages, looking into both formal requirements as well as linguistic variation, these findings can be the basis for the development of materials which are truly relevant for students.

Students need to be made aware of both international and local demands, as well as variations within each, to be able to reflect their own voice in their writing, while at the same time successfully completing their work in a way that meets the expectations of their different possible audiences. There is otherwise a danger that candidates will be unsure of which discourse patterns or approaches are appropriate or even required under different circumstances. This may have been less of a problem for the group selected for this study because they were highly proficient in their use of English, but it could pose serious problems for the increasing number of candidates from other fields of study who choose to or have to write in English, or those opting to study in Poland but coming from different cultural backgrounds.

A tension seems to exist between providing students with formulaic patterns to follow in their writing and encouraging them to express themselves and establish their own voice in their writing. The variability in the conclusions reported by Bunton (2005) as well as in this study suggests that there is no single pattern which leads to a successful conclusion or for that matter to a successful thesis. Though guidelines can and should be provided, students need to be accorded opportunities to work with theses in their field of study and to learn to assess their strengths and weaknesses in terms of readability and audience awareness. Even theses that have been successfully defended may have room for improvement and students need to appreciate this. The need to work with and on theses to learn how to go about writing one's own seems to add an additional dimension to the entire process of obtaining a research degree: one which is being addressed in some contexts through thesis writing support or thesis writing courses, but one that is not necessarily fully appreciated by students who see their research, rather than the writing up of that research, as all important.

Notes

[1] There is considerable confusion between the terms 'thesis' and 'dissertation'. In some countries there is a preference for using 'thesis' at master's level and 'dissertation' at doctoral level; in other countries, the reverse is true. Throughout this chapter, the term 'thesis' is used to refer to the long essay produced at either master's or doctoral level.

[2] In order to retain the anonymity of authors of the theses, the actual subject under investigation is not specified here or elsewhere in the text where it is not necessary for understanding the point being made.

References

Apanowicz, J. (2005). *Metodologiczne uwarunkowania pacy naukowej [The methodological features of academic writing]*. Warszawa: Difin.

Arulandu, M. (2006). A genre analysis of masters and doctoral dissertation introductions in the Sciences and Social Sciences. (Unpublished MA thesis). Universiti Putra Malaysia, Malaysia.

Böhm, A., Follari, M., Hewett, A., Jones, S., Kemp, N., Meares, D., Pearce, D., & Van Cauter, K. (2004). *Vision 2020. Forecasting international student mobility: a UK perspective*. London: The British Council.

Bunton, D. (1998). Linguistic and textual problems in PhD and MPhil theses: An analysis of genre moves and metatext. (Unpublished doctoral dissertation). The University of Hong Kong, Hong Kong.

Bunton, D. (2002). Generic moves in PhD theses introductions. In J. Flowerdew (Ed.), *Academic discourse* (pp. 57–75). Harlow: Longman.

Bunton, D. (2005). The structure of PhD conclusion chapters. *Journal of English for Academic Purposes, 4*(3), 207–224.

Cooley, L., & Lewkowicz, J. (2003). *Dissertation writing in practice: Tuning ideas into text*. Hong Kong: Hong Kong University Press.

Crystal, D. (2003). *English as a global language*. Cambridge: Cambridge University Press.

Devos, A. (2003). Academic standards, internationalisation, and the discursive construction of 'the international student'. *Higher Education Research and Development, 22*(2), 155–166.

Dudley-Evans, T. (1986). Genre analysis: An investigation of the introduction and discussion sections of MSc dissertations. In M. Coulthard (Ed.), *Talking about Text* (pp. 219–228). London: Routledge.

Duszak, A., & Lewkowicz, J. (2008). Publishing academic texts in English: A Polish perspective. *Journal of English for Academic Purposes, 7*(2), 108–120.

Ferguson, G., Pérez-Llantada, C., & Plo, R. (2011). English as an international language of scientific publication: A study of attitudes. *World Englishes, 30*(1), 41–59.

Higher education admissions and student mobility within the EU (Centre for Educational Research, Clare Market Papers No. 18). (2001). London: London School of Economics and Political Science, Centre for Educational Research.

Higher Education Statistics Agency. (2010). Students in higher education institutions, 2008/2009.

Hyland, K. (2004). Graduates' gratitude: The generic structure of dissertation acknowledgements. *English for Specific Purposes, 23*(3), 303–324.

Hyland, K. (2009). *Academic discourse*. London: Continuum.

Jordan, M. P. (1984). *Rhetoric of everyday English texts*. London: Allen & Unwin.

Lewkowicz, J. (2009). Concluding your Master's level thesis. *Revista Canaria de Estodios Ingleses, 59*, 63–72.

Lillis, T., & Curry, M. J. (2010). *Academic writing in a global context*. London: Routledge.

Marginson, S. (2006). Dynamics of national and global competition in higher education. *Higher Education, 52*(1), 1–39.

Mendel, T. (2009). *Metodyka pisania prac doktorskich [The methodology of writing a PhD thesis]*. Poznan: Wydawnictwo Uniwersytetu Ekonomicznego w Poznaniu.

Overseas students in the UK – a growing market. (2004). Retrieved from the Higher Education Careers Services Unit (HECSU), Prospects website: http://www.prospects.ac.uk/index.htm

Paltridge, B. (2002). Thesis and dissertation writing: An examination of published advice and actual practice. *English for Specific Purposes, 21*(2), 125–143.

Peters, S. (2011). Asserting or deflecting expertise? Exploring the rhetorical practices of master's theses in the philosophy of education. *English for Specific Purposes, 30,* 176–185.

Rasmeenin, C. (2006). A structural Move analysis of MA thesis discussion sections in applied linguistics. (Unpublished MA thesis). Mahidol University, Thailand.

Samraj, B. (2002). Introductions in research articles: Variations across disciplines. *English for Specific Purposes, 21*(1), 1–17.

Samraj, B. (2008). A discourse analysis of master's theses across disciplines with a focus on introductions. *Journal of English for Academic Purposes, 7*(1), 55–67.

Soler-Monreal, C., Carbonell-Olivares, M., & Gil-Salom, L. (2011). A contrastive study of the rhetorical organisation of English and Spanish PhD thesis introductions. *English for Specific Purposes, 30*(1), 4–17.

Starfield, S. (2003). The evolution of a thesis writing course for Arts and Social Sciences students: What can applied linguistics offer? *Hong Kong Journal of Applied Linguistics, 8,* 137–154.

Sudgen, J. (2009, Sept 24). British universities 'make £2bn selling degrees abroad'. *Times online.* Retrieved from http://www.timesonline.co.uk/tol/life_and_style/education/article6847524.ece

Swales, J. M. (1990). *Genre analysis.* Cambridge: Cambridge University Press.

Swales, J. M. (2004). *Research genres.* Cambridge: Cambridge University Press.

Swales, J. M., & Feak, C. (2004). *Academic writing for graduate students.* Ann Arbor: University of Michigan Press.

Swales, J. M., & Najjar, H. (1987). The writing of research article introductions. *Written Communication, 4*(2), 175–191.

Thompson, P. (2001). A pedagogically-motivated corpus-based examination of PhD theses: Macrostructure, citation practices and uses of modal verbs. (Unpublished doctoral dissertation). The University of Reading, UK.

Thompson, P. (2005). Points of focus and position: Intertextual reference in PhD theses. *Journal of English for Academic Purposes, 4*(4), 302–323.

de Vita, G., & Case, P. (2003). Rethinking the internationalisation agenda in UK higher education. *Journal of Further and Higher Education, 27*(4), 383–398.

Wojcik, K. (2005). *Piszę akademicką pracę promocyjną [Writing an academic thesis].* Warszawa: Placet.

Yang, R., & Allison, D. (2003). Research articles in applied linguistics: Moving from results to conclusions. *English for Specific Purposes, 22*(4), 365–385.

Zenderowski, R. (2009). *Praca magisterska licencjat* [The Masters' thesis diploma]. Warszawa: CeDeWu.

Zhao, M., & Jiang, Y. (2010). Dissertation acknowledgements: Generic structure and linguistic features. *Chinese Journal of Applied Linguistics, 33*(1), 94–109.

Chapter 7

EFL/ESL Writers and the Use of Shell Nouns

Hilary Nesi and Emma Moreton

1 Introduction

Many inanimate abstract nouns can perform a cohesive function, facilitating the creation of succinct, coherent texts. Such nouns only have a vague general meaning when taken out of context, but acquire a more specific and often attitudinally marked meaning with reference to other words in the text, whether they be in the same clause or in a previous or subsequent clause. Flowerdew's (2003a) overview of this phenomenon includes items previously referred to as *general nouns* (Halliday & Hasan, 1976), *type 3 vocabulary* (Winter, 1982), *anaphoric nouns* (Francis, 1986), *advance labels* (Tadros, 1994), *carrier nouns* (Ivanic, 1991), *shell nouns* (Hunston & Francis, 1999; Schmid, 2000), *enumerative* and *resultative nouns* (Hinkel, 2001) and *signalling nouns* (Flowerdew 2003a, b). Typical examples of inanimate abstract nouns which can perform a cohesive function are: *aspect, category, change, difficulty, fact, method, problem, process, reason, system* etc. The following example shows how a noun of this type (*system*) refers back to 'token economies that are used in mental institutions' discussed in the previous sentence.

One such idea that has received this criticism is the *token economies that are used in mental institutions*. Although not strictly a form of treatment this *system* can be used to generally encourage desired behaviour and eliminate abnormal behaviour.

(First year psychology assignment)

Some researchers have noted that nouns of this type are particularly common in academic writing. Flowerdew (2003b), for example, draws attention to their role in the evaluation and justification of claims in research articles and in argumentative writing generally, and also compares their frequency in biology lectures and in biology textbook writing, finding that they are more than twice as common in the written mode.

In this paper we shall use the term *shell noun*, following Hunston and Francis (1999) and Schmid (2000), who were influenced in turn by Sinclair's concepts of 'encapsulation' and 'prospection' (Sinclair, 1993).

Our study also draws on the work of Hinkel (2001), who compared cohesive markers in 895 short essays written by native speaker (NS) and non-native speaker (NNS) students, and Aktas and Cortes (2008), who examined shell nouns with reference to a corpus of 28 research papers produced by NNS graduate students, and a corpus of 166 published research articles.

Hinkel (2001) found that her NNS students tended to use nouns such as *fact, problem* and *reason* in a rather simplistic fashion, to generalize rather than to tie together the essay's main points. Inanimate abstract nouns performing a cohesive function were rare in both her NS and NNS data, however, per-haps because the essays were so short (about 300 words) and were personal opinion pieces rather than works of scholarship. Aktas and Cortes (2008) found that their NNS student writers used shell nouns in their research papers 'as frequently as published writers, and in some cases, more frequently' (p. 9), but that they also used these nouns in somewhat different ways.

Building on the work of Schmid (2000), Aktas and Cortes identified in their corpora seven lexico-grammatical patterns for *effect, result, fact, system, process* and *problem* as shell nouns. These patterns are summarized in Table 7.1.

Charles discusses two of these patterns, *th-* + *N* (2003) and *N* + *clause* (2007), in terms of their roles as major shell noun patterns in academic

Table 7.1 Lexico-grammatical patterns analysed by Aktas and Cortes (2008, p. 10, Table 7)

Pattern	Abbreviation	Example
Noun + post-nominal complement clause	*N* + clause	*Given **the fact** that no price differences exist*
Demonstrative determiner + Noun	*th-* + *N*	*It is interesting to note that …. **This fact** can be explained….*
Definite article + Noun	the + *N*	*…a mass concentration that contributes to the lensing properties of **the system***
Indefinite article + Noun	a(n) + Noun	*…the real option value exerts over the timing of price changes, **an effect** we interpret as retail price fixity*
Definite article + Noun + *of-* prepositional phrase	the + *N* + *of*	*…**the process of** administering the service was different for the two groups.*
Indefinite article + Noun + *of-* prepositional phrase	a(n) + Noun + *of*	*One way to begin **a process of** empowerment might be to create a space for …*
Definite article + *same* + Noun	*the same* + *N*	***The same result** was obtained with …..*

writing, the first functioning as a link to the preceding message and the second functioning as a link to the message that follows. These were the only two patterns used by both sets of writers in Aktas and Cortes' study, but their distribution constituted the biggest functional difference between the two corpora in terms of shell noun use. Aktas and Cortes (2008) found that their student writers were more likely to use *fact* with the pattern *th-* + *N*, where the shell noun follows a demonstrative adjective (*this* or *that*) and creates inter-sentential cohesion by referring back to the previous clause, whereas the published writers were more likely to use the pattern *N* + *clause*, conveying cataphoric reference in order to 'semantically characterize a piece of experience in a general way' (p. 11).

The two corpora Aktas and Cortes compared differed across a number of variables. Their published authors were presumably native or near-native users of English, whereas their graduate students were all attending an academic writing course because they had not passed a compulsory English placement test. We can assume that the published authors had greater research and disciplinary expertize, but we might also argue that graduate research papers and published research articles are somewhat different genres, with a different intended readership, even though Aktas and Cortes claimed that the student writing 'resembled those articles in the published corpus in their organization and language use' (p. 7). The shell noun use of the published authors was presented as 'the model for students to imitate' (p. 9), but because the circumstances of the students were so different from those of the published writers it is impossible to determine whether their differing use of shell nouns was due to lack of language skill and familiarity with research genres (deficits which can be addressed in the academic writing class), or whether they were due to general lack of disciplinary knowledge and differences in communicative purpose (a natural consequence of their status as graduate students rather than experts in the field).

For our own study we therefore set out to apply the methods of Aktas and Cortes to the study of two groups of students writing scholarly papers under more or less identical circumstances, distinguished solely by their status as users of English as a first or a foreign language. Our aim was to discover whether the student writers with first languages other than English used similar shell noun strategies to their native English speaker counterparts, or whether there was any evidence that they were not able to exploit the potential of the shell noun to its fullest extent, as the studies by Hinkel (2001) and Aktas and Cortes (2008) both suggest. To do this we compared native and non-native speaker contributions to the British Academic Written English (BAWE) corpus.

2 NNS Writing in the BAWE Corpus

The BAWE corpus contains 2,761 proficient student assignments, produced and assessed as part of university degree coursework, and fairly evenly distributed across 35 university disciplines and four levels of study (first year undergraduate to the Masters level). About half the assignments were graded by the students' subject tutors at a level equivalent to 'distinction' (D) (70% or above), and half were graded at a level equivalent to 'merit' (M) (between 60% and 69%). (For a more detailed description of the design and contents of the BAWE corpus see, for example, Alsop & Nesi (2009).) The majority of assignments in the corpus were written by 'native' or 'near-native' speakers of English: 1,953 were written by students who reported that English was their mother tongue, and a further 3 were written by one Welsh student, entirely educated in the UK, who claimed Welsh as his L1 but who was effectively bilingual.

This leaves 805 assignments written by non-native speaker (NNS) students who did not claim English as their L1. Table 7.2 summarizes the make-up of the NNS and NNS subcorpora referred to in this study.

The largest category of NNS assignments are the 245 written by speakers of Chinese languages (Cantonese, Mandarin and unspecified), but thirty-seven other languages are also represented, including relatively large numbers of languages spoken in Europe and East Asia. The distribution of these NNS assignments across level and disciplinary group is illustrated in Table 7.3. The table shows that 316 (39%) of the assignments were contributed by students at Level 4; this reflects the fact that the majority of international students in British universities are postgraduates. Arts and Humanities disciplines are the least popular for these students, and Social Science disciplines are the most popular, especially applied disciplines which prepare students for entry into employment, such as Business, Hospitality and Law.

Table 7.2 The two BAWE subcorpora

	NS	NNS
Type	89740	53831
Token	4616402	2029022

Table 7.3 The distribution of NNS assignments in the BAWE corpus by level and disciplinary grouping

Disciplinary grouping	Level 1	Level 2	Level 3	Level 4	Total
Arts & Humanities	15	25	44	30	114
Life Sciences	24	30	30	101	185
Physical Sciences	43	31	45	47	166
Social Sciences	82	55	61	138	340[1]
Total	**164**	**141**	**180**	**316**	**805[2]**

[1] with four of unspecified level
[2] with four of unspecified level

Although written by non-native speakers, these assignments are of a relatively high standard, as are all those included in the BAWE corpus. The majority are almost indistinguishable from the assignments submitted by native-speakers of English, and so they do not constitute a learner corpus of the type typically investigated through Contrastive Interlanguage Analysis (cf. Granger, 2002). For example, Granger and Rayson (1998) recorded very different part of speech (POS) profiles for samples of essays from the International Corpus of Learner English (ICLE) and the Louvain Corpus of Native English Essays (LOCNESS), with heavier use of personal pronouns in the NNS sample, and heavier use of nouns in the NS sample. Similarly, Arshavskaya (2009) found that the native speaker component of the BAWE corpus was significantly more nominal and contained fewer personal pronouns than the Montclair Electronic Language Database (MELD), an NNS learner corpus. However Arshavskaya found almost identical POS distribution in the NS and NNS components of the BAWE corpus, the only significant difference being the higher incidence of nouns in the NNS subcorpus. This greater use of nouns may be because there were proportionately more NNS BAWE submissions at the highest level of study.

3 Potential Shell Nouns in the BAWE Corpus

Since the NNS contributions to the BAWE corpus are so similar to the NS contributions, we must look beyond simple POS distribution if we wish to investigate any non-native-like characteristics in the NNS component of BAWE. One possible area of difference is in the patterns of shell noun use. Table 7.4 shows the frequency in the BAWE corpus of shell nouns which were identified by Hinkel (2001) as common cohesive abstract nouns, and which were also identified as signalling nouns in Flowerdew's (2003a, 2003b) 95,482 word biology

Table 7.4 The frequency per 100,000 words of selected nouns across levels of study

	Level 1	Level 2	Level 3	Level 4
approach	35	43	48	83
aspect	28	29	31	34
category	8	16	11	20
change	80	77	76	78
characteristic	22	21	18	26
circumstance	11	12	12	9
difficulty	12	10	15	17
effect	70	85	84	69
fact	72	68	58	54
factor	60	72	73	72
feature	25	27	27	33
form	69	75	57	67
item	23	8	8	17
manner	10	12	9	6
method	72	85	85	71
problem	82	80	87	98
process	64	79	94	110
purpose	21	21	23	19
reason	45	59	44	48
result	99	119	122	107
stage	34	38	41	42
subject	26	24	26	18
system	116	138	159	153
task	27	26	21	33
topic	9	7	10	10
trend	11	10	14	21
type	42	54	52	48
All listed words at this level per 100,000 words	**1177**	**1297**	**1306**	**1362**

textbook corpus. All but *approach, circumstance, item, result, topic* and *trend* were also found to function as signalling nouns in Flowerdew's 92,939 word biology lecture corpus. The 27 words in Table 7.4 are amongst those investigated by Aktas and Cortes, who took Hinkel's list as a starting point for their comparison of shell noun use by NNS graduate students and published writers.

The total number of words at level one in the BAWE corpus is 1,440,185, at level two 1,781,686, at level three 1,558,715 and at level four 1,704,015. (A small number of assignments were not assigned to a particular level, so these figures do not add up to the total size of the corpus (6,506,995 words).) Because numbers are different at each level the frequencies in Table 7.4 have been normalized to 100,000 words by dividing the raw frequency of each word at each level by the total number of words at that level, and then multiplying by 100,000. Here and in subsequent tables, normalized figures have been rounded to the nearest whole number.

Although it can be seen that there is a rise in the frequency of these nouns from level one (first year undergraduate) through to level four (masters level), a one way ANOVA revealed that the differences between levels were not statistically significant [p = 0.918].

Aktas and Cortes (2008) found that the most frequently used shell nouns in their corpus of published research articles were *effect, result, fact, system, process* and *problem*, all of which were used as shell nouns 15 or more times per 100,000 words. In their student corpus, *factor* and *method* were the most frequently used shell nouns, followed by *process, effect, result* and *approach*. As can be seen in Table 7.4, all of these words occur frequently in the BAWE corpus, although it should be noted that Table 7.4 merely indicates their frequency when used as nouns, and does not distinguish between their use as cohesive items (shell nouns) and their use with reference to entities outside the text. For example, *system*, which in the BAWE corpus is the commonest of the words taken from Hinkel's list, sometimes functions as a signalling noun, as in Examples One and Two, but often does not serve a cohesive function, as in Examples Three and Four.

Example One:

Realism solves this problem as it recognizes that society is an open **system** in which events are influenced by other contingencies, so the causal influence of emergent properties is not to consistently produce observable effects.

(0004b, Level 1, Sociology, English native speaker)

Example Two:

The circuit has now been set up with strain gauges to sense the stresses in the shaft, and these mechanical outputs have been converted into electrical ones and amplified to a sufficiently high level with the noise attenuated so the signal can be read by a voltage-measuring instrument. This **system** now needs to be able to be read and calibrated for data presentation.

(0018a, Level 2, Engineering, Cantonese speaker)

Example Three:

Having half of its roads, railways and public buildings destroyed during the Great War, and a continuing expenditure of over 50 per cent of the state budget on defense and the railway **system**, the government lacked the essential funds ....

(0003d, Level 2, History, Dutch speaker)

Example Four:

With such a huge genetic diversity within the human population the problem of tissue rejection must be discussed. Two solutions to this problem would be to either suppress the immune **system** of the patient or induce tolerance.

(0009d, Level 2, Biological Sciences, English native speaker)

4 Methodology

Using the online corpus query tool Sketch Engine[1], we examined shell noun patterns for the nine nouns in Hinkel's list that were the most frequent in the BAWE corpus and/or in the published corpus studied by Aktas and Cortes (2008). These were *change, effect, fact, factor, method, process, problem, result* and *system*. Most of these occurred 75 times or more per 100,000 words in the BAWE corpus. *Factor* occurred 68 times, but was one of the most frequently used shell nouns in the Aktas and Cortes corpus of student writing. *Fact* occurred 62 times, but was one of the most frequently used shell nouns in the Aktas and Cortes corpus of published research articles. Five of these nouns – *effect, fact, method, problem* and *result* – were also extremely common as shell nouns in Flowerdew's (2010) corpora of L1 and L2 students' argumentative essays.

Contexts were examined with reference to the lexico-grammatical patterns for shell nouns listed in Table 7.1, and a comparison was made between NS and NNS production. To facilitate this procedure, various corpus query techniques were used. The BAWE corpus has been tagged for Part of Speech using the UCREL CLAWS7 tagset, details of which can be accessed from the open Sketch Engine site. It was therefore possible to specify the parts of speech we wished to search for:

- [tag = "N.."] to select forms functioning as nouns, rather than verbs or adjectives.
- [tag = "AT.?"] to select occurrences where an article such as *the, a, an* preceded the noun.
- [tag = "DD.?"] to select occurrences where a determiner such as *this, that, these, those* preceded the noun.

Using Corpus Query language (CQL) we could thus create queries for the shell noun patterns identified by Aktas and Cortes (2008), where the shell noun under investigation is substituted for XXXX:

Table 7.5   Occurrences of the nine nouns in the NS and NNS corpora (raw data)

	effect	result	fact	factor	system	process	problem	change	method
NS	3664	5114	2898	2799	5100	3363	4050	3320	3493
NNS	1391	2164	1185	1749	4135	2321	1610	1754	1588

1. [lemma = "XXXX" & tag = "N.."] [word = "that|wh.*|to"] to identify the pattern *N* + *cl.*
2. [tag = "DD."] [lemma = "XXXX" & tag = "N.."] to identify the pattern *th-* + *N.*
3. [tag = "AT."] [lemma = "XXXX" & tag = "N.."] to identify the pattern *a/the* + *N.*
4. [tag = "AT."] [lemma = "XXXX" & tag = "N.."] [word = "of"] to identify the pattern *a/the* + *N* + *of.*
5. [tag = "AT"] [word = "same"] [lemma = "XXXX" & tag = "N.."] to identify the pattern *the same* + *N.*

In the 'View options' 'references' menu on the Sketch Engine concordance page, 'text l1' was highlighted in order to see the first languages of the student writers. By this means we can identify all the assignments produced by native speakers of English (and the three assignments written by the Welsh-English bilingual student). For convenience, view options were changed on the Sketch Engine concordance line page so that it was possible to view up to 3000 lines. Sketch Engine output with 100 character line lengths was copied and saved to Excel spreadsheets where it could be counted and sorted more easily.

5   Findings

Tables 7.5 and 7.6 show the overall frequency of the nine nouns in the NS and NNS components of the BAWE corpus.

   Some variation in the frequencies of NS and NNS use may be accounted for by the unequal distribution of NS and NNS writing across disciplines, genres and levels of study. *System* and *process*, for example, are proportionately

Table 7.6   Occurrences of the nine nouns in the NS and NNS corpora (normalized to 100,000)

	effect	result	fact	factor	system	process	problem	change	method
NS	79	111	63	61	110	73	88	72	76
NNS	69	107	58	86	204	114	79	86	78

much more frequent in the NNS data, but this may be due to the preponderance of NNS students in disciplines which place emphasis on the concepts of system and process (both words occur much more frequently in the Sciences and Social Sciences than in the Arts and Humanities disciplines). Table 7.6 shows that '*fact*' and '*method*' are the nouns which occur with the most similar frequency in the two corpora.

Tables 7.7 and 7.8 show the distribution of the seven lexico-grammatical patterns used by Aktas and Cortes (2008) with each of the nine nouns in the NS and NNS components of the BAWE corpus. Most of the nine nouns in the corpus occurred in other contexts, as a comparison of Tables 7.5 and 7.7 will reveal. *Effect*, for example, was used 3664 times by NS writers, but is recorded only 436 times in the lexico-grammatical patterns listed in Table 7.7. Thus although the seven lexico-grammatical patterns did not capture every instance of shell noun behaviour in the corpus, there were also certainly many instances in the corpus where the nine nouns did not perform a cohesive function.

From these tables it can be seen that the patterns *N + cl, th- + N* and *a/the + N* were the most frequent. The pattern *a/the + N + of* is, of course, a subcategory of *a/the + N* and must therefore be less frequent. Use of the pattern *the same + N* was negligible, especially by NNS students.

The shell noun *fact* was chosen for more detailed study because NS and NNS writers used it with much the same frequency, but in rather different

Table 7.7 Frequency distribution of lexico-grammatical patterns

Patterns	effect		result		fact		factor		system	
	NS	NNS	NS	NNS	NS	NNS	NS	NNS	NS	NNS
N + cl	163	49	138	52	1421	487	449	255	406	256
th- + N	136	33	229	71	72	72	223	162	172	70
a/the + N	118	20	1057	422	46	18	118	28	216	111
a/the + N + of	7	5	683	219	5	2	43	7	71	34
the same + N	12	6	26	7	1	0	4	2	0	1

Patterns	process		problem		change		method		TOTAL	
	NS	NNS	NS	NNS	NS	NNS	NS	NNS	NS	NNS
N + cl	236	135	261	105	309	79	254	127	3637	1545
th- + N	280	166	283	118	164	79	396	145	1955	916
a/the + N	198	107	296	83	249	66	149	28	2447	883
a/the + N + of	82	32	5	9	29	7	74	10	999	325
the same + N	11	5	19	6	2	0	27	4	102	31

Table 7.8 Frequency distribution of lexico-grammatical patterns (normalized to 100,000)

Patterns	effect		result		fact		factor		system	
	NS	NNS	NS	NNS	NS	NNS	NS	NNS	NS	NNS
N + cl	4	2	3	3	31	24	10	13	9	13
th- + N	3	2	5	3	2	4	5	8	4	3
a/the + N	3	1	23	21	1	1	3	1	5	5
a/the + N + of	0	0	15	11	0	0	1	0	2	2
the same + N	0	0	1	0	0	0	0	0	0	0

Patterns	process		problem		change		method		TOTAL	
	NS	NNS	NS	NNS	NS	NNS	NS	NNS	NS	NNS
N + cl	5	7	6	0	7	4	6	6	79	76
th- + N	6	8	6	0	4	4	9	7	42	45
a/the + N	4	5	6	0	5	3	3	1	53	44
a/the + N + of	2	2	0	0	1	0	2	0	22	16
the same + N	0	0	0	0	0	0	1	0	2	2

ways. Table 7.9 shows that the NS writers made proportionally greater use of the pattern $N + cl$ than the NNS writers, and the NNS writers made proportionally greater use of the pattern $th- + N$. This accords with the findings of Aktas and Cortes (2008). The tables also show, however, that in our study both sets of writers preferred the pattern $N + cl$, and in this respect our findings differ from those of Aktas and Cortes. We were expecting slightly higher frequencies in our study because, given the size of the BAWE corpus, we did not test each occurrence of each pattern to see if *fact* was functioning as a shell noun. However although the $th- + N$ pattern predicts shell noun function less strongly than the $N + cl$ pattern, our normalized figures for the $th- + N$ pattern are lower than those of Aktas and Cortes, whereas our normalized figures for the $N + cl$ pattern are much higher.

Example Five illustrates use of the $N + cl$ pattern, and Example Six illustrates use of the $th- + N$ pattern.

Table 7.9 Normalized frequencies for *fact*

Pattern	BAWE NS	BAWE NNS	Aktas & Cortes published	Aktas & Cortes student
N + cl	31	24	15	4.5
Th- + N	2	4	1.5	10.5
a/the + N	0	1	0.4	0

Example Five:

Emphasis was put on their undesirable behaviour, for example crime, and prostitution, despite **the fact that** much of this was not carried out by immigrants

(0001a, English, Level 1, Sociology)

Example Six:

Breast conserving surgery with radiation is the preferred form of treatment for early tumours, particularly as numerous RCTs have shown mastectomy to have no additional effect upon survival (30). Despite **this fact** the standard therapy for most patients is a modified radical mastectomy.

(0047a, English, Level 4, Medicine)

Further investigation revealed that in the NNS corpus 39% of all instances of the pattern *this/that/those/these FACT(s)* (*th-* + *N*) were in unmarked subject position, whereas only 20% were in this position in the NS corpus. This finding is comparable to that of Gardezi and Nesi (2009), who compared the placement of conjunctive adjuncts in assignments written by NS and Pakistani students of economics. This study noted a tendency amongst the Pakistani writers to place adjuncts in sentence-initial position, whereas the British writers were more likely to delay their placement, a tactic which has certain rhetorical advantages:

> Delayed placement allows for initial hedging, and enables other thematic elements to take up initial position, thus providing more scope for manipulation of the thematic structure of the text according to the perspective the writer wishes to take. (Gardezi & Nesi, 2009, p. 244)

There was also variation in the function of *fact* in unmarked subject position, as can be seen in Table 7.10.

In sentences where *fact* is the unmarked subject, as in Examples Seven, Eight and Nine, Function 1 presents the previous clause as a 'fact' and the shell noun is purely anaphoric. The shell noun does not explain the original entity or concept any further; instead the new clause evaluates the

Table 7.10 The functions of *th-* + *FACT(s)*

Function	NS raw	NS normalized to 100,000	NNS raw	NNS normalized to 100,000
1. Anaphoric	3	0.1	20	1.0
2. Both anaphoric and cataphoric	8	0.2	5	0.2

importance, validity or implications of the 'fact', often using an evaluative adjective (e.g. *major, very important*). All these examples could be made more succinct by reducing the number of clauses; we will return to the pedagogical implications of this in the discussion section at the end of this chapter.

Example Seven:

Nepal is literate, whether in the UK it is not a concern (appendix 2). **This fact** has a major impact over the human resources management, foremost for a service business where the required qualifications are higher than in the manufacture or agriculture industry.

(3121b, French, Level 4, Hospitality, Leisure and Tourism)

Example Eight:

A very important characteristic of peat is that not many changes occur to it during storage. **This fact** is very important for a growing media. An experiment which took place in Nottingham Trent University investigated changes in organic growing media during storage.

(6110b, Greek, level 4, Biological Sciences)

Example Nine:

Interestingly, Ahumada (1992, p. 343) found a greater speed of adjustment with a similar model for the period 1977 to 1988. **This fact** may suggest that the economic reforms implemented in Argentina in the 1990s affected the speed of adjustment of real cash balances to disequilibrium in the long run relation of the demand for money.

(0079d, Spanish, Level 4, Economics)

Function 2, on the other hand, presents the previous clause as a 'fact' but then elaborates and expands on this in the following clause, leading on to a fuller explanation of the concept or claim, or a demonstration of its validity. This makes the structure both anaphoric and cataphoric, as in Examples Ten to Fourteen:

Example Ten:

If the five grey levels that make the central peak were all described with short codes, and the other grey levels with longer codes, the result will obviously be more efficient. **This fact** applies even more to the lengths of the codes. The longest run in this particular image is 76 pixels, but the vast majority, as can be seen by the following histogram, are under 10.

(6101a, NS, level 3, Computer Science)

Example Eleven:

The case, a summons taken out by the trustees, arose out the payment of monies to one of the charities named in the settlement, and the subsequent refusal of the Chief Inspector of Taxes (Claims) to repay the income tax deducted at source. **These facts** give rise to three fiscal elements to the decision. Firstly, it highlights …

(0397b, NS, level 3, Law)

Example Twelve:

Some feminists have argued that rape is at near epidemic levels and that if official statistics do not reflect this, then it is because rape is the single most underreported major crime. **This fact**, as Estrich (1987) demonstrates, depends on the definition of rape used. If we use the definition of rape to involve strangers and/or weapons …

(0214b, NS, level 3, Sociology)

Example Thirteen:

As a result, controlling the presence and replication of L. pneumophila in potable water supplies is very difficult, as even residual treatment which may kill free bacteria can not remove cells carried by the highly tolerant amoebae. **These facts** can be shown by a study using water samples obtained from five hospitals in Paris. Of the samples taken, 71% contained amoebae and 47% showed presence of L. pneumophila.

(0009e, NS, level 2, Biological Sciences)

Example Fourteen:

The spread of infection is critically important in healthcare settings. **This fact** has been highlighted in recent years by epidemics of drug resistant organism such as methicillin-resistant staphylococcus aureus (MRSA).

(3143b, NS, level 2, Health)

One further tendency in the data was the use of phrases such as *because of the fact that* and *due to the fact that,* instead of *because.* Such redundancy was noted in both the NS and the NNS data, as can be seen in Table 7.11.

Table 7.11   Examples of redundant *fact* in NS and NNS data

Expression	NS raw	NS normalized to 100,000	NNS raw	NNS normalized to 100,000
because of the fact that	1	0.02	8	0.4
due to the fact that	151	3.3	45	2.2

Examples of this use are provided in Figures 7.1 and 7.2. In most cases '*the fact that*' seems to add nothing to the meaning or communicative effect, and is indicative of a lexically 'sparse' style, as opposed to the succinct dense style we associate with written text, and particularly written academic text (as noted by Stubbs, 1980 and Halliday, 1985, amongst others).

6 Discussion and Pedagogical Implications

The BAWE corpus was not designed to facilitate comparisons of NS and NNS student writing, and therefore the findings of such comparisons must be treated with caution. NS and NNS writing is not represented in equal quantity in the corpus, and the NNS assignments are not distributed evenly across disciplines and levels of study, as shown in Table 7.3.

The writing of both NS and NNS students in the BAWE corpus is of a standard required by their subject tutors, with respect to their disciplinary knowledge and level of study. From her analysis of cohesive devices in student essays, Hinkel (2001) concluded that her NNS students had problems with 'tying strings' in their writing, and needed to be taught that 'nouns such as *advantage, factor, problem, reason, stage, term, type* are expected to have identifiable referents in text, to which these nouns are "connected"' (pp. 129–130).

This problem is not apparent in our data; we did not find many dangling shell nouns which could not be linked to propositions earlier or later in the

and mind are distinct from each other **because of the fact** that he "can clearly and distinctly understand one the whole essence of our existence is **because of the fact** that we are thinking . This follows , that if we were neighbouring and unrelated products . **Because of the fact** that the Commission is considering conglomerate will be our competitor's main disadvantage, **due to the fact** that they will be anxious to main a good relations the majority was apathetic or hostile to it. **Due to the fact** that there can be many interpretations to a book, medicine to cure these problems . This is **due to the fact** that the economic processes of globalisation unde requirements, existing **due to and alongside the fact** that the keeping of PEAs is regulated by legislation

FIGURE 7.1   Examples of NNS use of *because of the fact that* and *due to the fact that*

---

alone in the midst of people, not only **because of the fact** of loneliness, but also for the fact of valuelessness
for all the short listed materials, purely **because of the fact** that lighter materials with the same strength
     is also fairly popular which may be **because of the fact** it contains materials to build nests, and may even
in Rome instead of Florence. This was partly **due to the fact** that, during the period at the beginning of the
organ in which energy is needed. Discussion **Due to the fact** that the person study is under the underweight
to compare data from 2004/5 and 2003/4, **due to that fact** that different standards have been employed.
than 5.04 the absorbance decreases. This is **due to the fact** that as the pH increases there are less hydrogen.

FIGURE 7.2 Examples of NS use of *because of the fact that* and *due to the fact that*

text, perhaps because the contributors to the BAWE corpus were more experienced academic writers. Moreover the NNS writer reliance on *th-* + *N* as an anaphoric linking device, documented by Aktas and Cortes (2008), was somewhat less pronounced in the BAWE corpus.

Nevertheless our study has implications for the teaching of academic writing, both to NNS and NS students. There is some evidence of the redundant use of shell nouns in both the NS and the NNS data, and there is also some evidence to suggest that the NNS writers did not utilize the cohesive potential of the pattern *th-* + *N* to the fullest extent, using it to evaluate a previous clause but not to carry forward their argument.

Unlike conjunctive adjuncts, and despite the growing body of research into their use, shell nouns have so far received very little attention in the academic writing class. Like Aktas and Cortes (2008), we would recommend the systematic teaching of shell noun structures. Even at an advanced level, students would benefit from greater awareness of their communicative potential and appropriate use.

One way of incorporating the study of shell nouns in the EFL/ESL classroom could be to encourage students who use shell nouns in the manner illustrated in Examples Seven, Eight and Nine to produce more succinct text with more immediate justification of claims and/or explanation of the concepts under discussion. A series of writing activities might be used to encourage writers to progress from the style of Example Eight A to the style of Example Eight D, for example.

Example Eight A:

A very important characteristic of peat is that not many changes occur to it during storage. **This fact is very important** for a growing media. An experiment which took place in Nottingham Trent [sic] University investigated changes in organic growing media during storage.

(6110b, Greek, level 4, Biological Sciences)

Example Eight B:

A very important characteristic of peat is that not many changes occur to it during storage. **This fact is very important** as has been demonstrated. An experiment which took place in Nottingham Trent University investigated changes in organic growing media during storage.

(rewritten text)

Example Eight C:

A very important characteristic of peat is that not many changes occur to it during storage. **This important fact** was demonstrated in an experiment at Nottingham Trent University which investigated changes in organic growing media.

(rewritten text)

Example Eight D:

A very important characteristic of peat is that not many changes occur to it during storage, as was demonstrated in an experiment at Nottingham Trent University which investigated changes in organic growing media.

(rewritten text)

In the original (Eight A) there are a number of repeated words and phrases: *very important, changes, during storage, growing media.* Students' attention could be drawn to any similar redundancies in their own writing. In Example Eight A, the shell noun *fact* functions solely as an anaphoric device, although the third sentence goes on to provide justification for the earlier claim (that not many changes occur to peat during storage). More proficient writers would probably incorporate this justification in the clause containing the shell noun, in the manner of Examples Ten to Fourteen discussed earlier.

Example Eight B begins the process of prospection (Sinclair, 1993), and Eight C collapses the information content still further. Eight D reduces all redundancy and the shell noun is removed, although of course it should be acknowledged that this final stage is not always appropriate, because elimination of the shell noun often renders the text too dense, resulting in loss of clarity of meaning.

Examples Fifteen and Sixteen, both produced by NNS writers in the early stages of academic study, are less than expert in their use of sentence-initial adjuncts, but effectively employ shell nouns to draw attention to key propositions, building on previous arguments and guiding readers towards new ones. As a classroom activity, learners might be asked to identify shell nouns in their own writing, and consider their potential to characterize, foreground and elaborate key propositions in similar ways.

Example Fifteen (where the shell noun 'factor' refers back to and encapsulates the idea that trade helps commercialization, and is used in a negative clause to predict that at least one other aid to economic growth will be identified)

Some people argue that imperialism played an important role in Britain's economic growth. However, although trade does help commercialization, it alone cannot be the only **factor** in stimulating economic growth. Furthermore, colonies are expensive to maintain, so free trade is a more ideal policy.

(0071a, Cantonese, level 1, Economics)

Example Sixteen (where the shell noun 'problem' in the third sentence provides an advance signal that the model introduced in the first two sentences will be evaluated in the sentences that follow)

The electrons who are charged negatively circle about the nucleus on orbits. This is why the model is also called the planetary model of the atom. However, there was one big **problem** with this model which couldn't be explained. Rutherford's model predicted that the electrons on circular or elliptical orbits circle about the nucleus and are therefore radial accelerated. However the classical Newtonians mechanic says that accelerating charges emit electromagnetic rays and therefore lose energy. As a result of this the electrons would circle towards the nucleus.

(6117a, German, level 1, Physics)

Finally, examples such as Seventeen and Eighteen, both produced by Masters level NS writers, might be used in the classroom to demonstrate that shell nouns remain an important resource for more experienced writers.

Example Seventeen:

Russell J. Lundholm in the article 'Reporting on the past: A new approach to improving accounting today proposes that financial reporting be amended to report on the expost accuracy of a firm's prior estimates. This will identify firms that have abused their reporting discretion. With a **system** to report on the expost accuracy, regulators might be more willing to allow the booking of difficult-to-measure assets, such as the value of R&D expenditures.

(0297a, English, level 4, Mathematics)

Example Eighteen:

Multiple pulse decoupling sequences such as TPPM (Two Pulse Phase Modulated) have proven to be much more effective than continuous wave (CW) decoupling methods. A disadvantage of the cross polarization technique is that results obtained via this **process** do not retain the quantitative nature of most single pulse NMR spectra.

(0306b, English, level 4, Physics)

Such examples show how shell nouns can be employed in sophisticated ways, to develop arguments over multiple clauses, and encapsulate meaning that is elaborated elsewhere in the text.

Acknowledgement

The British Academic Written English (BAWE) corpus was developed at the Universities of Warwick, Reading and Oxford Brookes under the directorship of Hilary Nesi and Sheena Gardner (formerly of the Centre for Applied Linguistics [previously called CELTE], Warwick), Paul Thompson (formerly of the Department of Applied Linguistics, Reading) and Paul Wickens (Westminster Institute of Education, Oxford Brookes), with funding from the ESRC (RES-000-23-0800).

Note

[1] See Kilgarriff et al. (2004). The Sketch Engine open site http://ca.sketchengine. co.uk/open/allows free access to the BAWE corpus.

References

Aktas, R. N., & Cortes, V. (2008). Shell nouns as cohesive devices in published and ESL student writing. *Journal of English for Academic Purposes, 7*(1), 3–14.

Alsop, S., & Nesi, H. (2009). Issues in the development of the British Academic Written English (BAWE) corpus. *Corpora, 4*(1), 71–83.

Arshavskaya, E. (2009, March). *Automatic profiling of learner corpora.* Paper presented at the CALICO conference: Language Learning in the Era of Ubiquitous Computing, Arizona State University.

Charles, M. (2003). 'This mystery...': A corpus-based study of the use of nouns to construct stance in theses from two contrasting disciplines. *Journal of English for Academic Purposes, 2*(4), 313–326.

Charles, M. (2007). Argument or evidence? Disciplinary variation in the use of the Noun *that* pattern in stance construction. *English for Specific Purposes, 26*(2), 203–218.

Flowerdew, J. (2003a). Signalling nouns in discourse. *English for Specific Purposes, 22*(4), 329–346.

Flowerdew, J. (2003b). Register-specificity of signalling nouns in discourse. In P. Leistyna & C. F. Meyer (Eds.), *Corpus analysis: Language structure and language use* (pp. 35–46). Amsterdam: Rodopi.

Flowerdew, J. (2010). Use of signalling nouns across L1 and L2 writer corpora. *International Journal of Corpus Linguistics, 15*(1), 36–55.

Francis, G. (1986). *Anaphoric nouns.* [Discourse Analysis Monograph. No. 11.] Birmingham: English Language Research, University of Birmingham.

Gardezi, S. A., & Nesi, H. (2009). Variation in the writing of economics students in Britain and Pakistan: The case of conjunctive ties. In M. Charles, D. Pecorari & S. Hunston (Eds.), *Academic writing: At the interface of corpus and discourse* (pp. 236–250). London: Continuum.

Granger, S. (2002). A birds-eye view of learner corpus research. In S. Granger, J. Hung & S. Petch-Tyson (Eds.), *Computer learner corpora, second language acquisition and foreign language teaching* (pp. 3–36). Amsterdam: John Benjamins.

Granger, S., & Rayson, P. (1998). Automatic profiling of learner texts. In S. Granger (Ed.), *Learner English on computer* (pp. 119–131). London: Longman.

Halliday, M. A. K. (1985). *Spoken and written language*. Oxford: Oxford University Press.

Halliday, M. A. K., & Hasan, R. (1976). *Cohesion in English*. London: Longman.

Hinkel, E. (2001). Matters of cohesion in L2 academic texts. *Applied Language Learning, 12*(2), 111–132.

Hunston, S., & Francis, G. (1999). *Pattern grammar*. Amsterdam: John Benjamins.

Ivanic, R. (1991). Nouns in search of a context: A study of nouns with both open- and closed-system characteristics. *International Review of Applied Linguistics in Language Teaching, 29*(2), 93–114.

Kilgarriff, A., Rychly, P., Smrz, P., & Tugwell, D. (2004). The sketch engine. In G. Williams & S. Vessier (Eds.), *Proceedings of the eleventh EURALEX congress* (pp. 105–116). France: Université de Bretagne Sud, Lorient.

Schmid, H. (2000). *English abstract nouns as conceptual shells*. Berlin: Walter de Gruyter.

Sinclair, J. M. (1993). Written discourse structure. In J. M. Sinclair, M. Hoey & G. Fox (Eds.), *Techniques of description: Spoken and written discourse* (pp. 6–31). London: Routledge.

Stubbs, M. (1980). *Language and literacy*. London: Routledge & Kegan Paul.

Tadros, A. (1994). Predictive categories in expository text. In M. Coulthard (Ed.), *Advances in written text analysis* (pp. 69–82). London: Routledge.

Winter, E. (1982). *Towards a contextual grammar of English*. London: Allen & Unwin.

Chapter 8

Writing in Tables and Lists: A Study of Chinese Students' Undergraduate Assignments in UK Universities

Maria Leedham

1 Introduction

Chinese people now comprise the 'largest single overseas student group in the UK' with more than 85,000 registered at UK institutions in 2009 (British Council, 2010). While there have been many studies carried out on short pieces of writing from this group (e.g. Chuang & Nesi, 2006) and Master's level theses (e.g. Hyland, 2008), there has been comparatively little corpus research carried out on Chinese students' undergraduate writing. This chapter explores the writing of 30 Chinese undergraduate students studying in UK universities in the first decade of the twenty-first century. A corpus of these students' assignments (n = 104) from five disciplines (Biological Sciences, Food Science, Engineering, Business and Economics) was extracted from the British Academic Written English corpus[1] (Nesi et al., 2005). Additionally, the assignments of 71 first language (L1) English undergraduate students from the same disciplines (295 texts) were also compiled from BAWE to provide a comparison corpus. Unlike many studies of second language (L2) English writing, however, the L1 English corpus is not intended to be normative since both sets of assignments are successful with scores of 60% or higher (equivalent to 2:1 or 1st class in the UK system).

This chapter concentrates on two features from the writing of each student group: the use of tables, figures, images and diagrams (henceforth collectively referred to as 'visuals') and the use of writing formatted as lists. These features were revealed to be of interest through a keyword analysis which indicated that lexical items such as *figure*, *refer* and *graph* and also numbers were employed significantly more frequently by the L1 Chinese students than by the L1 English students. Counts of tagged visuals and lists in the corpora confirmed this difference, and analysis of the two student corpora by year groups suggested that disparity in the use of lists in particular becomes more pronounced over the three years of undergraduate study. Following the corpus analysis, pairs of texts with the same assignment title by L1 Chinese and L1 English students in Biological Sciences and Economics (n = 4) were examined in detail to explore the ways in which visuals and lists are used in the writing. It is suggested that these are used by L1 Chinese students as strategies for meeting the many current challenges which confront all undergraduate students in UK universities today, and that these are useful strategies which could be employed by both L1 and L2 English students.

2 Current Challenges in Assessed Writing in UK Higher Education (HE)

Undergraduate students in UK Higher Education face a number of challenges in writing university assignments (Lea & Stierer, 2000). Difficulties include tutors' lack of articulation as to exactly what they require (Crème & Lea, 2003; Lea & Street, 1998; Lillis, 1997, 2001), tutors' and students' different conceptions of what a particular assignment entails (Lea, 2004), and different perceptions of what constitutes 'good writing' (Lea & Stierer, 2000). For all undergraduate students, a major strategic aim of assignment-writing is to display disciplinary knowledge in an appropriate form in order to gain marks and ultimately a university degree (Kaldor & Rochecouste, 2002). However, framing this knowledge is difficult since undergraduates are effectively required to write for a dual audience: assignment rubrics may necessitate writing for an audience with little knowledge of the discipline (the imagined reader of the essay/press release/case study), while the assessment actually involves writing for an audience with a high level of disciplinary knowledge (the discipline lecturer/assessor). (See ethnographic accounts of this difficulty in Lillis, 2001.)

Alongside the longstanding challenge of working out such 'rules of the academic achievement game' (Newman, 2001, p. 472), students are faced with more current challenges. In recent decades, UK Higher Education has altered from a 'conventional single route initiating a cohort of students into the practices of their discipline' (North, 2005, p. 517) to a model of increasing flexibility of degrees which allow students to combine courses from different areas. Recent research within the area of academic literacies has highlighted the difficulties involved in learning to write in ways prescribed by a particular discipline (e.g. Bazerman, 2001;

Hewings, 1999; Lillis, 2001; Rai, 2008). Corpus studies such as Hyland (2008), and ethnographic studies such as Prior (1998) have illustrated the extent to which academic writing varies between disciplines. Indeed, Harwood and Hadley (2004) suggest this variation extends beyond whole disciplines to practices in academic writing which differ 'from department to department, and even from lecturer to lecturer' (p. 366). Despite this, classes in English for Academic Purposes (EAP) frequently consist of students from a wide range of disciplinary areas, and do not have the resources to distinguish between or practise the writing required within each of these disciplines.

A further challenge for all undergraduate writers is the increase in new genres such as reflective blogs, website evaluations or press releases (Gibbs, 2006; Nesi & Gardner, 2006). While these may not be 'new' for all students, they are likely to be unfamiliar to many, and often entail writing in a different 'voice' and for a different audience to the 'default genre' of the essay (Andrews, 2003, p. 117). An example of an assignment rubric which would probably be new to all students is the following from a History of Mathematics module: 'It is the early 1830s. Write a letter of advice to a very good student of yours who is about to travel abroad to study Mathematics'. An effective response to this would entail the selection of appropriate disciplinary knowledge, the choice of suitably advisory language for the intended audience and an awareness of letter-writing conventions. This is very different to relaying the same information within an essay or report format. Among the reasons for the change to a broader range of genres are the widespread use of electronic resources, shifts in the exam: coursework balance, and increasing employer and student demands for real-life tasks (see Leedham (2009) for a fuller discussion).

The number of written genres that students are now expected to produce inevitably places a strain on them, and L2 English students from different cultural backgrounds are particularly likely to struggle. For example, the large cohort of L1 Chinese students with a secondary education from the People's Republic of China[2] are accustomed to short answer questions and the traditional written essay (Cross & Hitchcock, 2007) rather than the plethora of new genres encountered in UK universities. Challenges such as a lack of clarity in assignment rubric, the increase in interdisciplinary degrees and the rise in innovative assignment types present difficulties for all undergraduate students in the UK, and add significantly to the existing pressure of producing extended writing for L2 English students.

3 Data and Methodology

The majority[3] of the assignments in this study are taken from the British Academic Written English (BAWE) corpus (see Heuboeck et al., 2008). Both the L1 Chinese and L1 English corpora in this study contain proficient undergraduate assignments from five disciplines (see Table 8.1).

These five disciplines[4] were selected as they contain relatively high numbers of assignments by L1 Chinese students, from a range of individuals and across the undergraduate year groups. All five are towards the 'hard' end of the 'hard/soft' continuum of disciplines (Becher, 1989). One reason for L1 Chinese students favouring 'hard' disciplines when studying internationally is that language is perceived as playing a smaller role in such disciplines than in the 'soft' disciplines of, say, History or Philosophy. This view is expounded by Neumann et al. (2002) who point out that in the hard sciences, 'a skill with deploying facts and figures counts for more than elegance of writing style' and 'many students survive scientifically-based courses with very little need for skills in prose exposition' (p. 412).

The two corpora of L1 Chinese texts and L1 English texts can also be analysed by year group[5] (see Table 8.2). Table 8.2 shows how the average length of assignments, as counted by WordSmith Tools software (Scott, 2008a), rises for each successive year group, since students are required to write longer assignments over time. However, the average length of assignments by L1 English students is slightly longer than that of L1 Chinese students. It seems plausible that the latter group takes longer to write in prose and therefore tend to submit assignments of shorter lengths while still within an acceptable range (see also Mauranen, 1993).

Table 8.1 Number of texts wordcounts and average wordlengths in each discipline

	L1 Chinese corpus			L1 English corpus		
Discipline	**No. of assignments**	**No. of words**	**Average length**	**No. of assignments**	**No. of Words**	**Average length**
Biological Sciences	18	33633	1868	83	173412	2089
Business	20	33303	1665	37	82966	2242
Economics	20	38086	1904	22	52158	2371
Engineering	20	35627	1781	97	203782	2101
Food Science	26	30267	1164	55	73496	1336
Totals	104	170916		294	585814	

Table 8.2 Number of texts and wordcounts in each year group

Yeargroup	L1 Chinese corpus			L1 English corpus		
	No. of assignments	No. of words	Average length	No. of assignments	No. of words	Average length
Year 1	38	46212	1216	96	151675	1580
Year 2	31	51747	1669	118	240440	2038
Year 3	35	72957	2084	80	193699	2421
Totals	104	170916		294	585814	

In comparing the writing of the two student groups, this chapter makes use of corpus linguistics for keyword analysis and counts of tagged features in the sets of assignments overall, and employs close reading of two texts in Biological Sciences and two in Economics in order to examine visuals and lists in whole assignments more closely. Finally, information from discipline interviews collected alongside the BAWE corpus is considered as these give pertinent comments on the relevance of visuals and lists in assignment-writing.

In corpus linguistics, a word is described as 'key' if it 'occurs more often than would be expected by chance in comparison with the reference corpus' (Scott, 2008b), rendering 'keyness' a way of discovering differences between the corpora. The 'reference corpus' in this case is the larger collection of L1 English assignments from the same five disciplines. Keywords were extracted for each of the discipline subcorpora using Word-Smith with a setting of $p = .001$ (e.g. the writing of the L1 Chinese students in Biological Sciences was compared with the writing of L1 English students in Biological Sciences). The keyword analysis indicated that visuals and numbered lists are two areas of difference between the student groups. I then looked at these tagged features in the texts to confirm this difference.

In the BAWE corpus, certain non-prose features are 'tagged', that is, either the features are omitted and replaced by a computer-readable label or 'tag' (e.g. appendices) or the beginnings and ends of features are marked (e.g. headings). Of interest in this study are tagged tables, figures and lists. In BAWE tagging, a 'table' consists of any graphic presented using rows and columns while a 'figure' covers any graph, diagram, image, picture or drawing. Both tables and figures are omitted and are replaced with a tag when assignments are converted to plain text for inclusion in the corpus. Prose formatted as a list is tagged at the beginning and end of the list but the list items are left intact within the corpus. The BAWE mark-up distinguishes between prototypical 'lists' where each list item consists of a word or noun/verb phrase, and 'false' lists which consist of 'paragraphs of running text carrying listlike formatting' (Ebeling & Heuboeck, 2007). These 'false lists' are termed 'listlikes' and are

Conclusions
The experiment yielded the following conclusions: • The efficiency of a single stage centrifugal pump at high pump speed (3000 RPM) is better than at low pump speed (2000 RPM). • The input power with high pump speech increases faster than the one with low pump speed as discharge increases. • The relationship between total head and discharge is not affected by pump speed, but higher pump speed provides higher total head.

FIGURE 8.1 Example of text containing three listlike items from an Engineering assignment.

presented as a list in the assignment, yet contain larger units of text per list item (see example in Figure 8.1). Common to both lists and listlikes is the distinct formatting of items with bullets, numbers, hyphens or other means.

Following the extraction of keywords and tagged features from the corpora overall, the second stage in the analysis was carried out, namely a close comparison of pairs of assignments in Biological Sciences and Economics. Since BAWE texts were collected at just four universities (Warwick, Reading, Oxford Brookes and also at Coventry towards the end of the project), there are a small number of texts by L1 Chinese and by L1 English students from the same university, the same module and which answer the same assignment question. As all BAWE texts were awarded high marks, a comparison can be made of the proportion of visuals and lists to prose in each text.

Finally, the discussion is supported through data from selected semi-structured interviews with discipline lecturers. These were carried out alongside the collection of assignments for the BAWE corpus. Both interviews and corpus compilation are part of the ESRC-funded project 'An Investigation of Genres of Assessed Writing in British Higher Education' (Nesi et al., 2005). As a researcher on this project, I carried out almost one-third of the interviews and have access to data from all fifty-eight. Of these, 7 interviews are with Biological Sciences or Economics lecturers and provide some insider knowledge on student writing within these disciplines.

4 Findings and Discussion

4.1 Corpus analysis

The initial keyword analysis of each L1 Chinese discipline with the equivalent L1 English discipline as a reference corpus suggested visuals and lists to be fruitful areas for further exploration. Table 8.3 shows keywords relating to visuals and lists given in decreasing order of keyness for each discipline.

Table 8.3   Keywords relating to visuals and lists

L1 & discipline	Chi-Biol	Chi-Bus	Chi-Econ	Chi-Engin	Chi-Food
Selected keywords	#		*growth*	#	#
	table		*curve*	*eq.*	*curve*
	data		*refer*	*according*	*referring*
	equation		*model*	*figure*	*statistical*
	figure		*per*		*deviation*
	graph		*output*		*numbers*

A greater reliance on tables and figures by the L1 Chinese students was hypothesized from the presence of keywords such as *table*, *refer*, *figure* and *curve*. This was confirmed through examination of concordance lines (e.g. 'the raw data curve in figure 3.6', 'referring to diagram 4'). The greater use of numbers (indicated both in WordSmith and Table 8.3 through the hash symbol '#') was also followed up through concordance line searches and seemed to be in part due to the use of numbered lists in the L1 Chinese corpus (e.g. 'There are 3 generic ways of changing the structure of a market: 1. building a new or modified set of players in a market, 2. eliminating players in a market' (text 7021a)). Numbers are also used by both student groups and particularly the L1 Chinese group in the labeling of tables and figures, within equations, in reference denotations, and within percentages and other data.

The existence of this group of keywords, however, does not in itself mean that the L1 Chinese students use a greater number of visuals and lists in their assignments, and the next stage in the analysis was to count tagged features in order to determine comparative usage. Table 8.4 gives the number of tables, figures, lists and listlikes used by each student group in the five disciplines, with results normalized to counts per 10,000 words.

Table 8.4 suggests that there are both disciplinary differences in the use of visuals and lists, and also differences between the two student groups. Thus, it can be seen that tables are used most frequently in Food Science, Biological Sciences and Engineering, and in each case, it is the texts by L1 Chinese students that have a higher count than those by L1 English students (e.g. Chi-Biol has a normalized count of 15 tables per 10,000 words while Eng-Biol contains 5). For the category of 'figures', the disciplines of Biological Sciences, Engineering and Economics show the highest usage, and again the texts by L1 Chinese students contain identical or higher counts. The normalized counts for lists are lower, since a 'list' comprises a potentially lengthy sequence of short items. The clearest

Table 8.4 Use of tables, figures, lists and listlikes per 10,000 words

	Tables	Figures	Lists	Listlikes
Chi-Biol	15****	25****	1	4
Eng-Biol	5	13	2	6
Chi-Econ	1	14****	2*	25****
Eng-Econ	0	12	1	3
Chi-Bus	2	2	6*	129****
Eng-Bus	6**	6**	3	23
Chi-Food	20*	6	5	82****
Eng-Food	14	6	4	18
Chi-Engin	10*	21	7	53****
Eng-Engin	7	21	10	24

Note: Figures used are from Rayson's Log Likelihood calculator:
*   95th percentile; p < .05; critical value = 3.84
**   99th percentile; p < .01; critical value = 6.63
***   99.9th percentile; p < .001; critical value = 10.83
****   99.99th percentile; p < .0001; critical value = 15.13

picture of difference between the two student groups comes from the use of listlikes, where, in all disciplines excepting Biological Sciences, the number of listlikes used by each L1 Chinese discipline is significantly greater (p = .0001).

Disciplinary differences in these features are to be expected, since for example Biological Sciences entails the understanding of images of natural phenomena, and Business is likely to involve reports with list type writing, yet it is less clear why the student groups should also differ in their usage of these features. One possible explanation is that using a table, figure, list or listlike to present information in an assignment is an attractive option for L1 Chinese students as this reduces the quantity of connected prose required. A great deal of information may be given succinctly in a table or figure, resulting in shorter assignments. Lists and listlikes reduce the need for connecting chunks and again reduce the wordcount. The higher use of visuals and lists thus partly accounts for the lower wordcounts of L1 Chinese students' texts noted in section 3. More positive explanations for the differences are that visuals and lists are viable alternative means of giving the required information, that they do so concisely, and that they perhaps help more visual readers to process information. Since all assignments in this study are deemed by discipline lecturers to be of a proficient standard, the strategies of using tables, figures, lists and listlikes appears to be, at the very least, an acceptable way of presenting information.

Analyzing the corpora by year group shows the use of listlikes to be significantly higher for the L1 Chinese subcorpora in all year groups

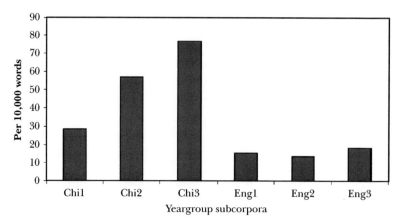

FIGURE 8.2   Listlikes by year group.

(p = .0001) and also reveals this way of presenting information to be used increasingly over the period of undergraduate study (Figure 8.2).

It seems that the L1 Chinese students increasingly write in bulleted or numbered items rather than paragraphs of connected prose as a presentation style in their writing. It may be that they adopt these strategies more and more in order to meet the challenge of writing increasingly lengthy assignments in a variety of genres. It is not possible, however, to ascertain from this corpus study whether L1 Chinese students tend to opt for assignments in which the rubric encourages this style of writing, or whether they simply choose to answer assignments in this way.

4.2 Close reading

Thus far, the use of visuals and lists in assignments has been contrasted through the total number of tables, figures, or lists used within a discipline by each student group. This is a very rough measure, as the number of occurrences of a feature does not indicate the length, complexity, or significance placed on these by the writer. The analysis in this section focuses on the space given to visuals and lists as a proportion of the whole assignment, in order to gauge their dominance. Two pairs of texts, from Biological Sciences and from Economics, were found which in each case answer the same question. The Biological Sciences texts illustrate the differing use of visuals in each student group, and the Economics texts show how similar answers to a series of questions can be given in list format or as connected prose. The pairs of texts are discussed below.

4.2.1 Biological Sciences

The two texts discussed in this section were written by third year Biological Sciences students from the same university, and are taken from a module entitled 'Development'. The title of each assignment is 'The role of maternal effect genes in the development of the nematode Caenorhabditis elegans'. Each text was awarded over 70%. Both texts contain an abstract, are written in an impersonal style, and one text is produced as two columns; these features suggest the writers may have wished to emulate a journal article. The two assignments contain approximately the same number of words when counted through Word-Smith (WS) after the removal of visuals and their captions (see Table 8.5).

Table 8.5 includes counts for the number of tables and figures in each assignment, and also gives an indication of the proportion of each assignment comprising visuals (as a percentage of the whole text). The figures for both texts are mainly in colour, though may have been printed out in black and white for submission to the tutor. The category of 'figures' includes images and cross-sectional diagrams of the organism and process diagrams of its lifecycle and the reproductive process. In both assignments, tables and figures are referred to in brackets at the end of information-giving sentences (e.g. 'both functions of somatic gene silencing in nuclei and stability and expression regulating of maternal RNAs in cytoplasm assist in preserve the germ cell fate. (Figure 17)' (text 0434a)).

Both writers seem to integrate visuals effectively with their writing, using them to both support and extend their prose descriptions. Some of the visuals in the two texts are labelled as adapted from secondary references. Others do not contain references, though this does not necessarily mean they are devised by the student. Frequently, particularly for text 0067b, a figure includes over 100 words of explanatory prose within the caption. However, captions are omitted in BAWE tagging, rendering the comparative word-counts achieved through WordSmith less accurate. While figures and tables appear to be an important part of each assignment, there is nevertheless a

Table 8.5 Comparison of two Biological Sciences assignments

	L1 Chinese, text 0434a	**L1 English, text 0067b**
No. of pages excluding refs	15.5	9
No. of tokens (in WS)	3,234	3,201
No. of tables	2	0
No. of figures	17	5
Visuals as proportion of whole text	48% (7.5 pp)	22% (2pp)
Layout	whole page	two columns

great difference in both the total number used and in the proportion of the assignment pages occupied by visuals.

The high use of tables and figures by the L1 Chinese writer increases the number of A4 pages filled to 15.5 (excluding 3.5 reference or blank end pages), compared to the 9 employed by the L1 English writer (though the use of two columns by this writer condenses the prose). Figure 8.3 shows the beginning of each assignment, with title, abstract and introduction.

In the case of these two assignments, it appears that texts 0434a and 0067b contain similar quantities of descriptive and explanatory prose, but that text 0434a more often extends these with illustrative figures. For example, in a section headed 'C. elegans maternal notch system' there are three figures in text 0434a and approximately 350 words of text, including captions. In the equivalent section in 0067b, there are no figures and approximately 400 words of text. Recent work within multimodal analysis has highlighted the role of non-linguistic resources such as images and layout in meaning making (for an overview of multimodal analysis, see Jewitt, 2009). More detailed analysis of the effectiveness of visuals would necessitate both lecturer and student's involvement in explaining the purpose and source of each table, figure, image or diagram.

4.2.2 Economics

The two texts in Economics are again from the same university, same module ('Econometrics 1') and have the same title ('Assignment 1'). The assignment asks students to analyse the exam marks of three undergraduate

Text 0434a, page 1, L1 Chinese writer   Text 0067b, page 1, L1 English writer

FIGURE 8.3   The first page of a Biological Sciences assignment by two writers.

Table 8.6 Comparison of two Economics assignments

	L1 Chinese, text 0155a	L1 English, text 0202j
No. of pages excluding refs	6	6
No. of tokens (in WS)	3,731	4,242
No. of formulae	19	6
No. of lists	2	0
No. of listlikes	28	0
Lists and listlikes as proportion of whole text	90%	0%

cohorts, and to answer six questions using the data tables provided. (Note that neither student reproduces these data tables in the body of their assignment.) The first question of the assignment asks for the main features of the data in a table of descriptive statistics. This is followed by sections requiring students to carry out tests such as regression analyses on the data (questions 2 to 5). Finally, students are asked to construct a model of exam performance, drawing on their answers to previous sections (question 6).

Both assignments contain appendices, though as these were not submitted to BAWE by the author of text 0155a they are not included in the current analysis. In line with the mean average wordcounts in Economics given in Table 8.1, the assignment by the L1 Chinese student is around 500 words shorter than the L1 English student's text (see Table 8.6). Each student's assignment was awarded over 70%.

The most notable difference on reading through the two texts is the layouts. The L1 Chinese student's work consists almost entirely of a series of lists and listlikes, organized under the 6 question headings, whereas the L1 English student's assignment is mainly written in connected prose, again beneath the 6 question headings.

Text 0155a is set out as a report, with a brief, 3-line 'introduction' followed by headings consisting of the question number and a meaningful title (e.g. '1. Main features of the data'). Within each of these sections, points are given as a bulleted list. Frequently this list includes further items given within lists. On occasion, list items are not separated by bullets or similar formatting (and so would not be included in the BAWE listlikes count), but consist simply of a series of sentences which each begin on a new line. The text is broken up throughout with the writer making use of italics or emboldening to highlight lines containing formulae. Bold is also used for subheadings and key concluding points. (See example text in Figure 8.4.)

The high use of lists throughout text 0155a serves to organize the assignment, reducing the need for connecting words and phrases. For example, in Figure 8.4, the possible ways of grouping the data are simply

---

• Comparisons of data across various groups

Pure Economics degree vs. non pure Economics degree: Students doing pure Economics degree scored 66.23 on average, while students doing a mixed-Economics degree scored 61.68 (very significant).

Female vs. Male: The average female students got 63.8, compared to 65.4 for male students.

UK students vs. non-UK students: On average, UK students gained 64.63 while non-UK students gained 66.38.

Number of parents who attended university: Those students whose parents never attended university achieved 64.12 on average, those with one parent atttended university achieved 64.99 averagely, and those with both parents attended university achieved 65.59 on average.

FIGURE 8.4   Extract from text 0155a.

listed as headings (e.g. 'Female vs. Male'). This use of headings and layout removes the need for linking phrases such as 'The next group considered is'. Sometimes, the reader has to interpret the relevance of each piece of information in a list; for example in the final list item of Figure 8.4, we have to compare the numbers given to extract the intended meaning that students with two parents who attended university achieved a higher score than those with one or none (cf. Hinds's (1987) notion of reader/writer responsibility). The final paragraph to this assignment is headed 'comments on the model' and impartially restates the main points and the evidence on which these are based. A more personal note is conveyed in the penultimate section to question 6 in which the writer says 'I am concluding, to the best of my ability, that the optimal function should be of a linear form'.

In contrast to the lists used in 0155a, text 0202j consists largely of paragraphs of sentences linked with *however, unfortunately, in all cases* and so on. There is a discursive introduction which sets out the rest of the text: 'in this project I shall firstly analyze various factors ... I shall then regress and analyse ... before concluding ....'. The main headings relate to the assignment outline (i.e. 'Question 1') and within these some limited use is made of subheadings. The prose is also punctuated by occasional formulae. However, the overall effect is of a continuous piece of writing with signposting used effectively to guide the reader through. Figure 8.5 shows an extract from the response to Question 1 given by the writer of text 0202j.

A comparison of Figures 8.4 and 8.5 illustrates the more discursive nature of 0202j. Text 0202j first introduces the need for 'sub-samples' within the results, and then guides the reader through these ('firstly we can break it up according to...'). Figure 8.5 also shows how the writer of 0202j broadens

> To make some comments about these results, we need to break this up into sub-samples. Firstly we can break it up according to sex, as Siegfried and Strand did. For males, table 2 shows that the mean score is 65.4%, which is higher than the corresponding score for females of 63.75%. This agrees with Siegfried and Strand's paper which claims males do better than females. However, the standard deviation for males is lower than for females, 12.64% compared to 14.02%.

FIGURE 8.5 Extract from text 0202j.

the discussion out from the given data, making links with other texts ('This agrees with Siegfried and Strand's paper ...'). While text 0202j brings in additional voices through citation, it displays a more minimal approach than 0155a to providing background information to calculations (see Table 8.6 to compare the number of formulae for each text).

The signposting shown in Figure 8.5 continues in later sections of 0202j (e.g. 'given my results from previous questions and previous research, I am now going to try and formulate a model of exam performance ...'). The final paragraph of this assignment begins 'in conclusion' and reiterates the writer's views on the model. Unlike the writer of text 0155a, the L1 English writer of 0202j restates the main results while also conveying the achievement of the assignment: 'I have calculated a model of exam performance based on a number of variables, as given above'. The writer relates these variables to 'theory from economists such as Romer' and also to their 'own experience', whereas the 0155a writer restricts their description to the provided data.

Overall, the L1 Chinese writer gives their responses to the 6 questions within the assignment succinctly and with little metatext or comment but focuses instead on the calculations. In comparison the L1 English writer guides the reader through the work and reflects more on the process (cf. Mauranen's (1993) discussion on Finnish and Anglo-American writers' strategies in addressing the reader). As with the Biological Sciences texts, it seems that the two Economics students have each achieved a creditable mark in the same assignment through different means, since giving an answer within bulleted lists is clearly acceptable, as is providing a response in prose form.

4.3 Interviews with lecturers

The BAWE lecturer interviews included questions relating to the role of assignment-writing in the department, valued features of undergraduate assignments, and the writing needs of L2 English students. Interviews with lecturers in Biological Sciences (n = 4) and Economics (n = 3) shed some light on the strategies employed by the students discussed in section 4.2, particularly with regard to the use of figures and tables. Lecturers in both disciplines commented on the importance of visuals, suggesting that typically at least one in three pages of an assignment should contain a visual of some kind. One Biological Sciences interviewee thought that including diagrams helps undergraduates to gain better marks since they can refer to these rather than having to describe everything and risking the introduction of errors. Students are, however, 'incredibly reluctant' to construct their own diagrams (Biol-int-2) and tend to use existing ones taken from websites. While this is acceptable, it is preferable if students at least devise their own accompanying caption. In both disciplines, mislabelled axes on graphs were mentioned as a particular dislike. The choice of data used in a report is seen as being of great importance since this tells the lecturer 'a great deal about what they are thinking' (Biol-int-1). Two of the three interviewees in Economics commented on the challenge involved in analyzing visuals in prose. While the pair of Economics assignments discussed in 4.2 do not include visuals, the main task appears to be the interpretation of a dataset given in graphs and other visual forms.

In Biological Sciences, the ability to be concise was mentioned, with one lecturer commenting that 'there's never been a penalty for an essay that's too short' (Biol-int-2). Echoing Neumann et al.'s (2002) remark on skill in 'deploying facts and figures count(ing) for more than elegance of writing style' (p. 412), one lecturer commented that it was easier to gain a good mark with a low language level in a laboratory report than in an essay. Interestingly, one interviewee stated that essential oral instruction on assignment tasks is often given out in lectures, meaning that a reliance on assignment rubric cannot give the whole picture as to how and why students construct their texts in particular ways.

The only comment given pertaining to lists was from one Economics lecturer who stated a dislike of written work in note format rather than in complete sentences. However, the lists and listlikes presented in text 0155a contain full sentences given as lists, rather than as sentence fragments, so would presumably not be viewed in this negative way.

5 Conclusion

This chapter has shown that there are differences in the use of visuals and lists between L1 Chinese and L1 English students in undergraduate assignments within the same disciplines in the BAWE corpus. There is a particularly stark difference in the use of listlikes between the two groups, and this difference increases further over time, with L1 Chinese students increasingly adopting this form of presentation. Employing visuals and lists may be strategies used by L1 Chinese students to meet the challenges of producing multiple, extended pieces of writing within unfamiliar genres in their L2. These strategies allow students to present their findings and views clearly and effectively, while reducing the quantity of connected prose required. Presenting ideas through visuals and within lists may also be a strategy used by other L2 English writers, though further research on students with different L2s and across disciplines would be needed to explore this.

Despite the widespread use of visuals in several disciplines within undergraduate writing by both student groups in this study, 'graphic literacy' is seldom taught or even discussed in EAP classes. This may be partly due to EAP tutors' lack of awareness of writing across the disciplines. Johns (1998) points out that most applied linguists are 'trained in the humanities, where words are central to disciplinary values and argumentation' (p. 183). (See also Woodward-Kron & Jamieson, 2007.) Thus in writing centers and EAP classrooms, tutors may 'find themselves relying on disciplinary norms they are familiar with' (Gardner & Holmes, 2009, p. 251). These norms are likely to include a concentration on 'linear text' (Johns, 1998, p. 183) rather than on the interaction of visuals with text. This privileging of continuous prose over the use of graphs, diagrams and images disadvantages not only those students who need to acquire competence in the production and comprehension of visuals in disciplines such as Biological Sciences and Economics (cf. Kaldor & Rochecouste, 2002), but also those who may be more visually-oriented or who may find it preferable to provide part of their response through graphical means. At the same time, with the advent of Web 2.0, interpreting visuals is becoming increasingly important as students are required to interpret data not only in their academic disciplines but also in newspapers, magazines, and other personal spheres (e.g. financial information) (Sorapure, 2010).

Writing an undergraduate assignment using lists and listlikes is seldom discussed. Again, this could be due, in part, to EAP tutors' backgrounds in discursive, essay-oriented disciplines. However, as both student groups in the corpora received high marks, this is clearly an acceptable strategy. While university writing workshops are provided for L2 English students in UK universities and a small group of often self-selected L1 English students, they are not routinely encouraged for all undergraduates. It is likely that all students could benefit from guidance in the transition from secondary school to university-level academic writing (see Gourlay's (2009) discussion of the 'struggle' of this transition). EAP classes could be used to provide help in enculturating all students into discipline-specific writing, to explore the ways in which genres may differ, and to equip students with strategies for coping with the increasingly varied assignment requirements at university level. Using visuals to present and extend data, and employing lists are two such strategies which both L1 and L2 English students could usefully acquire.

Notes

[1] The data in this study come from the British Academic Written English (BAWE) corpus, which was developed at the Universities of Warwick, Reading and Oxford Brookes under the directorship of Hilary Nesi and Sheena Gardner (formerly of the Centre for Applied Linguistics [previously called CELTE], Warwick), Paul Thompson (formerly of the Department of Applied Linguistics, Reading) and Paul Wickens (Westminster Institute of Education, Oxford Brookes), with funding from the ESRC (RES-000-23-0800).

[2] The student groups are termed 'L1 Chinese', to refer to students with a wide variety of Chinese dialects and who were educated at secondary level wholly or mainly within the People's Republic of China, Hong Kong or Taiwan, and 'L1 English', denoting students whose L1 is English and whose secondary school education was wholly or mainly within the United Kingdom.

[3] Ninety-five texts are BAWE assignments by L1 Chinese students within the 5 disciplines; these were supplemented by a further 9 texts from additionally-collected data (Leedham, 2011) in order to increase the number of L1 Chinese texts and thus the generalizability of the study.

[4] In the BAWE corpus a 'discipline' is framed in terms of a subject taught within one university department (Heuboeck et al., 2008).

[5] The L1 Chinese corpus does not contain sufficient variety of texts by individuals to warrant a division by both discipline and year group.

References

Andrews, R. (2003). The end of the essay? *Teaching in Higher Education, 8*(1), 117–128.

Bazerman, C. (2001). Distanced and refined selves: Educational tensions in writing with thepower of knowledge. In M. Hewings (Ed.), *Academic writing in context* (pp. 23–29). Birmingham: Birmingham University Press.

Becher, T. (1989). *Academic tribes and territories.* Milton Keynes: The Society for Research into Higher Education/Open University Press.

British Council. (2010). *China market introduction.* Retrieved August 17, 2010, from http://www.britishcouncil.org/eumd-information-background-china.htm

Chuang, F.-Y., & Nesi, H. (2006). An analysis of formal errors in a corpus of L2 English produced by Chinese students. *Corpora, 1*(2), 251–271.

Crème, P., & Lea, M. R. (2003). *Writing at university* (2nd ed.). Buckingham: Open University Press.

Cross, J., & Hitchcock, R. (2007). Chinese students' (or students from China's) views of UK HE: Differences, difficulties and benefits, and suggestions for facilitating transition. *The East Asian Learner, 3*(2), 1–31.

Ebeling, S. O., & Heuboeck, A. (2007). Encoding document information in a corpus of student writing: The British Academic Written English corpus. *Corpora, 2*(2), 241–256.

Gardner, S., & Holmes, J. (2009). Can I use headings in my essay? Section headings, macrostructures and genre families in the BAWE corpus of student writing. In M. Charles, D. Pecorari & S. Hunston (Eds.), *Academic writing: At the interface of corpus and discourse* (pp. 251–271). London: Continuum.

Gibbs, G. (2006). Why assessment is changing. In C. Bryan & K. Clegg (Eds.), *Innovative assessment in higher education* (pp. 11–22). New York: Routledge.

Gourlay, L. (2009). Threshold practices: Becoming a student through academic literacies. *London Review of Education, 7*(2), 181–192.

Harwood, N., & Hadley, G. (2004). Demystifying institutional practices: Critical pragmatism and the teaching of academic writing. *English for Specific Purposes, 23*(4), 355–377.

Heuboeck, A., Holmes, J., & Nesi, H. (2008). *The BAWE corpus manual*. Warwick: Warwick University.

Hewings, A. (1999). Disciplinary engagement in undergraduate writing: An investigation of clause-initial elements in geography essays. (Unpublished doctoral dissertation). University of Birmingham, UK.

Hinds, J. (1987). Reader versus writer responsibility: A new typology of language. In U. Connor & R. Kaplan (Eds.), *Writing across languages* (pp. 141–152). Reading, MA: Addison-Welsey.

Hyland, K. (2008). As can be seen: Lexical bundles and disciplinary variation. *English for Specific Purposes, 27*(1), 4–21.

Jewitt, C. (2009). *The Routledge handbook of multimodal analysis*. London: Routledge.

Johns, A. M. (1998). The visual and the verbal: A case study in macroeconomics. *English for Specific Purposes, 17*(2), 183–197.

Kaldor, S., & Rochecouste, J. (2002). General academic writing and discipline specific academic writing. *Australian Review of Applied Linguistics, 25*(2), 29–47.

Lea, M. R. (2004). Academic literacies: A pedagogy for course design. *Studies in Higher Education, 29*(6), 739–756.

Lea, M. R., & Stierer, B. (2000). Editor's introduction. In M. R. Lea & B. Stierer (Eds.), *Student writing in higher education*. Buckingham: Open University Press.

Lea, M. R., & Street, B. (1998). Student writing in higher education: an academic literacies approach. *Studies in Higher Education, 23*(2), 157–172.

Leedham, M. (2009). From traditional essay to 'Ready Steady Cook' presentation: Reasons for innovative changes in assignments. *Active Learning in Higher Education, 10*(2), 191–206.

Leedham, M. (2011). A corpus-driven study of features of Chinese students' undergraduate writing in UK universities. (Unpublished doctoral dissertation). The Open University, Milton Keynes.

Lillis, T. (1997). New voices in academia? The regulative nature of academic writing conventions. *Language and Education, 11*(3), 182–199.

Lillis, T. (2001). *Student writing.* London: Routledge.

Mauranen, A. (1993). Theme and prospection in written discourse. In M. Baker, G. Francis & E. Tognini-Bonelli (Eds.), *Text and technology* (pp. 95–114). Philadelphia: John Benjamins.

Nesi, H., & Gardner, S. (2006). Variation in disciplinary culture: University tutors' views on assessed writing tasks. In R. Kiely, P. Rea-Dickins, H. Woodfield & G. Clibbon (Eds.), *Language, culture and identity in Applied Linguistics* (British Studies in Applied Linguistics vol. 21) (pp. 99–107). London: Equinox Publishing.

Nesi, H., Gardner, S., Forsyth, R., Hindle, D., Wickens, P., Ebeling, S., Leedham, M., Thompson, P., & Heuboeck, A. (2005, July). *Towards the compilation of a corpus of assessed student writing: An account of work in progress.* Paper presented at the Corpus Linguistics 2005 Conference, Birmingham, UK. Available from http://www.corpus.bham.ac.uk/pclc/

Neumann, R., Parry, S., & Becher, T. (2002). Teaching and learning in their disciplinary contexts: A conceptual analysis. *Studies in Higher Education, 27*(4), 405–417.

Newman, M. (2001). The academic achievement game: Designs of undergraduates' efforts to get grades. *Written Communication, 18*(4), 470–505.

North, S. (2005). Different values, different skills? A comparison of essay writing by students from arts and science backgrounds. *Studies in Higher Education, 30,* 517–533.

Prior, P. (1998). *Writing/Disciplinarity.* Mahwah, NJ: Lawrence Erlbaum.

Rai, L. (2008). Student writing in social work education. (Unpublished doctoral dissertation). The Open University, Milton Keynes.

Scott, M. (2008a). WordSmith Tools version 5. Liverpool: Lexical Analysis Software.

Scott, M. (2008b). WordSmith Tools version 5, help pages. Liverpool: Lexical Analysis Software.

Sorapure, M. (2010). Information visualization, Web 2.0, and the teaching of writing. *Computers and Composition, 27,* 59–70.

Woodward-Kron, R., & Jamieson, H. (2007). Tensions in the writing support consultation: Negotiating meanings in unfamiliar territory. In C. Gitsaki (Ed.), *Language and languages: Global and local tensions* (pp. 40–60). Newcastle: Cambridge Scholars Publishing.

Part Three

Identity Work and Professional Opportunities in Academic Writing

Chapter 9

Writing and Researching Between and Beyond the Labels

Hanako Okada and Christine Pearson Casanave

I am a Japanese citizen. I am Japanese by blood and by nationality. I have been living in Japan for most of my life. I look Japanese, I have a common Japanese name, and I am a highly proficient speaker of the language. I feel that I understand Japanese norms, customs, and culture. I feel that I am capable of fitting into these norms, customs, and culture as well. By all such criteria, I appear to be 'Japanese.' On the other hand, I spent six years of my childhood abroad. I have been speaking English since age five. I have been completely educated in English in international schools all my life and it is my dominant academic language. English is not just a foreign language to me. Although I do not consider myself a 'native' English speaker, I feel that this language that I have been speaking from a young age has become a fundamental and inseparable part of me. I cannot imagine life without speaking English. I believe that a large part of my identity has been constructed around being an English speaker.

(Okada, 2009, p. 2)

1 Introduction

In the field of second language education, we are trapped by labels that dichotomize who people are: L1 and L2 users, native and non-native speakers, mainstream and minority students, standard and nonstandard English speakers. This continues to be the case even though increasing numbers of students and scholars do not fit comfortably within these labels, nor within the 'generation 1.5' label that applies to certain kinds of immigrant students (Harklau et al., 1999; Roberge et al., 2009). The issue of labels affects many aspects of second language educators' lives, but, in particular, how we write about and construct identities for ourselves, our research participants, and our students. We are particularly interested in the experiences of scholars and students whose dominant academic language is English and who write nearly exclusively in English but whose mother tongue is not English, such as some of the writers in edited collections in the second language education field (e.g. Belcher & Connor, 2001; Braine, 1999; Casanave, 1998; Casanave & Li, 2008; Casanave & Vandrick, 2003; Novakovich & Shapard, 2000) and authors of articles and dissertations (e.g. Liu, 1999; Okada, 2009; Pavlenko, 2007).

Our discussion centers around the research and writing experiences of Hanako in her doctoral program in TESOL at an American university campus in Japan, and Christine's experiences teaching and advising in the same program. Hanako found it impossible in her doctoral program to fit herself into either an L1 or L2 category. Her 'in-between' status as a Japanese national educated solely in English caused her to question the native speaker/nonnative speaker labels, which did not apply to her, and to question her identity in relation to the work in applied linguistics on bilingualism. Thus, she located herself centrally in her own writing in her doctoral dissertation, where she studied Japanese international school students like herself who were educated only in the medium of English and were unsure how to identify themselves and their native languages. Her study therefore not only interrogated the dichotomous L1-L2 labels that pervade research on bilingualism and the TESOL field, but also explored her own experiences and identity and how she represented these in writing in her doctoral dissertation.

Labeling students and scholars like Hanako exclusively as first or second language speakers, or as native or nonnative writers of English, and presuming that they are competent academic writers in their mother tongue languages, oversimplifies a complex academic literacy situation. From our experiences in this doctoral program and in the field as well as from our reading, we believe that a growing number of researchers and research participants in the second language education and TESOL fields do not fit easily into the dichotomous categories that we so often force upon them and upon ourselves. How do we represent such individuals and their identities in our researching and writing? How do we escape the pernicious influence of the idealized native speaker concept in the TESOL field?

In this chapter, we first lay out the issues about labeling that motivate our discussion. We then discuss why Hanako chose her dissertation topic and how she used her own experiences to go beyond the native speaker-nonnative speaker dichotomy in writing about herself and her case study participants. Christine's perspective as one of Hanako's dissertation advisors highlights some of the dilemmas that advisors face when guiding students in their research and writing on topics such as that chosen by Hanako. We conclude with a summary of issues for second language educators to consider when they write and research about multilingual-multicultural people, urging them when appropriate to go beyond dichotomous and inevitably misleading labels.

2 The Basic Labeling Problem

When we write and talk about ourselves and participants in our research projects, we inevitably face a labeling problem. Labels characterize aspects of people that are the focus of our research interests (or political projects); we rarely describe our participants simply as 'people.' They are second language speakers, bilinguals, native speakers of Chinese, middle class adolescents, low proficiency English users, insiders and outsiders, and so on. We use such labels to describe ourselves as well, but usually recognize the multiplicity and fluctuating nature of labels in real life. However, in conducting and writing up our research, given the narrow focus of most projects, labels are restricted to those that suit our needs. In our field and in institutional and political discourse, labels are often linked to stereotypes of language and race (Kubota & Lin, 2006) and to stereotypical notions of culture, such as 'Asian' and 'Chinese' (Kumaravadivelu, 2003). Stereotypes of learners, noted Kumaravadivelu (2003), may help us 'reduce an unmanageable reality to a manageable label' (p. 716).

Labels, and hence identities and ethnicities, get reified and perpetuated, obfuscating the complex, contextual and shifting nature of who we and our participants are (Leung et al., 1997; Spack, 1997; Zamel, 1997). In some cases, we are 'acquired by' a label, as McDermott (1993) found in his study of how children with disabilities are described in written documents. In the applied linguistics field, learners of many different kinds are inappropriately 'acquired' by the 'ELL' (English Language Learner) label. Exacerbating this problem is the fact that our research and writing continues to be dominated by the constructs of the idealized native speaker (L1) and the nonnative speaker (L2), who is always measured against the idealized L1 speaker (Davies, 2003; Leung et al., 1997). We simply have not yet found a satisfactory (meaning simple and efficient) way of capturing the complexities with our labels. Rampton (1990), for one, made headway with his suggestion that we replace the native speaker label with more complex and flexible descriptions about people's language expertise, affiliation and inheritance, but these terms have not caught on as hoped. This is in spite of the fact that we generally agree that 'identities are not given entities, static properties, or finished projects' (Georgakopoulou, 2006, p. 83; Hall, 1990, 1996; Leung et al., 1997; Rampton, 1990).

Although we recognize that there are many users of L2s who are clearly L1 dominant and can be called native users of language X and second language users of language Y, we believe that an increasing number of scholars and of students throughout the world fall into more ambiguous categories. Such ambiguity startles us into rethinking stereotypes. A clear example is Leung et al.'s (1997) descriptions of urban immigrant youth in London. The students' multiethnic backgrounds and various levels and kinds of language expertise and affiliations do not fit at all well within native-nonnative speaker categories. At the professional level, Liu (1999) consulted with seven multilingual scholars who write in both English and their mother tongues. He wished to learn how they identified themselves. Many were not able to state unambiguously what they considered their native languages to be. Their responses differed according to 'the sequence in which languages [were] learned, competence in English, cultural affiliation, self-identification, social environment, and political labeling' (Liu, 1999, p. 100). Liu concluded that it was not their status as native or nonnative speakers that counted, but their professional qualifications in the TESOL field.

Similarly, some of the scholars represented in Belcher and Connor (2001), Braine (1999), Casanave and Li (2008), and Casanave and Vandrick (2003) cannot clearly be unambiguously labeled L1 or L2 dominant. Many of the scholars represented in these collections in the second language education field were born outside English dominant countries yet their dominant scholarly languages are English. Their complex linguistic and literacy histories require that we specify particular contexts, genres of writing, senses of identity and affiliation, and purposes for writing.

To give one concrete example, in Hanako's own doctoral program are a handful of such people, including Xiaorui Zhang, another of Christine's former advisees. We cannot apply any of the conventional labels to her. Xiaorui was born in China, speaks three dialects of Chinese, studied English and English literature there and then became fluent in scholarly academic English as part of her MA and EdD study at her American university in Japan. Married to a Japanese who also uses some Chinese and English, she acquired Japanese to an advanced proficiency level, eventually using it as her working language at her Japanese university after she graduated with her EdD. In trying to describe herself and her identities (plural) she said that she cannot imagine writing scholarly works in Chinese – English is her dominant language for this kind of activity, and she has even written a few academic papers in Japanese. Her spoken English self is confident and assertive in an English dominant university environment, and less assertive in an international English speaking environment, such as in Europe, where, with her good ear, she tends to pick up the accents of those around her. Japanese, as her working language, feels natural in her university environment, but she feels less 'close' to it than to English or Chinese in terms of identity. Interacting with other Chinese people who live in Japan, she liberally mixes Chinese and Japanese. On frequent trips to China, though Chinese is technically her mother tongue, she now struggles sometimes to find precise words in Chinese. Still, she observed that *none of these languages feels like a foreign language to her* – they are simply part of who she is (Xiaorui Zhang, personal communication, November 28, 2009).

How do we label someone like Xiaorui when we wish to design research instruments such as questionnaires and interviews and to comprehend and write about her responses? If we ask our participants questions that presume dichotomous categories, as we will see in Hanako's dissertation work, participants may not be able to answer questions clearly that ask about their 'native' and 'second' languages because the dichotomous labels might not be meaningful to them. Their responses and our writing will reflect these dichotomies, and thus misrepresent them as multicompetent languages users who in fact have inevitably ambiguous and shifting identities. How then do we represent participants like Xiaorui, Hanako and Hanako's multicompetent participants accurately in our academic writing? As much as scholars wish to describe participants unambiguously in a research report, ambiguity may reflect the reality of our participants' lives. All dichotomous and unambiguous labels will therefore be inaccurate. How do we avoid the monolingual bias of so much applied linguistics research that results in so much inaccurate labeling? Let us turn now to Hanako's dissertation work and see how these complexities played out in her writing.

3 Hanako

3.1 Choosing a dissertation topic: Surrounded by dichotomies

As a child of an expatriate, I spent my early childhood in Europe. At the age of five, I was sent to an American School in Rotterdam, the Netherlands. Since then, I have been educated in English medium schools all my life – upon my return, I attended an international school in Tokyo and then continued my studies in an all-English department in a Japanese university, where there were many international students and Japanese students who were educated abroad or in international schools.

Having grown up and been educated in such environments, it was natural for me to be surrounded by diversity – we were *all* different. We came from different countries, we spoke different languages at home, and we all looked different. We all spoke English at school because that was the language of instruction of the schools we had attended. The majority of us spoke at least two languages. I spoke both English and Japanese, and I never really thought about which one was my first or second language. It was not until I entered an applied linguistics graduate program of an American university in Japan that I came to face labels and dichotomies about language squarely.

Perhaps this was, at least partially, inevitable for two reasons: First, the majority of the students in the program could be grouped into one of two categories: Japanese or 'native' English speakers. The majority of the Japanese students who were enrolled in the program were educated entirely in Japanese schools, and Japanese was their dominant spoken and academic language at least through undergraduate level, and they identified English as their second language, even though all of their graduate work was done in English. The majority of the foreign students were 'native speakers' from English dominant countries. I did not fit into either category. Professors' reactions toward me suggested that I was different too. Most professors advised that 'nonnative speakers' get their papers checked by a 'native speaker' before submitting them. When I asked, the professors told me that was not necessary for me. One professor wrote the following comment on an assignment I submitted: 'Your English is so good, I thought you were a Japanese-American.' Another American professor told me later on that he did not know what to make of me when I took his class for the first time. He said 'You looked completely Japanese, but when you opened your mouth, you were speaking *my* language!' Some of my Japanese classmates referred to me as a 'native speaker', but I felt uncomfortable and complex – I knew my English was not on a par with that of my 'native speaker' classmates.

The second reason why I felt that labels and categories were inevitable was because of the nature of the field I was studying. What Davies (2003) said may summarize the point I wish to make:

> Applied linguistics makes a constant appeal to the concept of the native speaker. This appeal is necessary because of the need applied linguistics has for models, norms, and goals, whether the concern is for teaching or testing a first, second, or foreign language, with the treatment of a language pathology, with stylistic discourse and rhetorical analysis or with some other deliberate language use. (p. 1)

Along with the 'constant appeal to the ... native speaker,' historically, there has been a monolingual bias throughout the fields that study languages and their relationship to individuals, from linguistics to anthropology

(Block, 2003; Grosjean, 1989; Koven, 1998; Valdés, 2005). In the applied linguistics and TESOL fields, this bias plays out as a persistent 'native-speakerism,' in which the idealized native speaker of English (always a speaker of British or North American varieties) dominates our perspectives of ESL/EFL scholarship and teaching (see Waters, 2007, and Kabel, 2009, for different views on this problem).

At first I was appalled at the dichotomous labels and categories. My identity had never been challenged like this before. I then thought that the situation was inevitable given the nature of the field. But then, the more I studied and the more I thought, the more I began to question such dichotomous labels and categories.

3.2 Needing to escape from dichotomies

I encountered more and more literature that problematized the native speaker bias (e.g. Braine, 1999; Leung et al., 1997; Liu, 1999; Medgyes, 1992; Paikeday, 1985a, 1985b), and that celebrated bi/multilingual speakers as multicompetent (e.g. Cook, 1992, 1995, 2002; Kramsch, 1997, 1998). However even within such work, it appeared that there was a default assumption that one has a *first* language. For example, in the literature of multilingualism/multicompetence (e.g. Belz, 2002a, 2002b; Cook, 1995), despite the authors' description of their participants as multilingual and multicompetent engaging in language play, the participants were always associated with their first language. I found that concepts such as multicompetence were more suitable in conceptualizing language *learners*, and not for those who have been exposed to multiple languages simultaneously, i.e. multiple language *users*. I wondered whether all bilinguals and multilingual individuals could place their languages on a hierarchy. Is the hierarchy of languages something so clear cut? It certainly wasn't for me …

3.2.1 Self

As I expanded my reading, I noticed that more and more up-to-date literature was problematizing dichotomies and hierarchical views within our field (e.g. Canagarajah, 2007; Kramsch & Whiteside, 2008; Valdés, 2005). To give a specific example, in discussing language identity, Canagarajah (2007) mentioned the following:

> People develop simultaneous multilingualism, making it difficult to say which language comes first …. Language identity is relative to the

communities and languages one considers salient in different contexts. Therefore, the label [of first language] is applied in a shifting and inconsistent manner. (p. 931)

This is particularly salient for childhood bilinguals who have been exposed to two (or more) languages from birth or at a very young age (Davies, 2003; Koven, 1998; Valdés, 2005). However, unlike studies focusing on language and identity of immigrants (and others who have crossed borders for varying reasons) and/or their children (e.g. Block, 2006; Day, 2002; Kanno, 2003; Norton, 2000; Toohey, 1998, 2000), childhood bilinguals, particularly within EFL contexts, remain under-researched.

As a childhood bilingual, and as a student and later a teacher in international schools, I was always surrounded by other childhood bilinguals. Dichotomies and hierarchies among languages were not salient within the multilingual environment I was brought up in (cf. Canagarajah, 2007). My experiences led me to question dichotomous labels and hierarchies about languages. Such questioning further led to a desire to inquire and reflect upon my own experiences. This was one of the primary reasons for choosing my dissertation topic: languages and identities of Japanese international school students (Okada, 2009). I hoped that my topic would guide my thinking, and at the same time, create some commotion about the ongoing use of static dichotomous labels and hierarchies in our research and writing.

3.2.2 Participants

My dissertation was a naturalistic long-term case study about the language and identity of three Japanese international school students, Jun, Ayako and Kenji (pseudonyms). The participants were Japanese nationals who attended international schools from kindergarten all the way through high school. Unlike most local students in international schools, these students did not have any foreign heritage or experience of living abroad. I was curious to explore the language and identity of those who had not left their country, as most studies focusing on language and identity dealt with those who have crossed borders. I also wanted to know what it was like for these participants to be educated entirely in English while living in their home country: Japan – a society that is largely perceived as monolingual.

All three of my participants said 'that's a hard question …' when I asked them which language was their stronger language. They identified with both Japanese and English, and making either-or choices between languages was extremely challenging for them. It was so natural for them to be using both English and Japanese, and they code-switched liberally. Japanese-English code-switch was a 'language' that they felt most comfortable speaking. But this wasn't a compensatory strategy; it was more of an identity marker (cf. Kanno, 2008; Kite, 2001). Here is a sample quote that indicates their feelings and the kind of *language* they spoke: 'It's really like "*docchi no hou ga umai*" *tte kikaretara* (if I'm asked which I'm better in), I can't answer' (Okada, 2009, p. 231).

My participants felt they were in between languages and cultures. They referred to themselves as being 'in between'. They could not place their languages in a hierarchical order. They were not sure what their first language was. Neither were they sure what their native language was. When they tried to choose one, it was often followed by a contradictory remark. Ayako and Kenji were not sure if they were native speakers of any language. Kenji, who mentioned that he was not sure which language he was better in, said if he *had* to choose one language as his native language, he would say it was Japanese just because he was Japanese by blood and passport. I also thought it was interesting that Ayako strategically used the spatial expression 'home language' instead of native language or first language, because she tends to use more Japanese at home with her family. Jun, who seemed to have a more solid view about his language, said he was not a native speaker of English despite his confidence in the linguistic aspects of the language. He reasoned that he lacked some cultural understanding of the language because he had only lived in Japan.

3.3 Dealing with labels in writing the dissertation

It wasn't just I who struggled with labels. In order to differentiate themselves from others, the three participants used marked expressions. For example, to refer to Japanese people who were educated in Japanese, the students used expressions such as 'Japanese-Japanese', 'mainstream Japanese', 'normal Japanese people', or '*Nihon-jin*' (Japanese). In referring to native English speakers, they used terms and phrases such as 'native speakers born and raised in... [an English dominant country]', or 'Americans in the US'. One participant used the expression '*true* natives' to refer to such people. In referring to themselves and those like themselves, they used expressions such as 'in between types', 'members of the international school community' and '*intaa* people' or '*intaa* types', with *intaa* as a shortened term for international school.

I, however, could not simply use '*intaa* type' to capture my participants' complex language and identity in writing, as this was insiders' jargon only fully understood by the members of the Japanese international school community. I was left with further problems as in some ways some of the expressions they used seemed to perpetuate dichotomies. I struggled to find ways to describe and conceptualize them for a larger audience, in a more sophisticated and scholarly perspective. One term used by some international school administrators I interviewed to refer to their students was the 'third culture kids (TCK)' (Pollock & Van Reken, 2009; Useem, 1993). However, it wasn't sufficient for my research context as it referred to 'children who accompany their parents into another society' (Useem & Cottrell, 1996, p. 24), and my participants had not crossed borders. Moreover, the literature on TCK was also largely non-academic, based on anecdotes of TCKs.

In order to portray my participants' complex language and identity and to show that languages and cultures are not pure or discrete but always in contact with another, I used the notion of hybridity (Bhabha, 1994, 1996) as part of my conceptual framework. My participants' accounts reassured me that labels such as 'first language', 'second language', and 'native language' were problematic and often inappropriate. However, using the notion of hybridity was not a simple way to escape the problems of static and monolithic labels.

3.3.1 Hybridity

The term hybridity originated in agriculture and animal breeding, where crossing of type A with B leads to a biological hybrid composed of half type A and half type B (Block, 2007). However, the notion of hybridity in social and cultural theories is more ambivalent, and hybrids are not perceived as clear half-and-half propositions as in agriculture and animal breeding (Block, 2006, 2007). It emerged from the postmodern view that culture is not pure, and one of its achievements was to liberate the individual from fixed and 'pure' origins (Papastergiadis, 1997; Rutherford, 1990; Werbner, 1997b). However, hybridity, which is often understood as a mix of two or more different types, also makes sense for modernist theories where culture is seen as made up of bounded and systematic categories (Friedman, 1997; Werbner, 1997b). Thus, hybridity carries the danger of being understood as another systematic category, or the *third* category.

Given this risk, the term hybrid to represent people like me and my participants may be a misnomer. In fact, extended debates on how hybridity should be understood and used in the postmodern/global age have taken place within cultural theory (e.g. Friedman, 1997; Papastergiadis, 1997; Werbner, 1997a; Wicker, 1997; Young, 1995). Homi K. Bhabha, the popularizer of this term through his work in postcolonial theory, emphasized that the importance of hybridity is not in tracing the (essentialist's view of) originals, but in its location or spatial condition, i.e. the third space where new forms of meaning are enacted:

> All forms of culture are continually in a process of hybridity. But for me, the importance of hybridity is not to be able to trace two original moments from which the third emerges, rather hybridity to me is the 'third space' which enables other positions to emerge. (Interview with Bhabha, Rutherford, 1990, p. 211)

It appeared to me that even Bhabha struggled with the conventional connotation that the term carried. I saw its potential dangers, and Chris, who was one of my co-advisors, pointed out her discomfort with the term. She found my dissertation title, 'Somewhere in between', to be problematic as well, because the term *in between* suggested a location between two clearly defined poles. I well understood her concern, but I did not know how else to capture my participants' identities. I could have simply used descriptive language, but I also had the urge and need to speak to a larger audience, and I simply did not know how to do that without borrowing conceptual terms that are already widely used. I completed my dissertation without resolving to my satisfaction how to represent either myself or my participants in my academic writing or knowing what to suggest to others when we do research with multicompetent language users. I wondered whether it was my problem of not knowing the right theoretical concepts that might capture my participants' experiences, or if such concepts/language simply did not exist.

4 Christine

4.1 Challenges for an advisor

As an advisor of doctoral students, one of my duties has been to help students conceptualize and plan a project and to support them during data collection. But the other duty, more fraught with uncertainty, especially with a qualitative, narratively-oriented project, has to do with writing. And by 'writing' I don't mean grammar, sentences and words. From that perspective, I don't consider that writing a doctoral dissertation will be significantly more difficult for an L2 user of English than for the so-called native speaker of

English. To have gotten as far as they have (graduate course work, comprehensive exams and dissertation proposal all done in English), most students have enough facility with academic English to put words and sentences and sections and chapters together that look like a dissertation. This is not to underplay how challenging and stressful it is to try to write a book-length piece of research in an L2. I cannot imagine doing this in my strong L2, Spanish, but perhaps I could with many years of doctoral level graduate work in Spanish under my belt. And the linguistic and lexical infelicities are, after all, correctable for all writers.

Instead, the hard part of writing a qualitative dissertation has to do with other matters in writing, which turn out to be hard for everyone. One of these challenges is to figure out how to transform difficult nonlinear ideas (such as conceptualizations of identity) into lines of words (Casanave & Sosa, 2008). For the doctoral student, whether an L1, L2, or 'in-between' language user, concepts, theories and abstractions are just plain difficult to talk and write about. Another challenge is to figure out how to talk and write about ourselves and our participants in ways that do not put people into the boxes, bins and categories that applied linguists and other social scientists often use: the 'If you are not A, then you must be B' mandate. The easy labels for language users, as we have argued so far, just don't work to encompass the complexities of some people's language proficiencies and identities, particularly in projects like Hanako's whose very purpose is to dismantle dichotomies. Finally, seeing writing as something profoundly implicated in the research itself, not just a linguistic representation of it (Casanave, 2010; Richardson & St. Pierre, 2005; Van Manen, 1990), complicates greatly my negotiations with doctoral students.

4.2 Hanako's dissertation

In Hanako's case, I was deeply involved in the stories of her participants. Over many months of talking together and writing back and forth and reviewing pieces of writing, I felt I was getting to know not just Hanako better, but the three young people she was writing about. The dilemmas she faced in writing about them, and that they faced in trying to talk about themselves, became ever more salient, particularly as we realized over time that the very way that she posed questions to her participants may have perpetuated certain kinds of labeling. What she did not want to do was to invent new categories and labels that would continue to constrain her written descriptions of these extraordinarily complex people (herself included).

Hanako was the expert on notions of 'hybridity', 'third space' and 'in-betweenness' as she has discussed above, given that she had read post-modern literature on these ideas that I had not. My response to the label 'hybrid' came from what I learned from her, from my meager knowledge of biology (a 'pure' A mixes with a 'pure' B to make a hybrid C), and from parallel debates that were going on in the field of composition studies. Patricia Bizzell (2002) rejected her own earlier usage of the term *hybrid* to refer to nontraditional, 'new' forms of academic discourse, including students' home dialects. She felt that the label 'hybrid' was both too abstract and too concrete, and that it did not really upset dichotomies because it implies at least two clear 'parents' in a biological sense (p. 4). She instead opted for the terms *new, alternative* and *mixed.* In the same volume, Sidney Dobrin (2002) asserted that 'all discourses are hybrids, mixed, alternative, and none are codifiable in any way that allow us to identify any as parent or hybrid' (p. 52). In other words, the danger of the hybrid label for both scholars was that the conventional ways we talk about language presumes a relatively static and definable entity, when in reality, change and diversity characterize even traditional academic discourse.

If we use a label such as 'hybrid' or 'in-between' for Hanako's participants, we inevitably imagine definable 'sides' as a default – Japanese parents who could be considered typical Japanese on one side, and American teachers and curri-cula that might be considered typical American on the other. Given Hanako's goal of breaking down stereotypes by challenging the labels in applied linguis-tics, she may have stepped into the quagmire of representing the 'sides' in dichotomous ways that misrepresented the complex language backgrounds and identities of the people and contexts around her participants. I wonder, for example, if the parents of Hanako's participants could be considered typical Japanese, by any stretch of the imagination. They had lived abroad, were profi-cient to varying degrees in English, and had chosen to send their children to a school where they would be educated entirely in English. Such a decision is still rare in Japan. Likewise, in what sense could we consider that the American teachers at the international schools were typical? Something had brought them to Japan, some may have learned some Japanese or other languages, and they may have been familiar with the *intaa* language (the international school code-switching) and cultural practices at the school. At least some of them were probably not typical Americans, if any such beast even exists.

A further complication in writing about research participants who talk about themselves at length is that they themselves may use the very labels that we are trying to avoid. This can happen whether or not the researcher has offered labels through the way she asks questions. In Hanako's case, it is not likely that the young people in her project would have described themselves as 'hybrid' or as being in a 'third space,' although the 'in-between' label seemed to suit them, as did 'Japanese side' and 'English (= American) side'. In writing about participants, we are ethically obligated to honor their voices and their characterizations of themselves. Their self-descriptions are in some sense their truths. But as researchers who are writing their stories, we need to say 'Sorry, but things aren't so simple', without denying them their perspectives. And in many cases, Hanako's participants were not able to describe their languages and identities clearly at all. How do we address these issues in research writing?

4.3 Audience considerations and representations of self

Moreover, in helping students write a doctoral dissertation, advisors are ethically obligated to help the writers communicate with a very particular audience. In the ESL/EFL field, this audience is likely to be made up of applied linguists. As Hanako said at the end of her section, she could perhaps have solved some of the labeling problems in her writing with a more exclusively descriptive approach, but her audience might have preferred the clarity that a label brings. Hybrid? In-between? Mixed? Multicompetent? None seems satisfactory because the dissertation writer instantly gets boxed in. Are we left without labels altogether when we write about the languages and cultures of people such as Hanako and her three participants? Could a richly descriptive approach to writing these stories, without the labels, achieve Hanako's purpose? Could Hanako have written at length about language expertise, language affiliation and language inheritance, following Leung et al. (1997) and Rampton (1990), among other complex descriptions? And closer to home, as multilingual applied linguists and second language educators, how do we represent ourselves in writing? We would not want to represent ourselves in writing simplistically. If we do some perspective taking (Casanave, 2009), we can see how challenging it is to write about ourselves in efficient ways that capture our own complex identities. Unfortunately, the dichotomous labels are efficient umbrella terms, but ones that hide complex realities about ourselves as well as about our research participants. More description and less categorization seem essential.

We do not have firm answers to our own questions. Still, we remain committed to the goal of helping student and faculty writers in graduate programs of TESOL or applied linguistics recognize, articulate and avoid the monolingual bias of so much research in our field. This exercise, regardless of who our research participants are, or what our approaches and designs are, probably begins best at home. How do we, as writers and researchers, describe the complexities of our own language expertise, affiliations and inheritances? How do the traditional labels suit the realities of our own lives when we look beyond the surface? What additional complex descriptions are needed in order to portray these deeper realities? How, then, can we devise ways to design our research and to write about ourselves and our participants that avoid the dichotomies? We hope that this exploration will have many layers, and no fixed answers, for all writers.

5 Conclusion: Summary of Issues on Researching and Writing about Multicompetent English Language Users

Labels and categories may be an inevitable part of our lives – we take on various roles and personas, and we position others through labels and categories to understand those around us and our worlds in manageable ways. This is an argument made by Waters (2007). However, research and writing about multicompetent language users that uses such labels and categories tends to obscure some of the very complexities we are interested in. Worse, such labels risk stereotyping and stigmatizing our participants (cf. Kabel, 2009). The labels and categories at hand are limited (and also limiting), and there are consequences if we use them. In addition to misportraying ourselves and our participants, we end up perpetuating the sense that the fields of applied linguistics and second language education are characterized by biases and static models.

Recent work in applied linguistics and SLA problematizing the monolingual bias has turned to the field of bilingualism as a way out of such bias (Ortega, 2010; Ortega & Carson, 2010; Valdés, 2005), referring to a 'bilingual turn in applied linguistics' (Ortega & Carson, 2010, p. 50). According to Ortega and Carson (2010):

> the bilingual turn began with the realization that, just as applied linguistics research can no longer stand on the native speaker as a model and norm, so it is no longer tenable to hold monolingualism as the starting point of inquiry. (p. 50)

This view is based on the understanding that:

> the bilingual is an integrated whole which cannot easily be decomposed into two separate parts. The bilingual is NOT the sum of two complete

or incomplete monolinguals; rather, he or she has a unique and specific configuration. The coexistence and constant interaction of the two languages in the bilingual has produced a different but complete entity. (Grosjean, 1989, p. 6)

Many researchers, whether graduate students or established scholars, are themselves bilingual and multicompetent users of different languages. Asking how we ourselves might wish to be portrayed in writing can provide insights into how we can conduct and write up research without resorting to misleading labels and dichotomies. This kind of reflection has been done in such work as autobiographic border-crossing narratives (e.g. Belcher & Connor, 2001; Danquah, 2000; Novakovich & Shapard, 2000), but it appears that such reflections, and published descriptions based on the reflections, are rare in applied linguistic research on second language education. More description and much more thought and care in how we use categories and labels are fundamentally necessary in writing not only about multilingual-multicultural people, but any people. By resisting, when appropriate, the convenient shorthand of the ubiquitous conventional labels and their monolingual bias in TESOL and applied linguistics, we can go between and beyond them in ways that contribute to more sophisticated scholarship and to more accurate and ethical portrayals of the people we write about.

References

Belcher, D., & Connor, U. (Eds.). (2001). *Reflections on multiliterate lives.* Clevedon, England: Multilingual Matters.

Belz, J. A. (2002a). The myth of the deficient communicator. *Language Teaching Research,* 6(1), 59–82.

Belz, J. A. (2002b). Second language play as a representation of the multicompetent self in foreign language study. *Journal of Language, Identity, and Education,* 1(1), 13–40.

Bhabha, H. K. (1994). *The location of culture.* London: Routledge.

Bhabha, H. K. (1996). Culture's in-between. In S. Hall & P. du Gay (Eds.), *Questions of cultural identity* (pp. 37–52). London: Sage.

Bizzell, P. (2002). The intellectual work of 'mixed' forms of academic discourses. In C. Schroeder, H. Fox & P. Bizzell (Eds.), *ALT DIS: Alternative discourses and the academy* (pp. 1–10). Portsmouth, NH: Boynton/Cook Heinemann.

Block, D. (2003). *The social turn in second language acquisition.* Washington, DC: Georgetown University Press.

Block, D. (2006). *Multilingual identities in a global city: London stories.* Hampshire, England: Palgrave MacMillan.

Block, D. (2007). *Second language identities.* London: Continuum.

Braine, G. (Ed.). (1999). *Non-native educators in English language teaching.* Mahwah, NJ: Lawrence Erlbaum.

Canagarajah, A. S. (2007). Lingua franca English, multilingual communities, and language acquisition. *Modern Language Journal, 91*(5), 923–939.

Casanave, C. P. (1998). Transitions: The balancing act of bilingual academics. *Journal of Second Language Writing, 7,* 175–203.

Casanave, C. P. (2009). Perspective taking. *The Language Teacher, 33*(7), 3–6.

Casanave, C. P. (2010). Taking risks? A case study of three doctoral students writing qualitative dissertations at an American university in Japan. *Journal of Second Language Writing, 19,* 1–16.

Casanave, C. P., & Li, X. (Eds.). (2008). *Learning the literacy practices of graduate school.* Ann Arbor: University of Michigan Press.

Casanave, C. P., & Sosa, M. (2008). Getting in line: The challenge (and importance) of speaking and writing about difficult topics. In D. Belcher & A. Hirvela (Eds.), *The oral/literate connection* (pp. 87–109). Ann Arbor: University of Michigan Press.

Casanave, C. P., & Vandrick, S. (Eds.). (2003). *Writing for scholarly publication: Behind the scenes in language education.* Mahwah, NJ: Lawrence Erlbaum.

Cook, V. (1992). Evidence for multicompetence. *Language Learning, 42*(4), 557–591.

Cook, V. (1995). Multicompetence and the learning of many languages. *Language, Culture, and Curriculum, 8*(2), 93–98.

Cook, V. (Ed.). (2002). *Portraits of the L2 user.* Clevedon, England: Multilingual Matters.

Danquah, M. N. (Ed.). (2000). *Becoming American: Personal essays by first generation immigrant women.* New York: Hyperion.

Davies, A. (2003). *The native speaker: Myth and reality.* Clevedon, England: Multilingual Matters.

Day, E. M. (2002). *Identity and the young English learner.* Clevedon, England: Multilingual Matters.

Dobrin, S. I. (2002). A problem with writing (about) 'alternative' discourse. In C. Schroeder, H. Fox & P. Bizzell (Eds.), *ALT DIS: Alternative discourses and the academy* (pp. 45–56). Portsmouth, NH: Boynton/Cook Heinemann.

Friedman, J. (1997). Global crises, the struggle for cultural identity and intellectual porkbarrelling: Cosmopolitans versus locals, ethnics and nationals in an era of de-hegemonisation. In P. Werbner & T. Modood (Eds.), *Debating cultural hybridity* (pp. 70–89). London: Zed.

Georgakopoulou, A. (2006). Small and large identities in narrative (inter)-action. In A. de Fina, D. Schiffrin & M. Bamberg (Eds.), *Discourse and identity* (pp. 83–102). Cambridge: Cambridge University Press.

Grosjean, F. (1989). Neurolinguists, beware! The bilingual is not two monolinguals in one person. *Brain and Language, 36,* 3–15.

Hall, S. (1990). Cultural identity and diaspora. In J. Rutherford (Ed.), *Identity: Community, culture, difference* (pp. 223–237). London: Lawrence & Wishart.

Hall, S. (1996). Introduction: Who needs 'identity'? In S. Hall & P. du Gay (Eds.), *Questions of cultural identity* (pp. 1–17). London: Sage.

Harklau, L., Losey, K. M., & Siegal, M. (Eds.). (1999). *Generation 1.5 meets college composition: Issues in the teaching of writing to U.S.-educated learners of ESL.* Mahwah, NJ: Lawrence Erlbaum.

Kabel, A. (2009). Native-speakerism, stereotyping, and the collusion of applied linguistics. *System, 37,* 12–22.

Kanno, Y. (2003). *Negotiating bilingual and bicultural identities.* Mahwah, NJ: Lawrence Erlbaum.

Kanno, Y. (2008). *Language and education in Japan: Unequal access to bilingualism.* Hampshire, England: Palgrave Macmillan.

Kite, Y. (2001). English/Japanese codeswitching among students in an international high school. In M. G. Noguchi & S. Fotos (Eds.), *Studies in Japanese bilingualism* (pp. 312–238). Clevedon, England: Multilingual Matters.

Koven, M. E. (1998). Two languages in the self/the self in two languages: French-Portuguese bilinguals' verbal enactments and experiences of self in narrative discourse. *Ethos, 26*(4), 410–455.

Kramsch, C. (1997). The privilege of the nonnative speaker. *PMLA, 112*(3), 359–369.

Kramsch, C. (1998). The privilege of the intercultural speaker. In M. Byram & M. Fleming (Eds.), *Language learning in intercultural perspective* (pp. 16–31). Cambridge: Cambridge University Press.

Kramsch, C., & Whiteside, A. (2008). Language ecology in multilingual settings: Towards a theory of symbolic competence. *Applied Linguistics, 29*(4), 645–671.

Kubota, R., & Lin, A. (2006). Race and TESOL: Introduction to concepts and issues. *TESOL Quarterly, 40*(3), 471–493.

Kumaravadivelu, B. (2003). Problematizing cultural stereotypes in TESOL. *TESOL Quarterly, 37*(4), 709–718.

Leung, C., Harris, R., & Rampton, B. (1997). The idealized native speaker, reified ethnicities, and classroom realities. *TESOL Quarterly, 31*(3), 543–560.

Liu, J. (1999). Nonnative-English-speaking professionals in TESOL. *TESOL Quarterly, 33*(1), 85–102.

McDermott, R. (1993). The acquisition of a child by a learning disability. In S. Chaiklin & J. Lave (Eds.), *Understanding practice: Perspectives on activity and context* (pp. 269–305). Cambridge: Cambridge University Press.

Medgyes, P. (1992). Native or nonnative: Who's worth more? *ELT Journal, 46*(4), 340–349.

Norton, B. (2000). *Identity and language learning.* Harlow, England: Pearson Education.

Novakovich, J., & Shapard, R. (Eds.). (2002). *Stories in the stepmother tongue.* Buffalo, NY: White Pine.

Okada, H. (2009). Somewhere 'in between': Languages and identities of three Japanese international school students. (Doctoral dissertation). Temple University. *Dissertation Abstracts International, 70*(06).

Ortega, L. (2010, March). *The bilingual turn in SLA.* Plenary delivered at the Annual Conference of the American Association for Applied Linguistics, Atlanta, GA.

Ortega, L., & Carson, J. (2010). Multicompetence, social context, and L2 writing research praxis. In T. Silva & P. K. Matsuda (Eds.), *Practicing theory in second language writing* (pp. 48–71). West Lafayette, IN: Parlor Press.

Paikeday, T. M. (1985a). May I kill the native speaker? *TESOL Quarterly, 19*(2), 390–395.

Paikeday, T. M. (1985b). *The native speaker is dead! An informal discussion of a linguistic myth with Noam Chomsky and other linguists, philosophers, psychologists, and lexicographers.* Toronto, Canada: Paikeday.

Papastergiadis, N. (1997). Tracing hybridity in theory. In P. Werbner & T. Modood (Eds.), *Debating cultural hybridity* (pp. 257–281). London: Zed.

Pavlenko, A. (2007). Autobiographic narratives as data in applied linguistics. *Applied Linguistics, 28*(2), 163–188.

Pollock, D. C., & Van Reken, R. E. (2009). *Third culture kids* (Revised ed.). Boston: Nicholas Brealey.

Rampton, M. B. H. (1990). Displacing the 'native speaker': Expertise, affiliation, and inheritance. *ELT Journal, 44*(2), 97–101.

Richardson, L, & St. Pierre, E. A. (2005). Writing: A method of inquiry. In N. K. Denzin & Y. S. Lincoln (Eds.), *The Sage handbook of qualitative research* (3rd ed.) (pp. 959–978). Thousand Oaks, CA: Sage.

Roberge, M., Siegal, M., & Harklau, L. (Eds.). (2009). *Generation 1.5 in college composition: Teaching academic writing to U.S.-educated learners of ESL.* New York: Routledge.

Rutherford, J. (1990). Interview with Homi Bhabha: The third space. In J. Rutherford (Ed.), *Identity: Community, culture, difference* (pp. 207–221). London: Lawrence & Wishart.

Spack, R. (1997). The rhetorical construction of multilingual students. *TESOL Quarterly, 31*(4), 765–774.

Toohey, K. (1998). 'Breaking them up, taking them away': ESL students in grade 1. *TESOL Quarterly, 32*(1), 61–84.

Toohey, K. (2000). *Learning English at school: Identity, social relations, and classroom practice.* Clevedon, England: Multilingual Matters.

Useem, R. H. (1993). Third culture kids: Focus of major study. *Newspaper of the International School Services, 12*(3), 1.

Useem, R. H., & Cottrell, A. B. (1996). Adult third culture kids. In C. D. Smith (Ed.), *Strangers at home: Essays on the effects of living overseas and coming 'home' to a strange land* (pp. 23–35). Bayside, NY: Aletheia.

Valdés, G. (2005). Bilingualism, heritage language learners, and SLA research: Opportunities lost or seized? *Modern Language Journal, 89*(3), 410–426.

Van Manen, M. (1990). *Researching lived experience.* Albany: State University of New York Press.

Waters, A. (2007). Native-speakerism in ELT: Plus ça change...? *System, 35,* 281–292.

Werbner, P. (1997a). Essentialising essentialism, essentialising silence: Ambivalence and multiplicity in the constructions of racism and ethnicity. In P. Werbner & T. Modood (Eds.), *Debating cultural hybridity* (pp. 226–254). London: Zed.

Werbner, P. (1997b). Introduction: The dialectics of cultural hybridity. In P. Werbner & T. Modood (Eds.), *Debating cultural hybridity* (pp. 1–26). London: Zed.

Wicker, H.-R. (1997). From complex culture to cultural complexity. In P. Werbner & T. Modood (Eds.), *Debating cultural hybridity* (pp. 29–45). London: Zed.

Young, R. J. C. (1995). *Colonial desire: Hybridity in theory, culture and race.* London: Routledge.

Zamel, V. (1997). Toward a model of transculturation. *TESOL Quarterly, 31*(2), 341–352.

Chapter 10

Identity Without the 'I': A Study of Citation Sequences and Writer Identity in Literature Review Sections of Dissertations

Suganthi John

1 Introduction

Research has often associated the construction of writer identity in academic writing with particular rhetorical choices writers make when they construct their texts. One of the rhetorical choices often highlighted is the first person pronoun, which has been identified by many as the most obvious realisation of writer identity in a text (e.g. Harwood, 2005; Hewings & Coffin, 2007; Hyland, 2002a; Ivanič, 1998; Ivanič & Simpson, 1992; Kuo, 1999; Ramanathan & Atkinson, 1999; Sheldon, 2009; Starfield & Ravelli, 2006; Tang & John, 1999). At the same time, there have also been other studies that shed light on the construction of writer identity in texts, such as studies on stance (Charles, 2003, 2006; Hyland, 1999; Vassileva, 2001), evaluation (Hunston & Thompson, 2000; Swales & Burke, 2003), hedging (Hyland, 1996, Salager-Meyer, 1994; Varttala, 2003), and voice (Hirvela & Belcher, 2001; Ivanič & Camps, 2001; Shaw, 1992). These studies have usefully sought to identify and discuss ways in which language works to enable writers to enact interpersonal and ideational positioning in their writing and have helped to highlight the fact that negotiating an 'identity' for oneself is a central, not extraneous, part of successful academic writing (Hyland, 2002a).

The usefulness of linking abstract concepts such as writer identity, stance and voice to corresponding linguistic realisations lies in the benefits this would have for second language (L2) writers learning to write academic English, as there is a significant amount of research identifying identity construction as a particular challenge for L2 writers (Bartholomae, 1995; Bizzell, 1992; Casanave, 2002; Elbow, 1995a, 1995b; Hirvela & Belcher, 2001; Hyland, 2001, 2002a, 2002b; Ivanič & Camps, 2001; Ivanič & Simpson, 1992; Lillis, 1997, 2001; Matsuda, 2001; Ramanathan & Atkinson, 1999; Stapleton, 2002; Zamel & Spack, 1998). Phan Le Ha (2009) summarizes the various views on this issue well when she says 'ESL/EFL writing brings to the fore issues of identity and voice, as it involves processes of negotiation, adaptation, appropriation and resistance that can occur during the acts of conceptualisation, drafting and writing' (p. 136).

Research on the connection between the construction of writer identity and the use of the 'I' in academic writing is extensive, as pointed out earlier, and in fact, it has been claimed that 'by avoiding the use of author pronouns, and failing to stand behind their interpretations, ... emerging writers run the risk of not establishing an effective authorial identity, and failing to create a successful academic argument' (Hyland, 2002b, p. 354). However, while I recognise the complex use of the first person pronoun in academic writing (John, 2009; Tang & John, 1999) and its importance in constructing an essential authoritative identity for the writer, this chapter proposes that writers have other linguistic options, besides the first person pronoun, to display their identity in written academic texts. These other options may not allow the writer to be as overtly present in the text as the first person pronoun does, but they are nonetheless signals of the writer's visible presence in the text and contribute to a successful academic argument.

This study uses the literature review sections of 17 master's level dissertations in the field of applied linguistics as data. These were written by L2 writers enrolled at a UK university. All the writers are from countries in the Far East (China, Japan, Hong Kong, Taiwan) or South East Asia (Malaysia and Thailand). Examples from draft and final versions of the dissertations are used throughout this chapter and they are referenced as [name of writer: stage of writing (draft or final): page number] as in [SMY:F:36].

Drawing on these data, I argue that writers are able to express their academic identities in their texts through attention to linguistic features other than the first person pronoun. In literature review sections, one such feature is the citation. Examples from student texts are used to illustrate how citations influence writer identity in the text due to the inherent evaluative quality of some types of citations and how these are used in the writer's argument. I put forward the idea that evaluation signals the writer's presence in the text as it is an obvious marker of the writer's opinion on the cited information or the sourced author. As Hunston and Thompson (2000) point out, citing references is one out of many ways through which writers 'lay claim to their own academic credibility' (p. 8). A writer's evaluation of the cited information or the sourced author thus contributes to the success of the academic argument that he/she is constructing in the text.

The final part of the chapter looks closely at two short extracts – one each from the draft and final versions of a dissertation written by one of the writers in this study. The discussion highlights the need for second language writers to be made aware of the evaluative nature of citations and how these might affect the visibility of the writer's academic identity (hereafter referred to as academic visibility) and the argument being constructed. The discussion also proposes that revision provides an excellent opportunity for writers to make clear the relationship between the writer, the sourced author and the cited material in the on-going development of the argument.

Before illustrating the ways in which citations may impact the academic visibility of the writer in the text, it is useful to briefly consider the evaluative quality of citations.

2 The Nature of Citations as Evaluative Acts of the Writer

An important practice for an academic writer is situating one's research within the academic discourse community and drawing on external sources to support and evaluate one's ideas. As Hyland (1999) says, '[t]he inclusion of explicit references to the work of other authors is ... seen as a central feature of academic research writing, helping writers establish a persuasive epistemological and social framework for the acceptance of their arguments' (p. 344). Any useful guide for a student engaging in academic writing is likely to have a section devoted to the ways in which writers can incorporate sources into their texts, whether this is referred to as 'attribution', 'referencing' or 'citation'. (See, for example, Bitchener, 2010; Coffin et al., 2003; Creme & Lea, 1999; Hacker, 1999; Stott et al., 2001.) This activity of using external sources in one's own text occurs throughout the dissertation but is especially concentrated in literature review sections of the dissertation.

There have been several studies which have looked at the different aspects of citations in academic discourse. Researchers have argued for the evaluative nature of citations, with several studies focussing on reporting verbs in particular (e.g. Hunston, 1993; Hyland, 1999; Shaw, 1992; Thompson & Ye, 1991). There have also been comparative studies on citation use in different disciplines (Charles, 2006; Harwood, 2009) and how citations are revealing of the discourse practices of multilingual scholars across the world (Lillis et al., 2010). Other studies argue for the value of teaching student writers how to manipulate citations in their writing (Hyland, 2002a; Petric,

2007). Drawing on the extensive work that has already been done on the complex nature of citations and their functions and uses in academic discourse, this paper extends several of these studies by focussing on the evaluative quality of a citation.

Generally, evaluation of the information within a citation presents three options for a writer: the writer can agree with the information, the writer can disagree with the information, or the writer can remain neutral about the information. Social science research (Chubin & Moitra, 1975; Moravcsik & Murugesan, 1975) has termed citations which signal agreement or neutrality 'affirmative citations' and those which signal disagreement 'negational citations'. For her part, Hunston (1993) expresses these options in terms of an evaluation of the commitment to the truth value of the cited information. She describes reporting verbs as signalling one of three main things – (i) both the sourced author and citing writer are committed to the truth value of the cited information (such as the verb *point out*), (ii) both the sourced author and citing writer are uncommitted to the truth value of the cited information (such as the verb *suggest*), or (iii) the sourced author is presented as being committed to the truth of the information presented but the citing writer remains uncommitted (such as the verb *claim*).

Hunston's (1993) research usefully highlights the fact that citations involve two parties – the citing writer and the quoted author. A similar idea is reflected in Thompson and Ye (1991), where the evaluative potential of reporting verbs is divided into three main categories – *author stance, writer stance* and *writer interpretation*. (Thompson and Ye 'arbitrarily but consistently' (p. 366) use the terms 'author' and 'writer' to refer to 'the person who is being reported' and 'the person who is reporting' respectively, a practice which has been adopted by many others in the field.) There are two points to note about these categories. First, the categories 'author stance' and 'writer stance' distinguish the two people, the cited author and the citing writer, involved in most acts of reporting. Secondly, the categories 'writer stance' and 'writer interpretation' distinguish between the 'two basic modes of evaluation' available to the writer (Thompson & Ye, 1991, p. 372). Their discussion highlights the complexity of the relationship between reporting verbs and evaluation, what they refer to as 'layers of report'. (See Thompson & Ye, 1991, pp. 377–380 for further details.) Myers (1989) raises this same point by stating that 'two different authors – the voice we take as speaking in the text, and the researcher whose work is described' (p. 4) need to be considered. This distinction is also well explained through the concepts of text averral and text attribution (Tadros, 1993). Text averral is manifested when a writer takes responsibility for the proposition(s) put forward in his/her text. This can be seen in a text in two ways – where there are no attributions or where there are positive signals of a writer's presence (Tadros, 1993). Text attribution is the marked part of the text and is defined as 'reports in the text which have the effect of transferring responsibility for what is being said' (Tadros, 1993, p. 104). In other words, when writers aver, they take responsibility for the proposition(s) being put forward, and when writers attribute, they transfer responsibility for those proposition(s) to another source. It is important to point out, however, that while the responsibility for the truth value of a statement may be transferred to some other attributed author, the writer is still responsible for the attribution itself (Hunston, 1995). As Groom (2000) says, 'it is the writer who has chosen the words that represent (and thus inevitably interpret) the views of the attributed author' and attributive forms can 'predict, or incorporate within themselves, an indication of the writer's own stance in relation to the attributed proposition' (p. 17).

In the next section, I will look at some of the common types of citations in my data to illustrate how different citations can influence the academic visibility of the writer in the text. I suggest that citations that carry or prospect evaluation by either the writer or the sourced author lead to greater academic visibility for the writer.

3 Citations and Writer Visibility

Table 10.1 illustrates the most common types of citations in my data. Because my primary interest in the rest of this chapter is to discuss how reporting verbs and the language structures in which these verbs are embedded may have an impact on academic visibility, it will be noticed that only integral citations are reflected in the table.

It can be seen from Table 10.1 that integral citations are used in a variety of different ways in my data. The relationship between reporting verb citations and academic visibility is fairly complex and an awareness of how these sequences construct visibility for the writer is invaluable for a second language writer. Aside from the different degrees of visibility carried or prospected by different reporting verbs, citations with modifying adverbs and *as* structures may further influence visibility, and some examples of these will be discussed later.

Table 10.1   Common types of citations in my data

Linguistic structure of citation	Examples from the data
As + X + verb	**As Hervey and Higgins (1992) suggests** cultural transplantation is …[SMY:F:56]
As + X + adverb + verb	However, **as Aixela aptly points out,** the difficulty of this definition is … [SMY:F:5]
X + verb + that-clause	**Coulthard suggests that** when an author is writing … [SMY:F:17]
X + verb + noun + that-clause	**Nida and Reyburn reminds us that** 'some historical events…meaningless.' [SMY:F:6]
X + verb + noun phrase	**Swain (1985, 1996) counter-argues the importance of output in SLA.** [HE:F:5]
noun phrase + be + verb + by + X	In addition, **the more detailed definition is given by Rost** (1990:152–153) … [YS:F:11]
it + be + verb + by + X + that	**It has been claimed by Granger (1998:13) that** NL/IL comparisons aim to uncover … [MD:F:9]
X + adverb + verb + that-clause	**Tsuda (1990) strongly suggests that** the English language is a device … [TS:F:10]
X + adverb + verb	**Phillipson (1992) also critically analyses** Wardhaugh's views … [TS:F:9]

In the next section, I briefly discuss a series of reporting verbs to illustrate how two factors impact academic visibility: (i) the identity of the source responsible for the action in the reporting verb (i.e. sourced author or writer) and (ii) the kind of evaluation the reporting verb carries or prospects (i.e. agreement, disagreement or neutrality). I propose that citations which indicate any kind of evaluation (agreement or disagreement) by the writer and/or the sourced author show a more visible writer in the text and citations which display neutrality show a less visible writer in the text and I will illustrate this with examples from my data. It is important to note that the examples used in the following discussion were produced by L2 writers. The patterns of usage of particular reporting verbs that we see here then may not be generalizable across all academic discourse. However, I would suggest that my conclusions from this data about the ways in which citation behaviours have the potential to impact academic visibility do hold across wider academic contexts.

3.1 The reporting verbs *find, suggest, claim* and *point out*

3.1.1 *Find*

In my data, when *find* is used as a reporting verb, the identity of the source responsible for the activity of 'finding something' is the sourced author. No information is provided about the opinion of the sourced author or the writer.

Example 1

They [Dulay and Burt] *found* that this sequence did not match the order which was found for first language. [CHL:F:14]

Example 2

Long (ibid.) *finds* that there is a difference between native talk directed toward a second language learner and native talk through interaction with a second language learner. [YXW:F:8]

Because there is no inherent evaluation contained in the reporting verb itself, and the contexts in which it is used in the data do not provide any added evaluation, it is reasonable to suggest that, in the data for this study, *find* as a reporting verb is used in ways that lead to low visibility for the L2 writers.

3.1.2 Suggest

The reporting verb *suggest* is found frequently in my data. This is not surprising as Hyland (1999) observed that *suggest* was one of the most frequent verbs in his corpus of 80 research articles in the field of Applied Linguistics, the same field from which the data for this chapter comes. Thompson and Ye (1991) point out that *suggest* is used by writers when they present 'the information/opinion as neither true nor false at that point in [their] work' (p. 372). In the current study as well, it appears that *suggest* is used to reflect a neutral stance where the writer's evaluation of the cited information is not apparent:

Example 3

Coulthard (1992:9) *suggests* that when an author is writing a text, he or she does not write it for real readers out there, but for an "ideal reader" who is constructed in his or her mind. [SMY:F:17]

Example 4

Also, Lamb *suggests* that the British educational system (before the new National Curriculum in 1993) is the cause of the unsatisfactory teaching of English in schools. [UY:F:15]

As we can see, with the verb *suggest*, the proposition in the text is signalled as belonging to some other sourced author, although the sourced author's commitment to that proposition is not strong. The writer himself/herself does not interpolate an opinion on what has been reported, but yet, because the writer represents the sourced author as having a stance (albeit a non-committal one), it could be said that the use of this verb constructs slightly more visibility for the academic writer than the use of a verb such as *find*.

3.1.3 Claim

The verb *claim* stands in contrast to the verbs we have discussed thus far as this verb has a strong potential for carrying the citing writer's evaluation of the reported information. The following is an example of the use of the reporting verb *claim* in my data:

Example 5

In the market there have appeared some teacher resource books which offer a great many dramatic activities for classroom use, such as Drama Techniques in Language Learning (Maley and Duff, 1996), Drama (Wessels, 1987), and Drama with Children (Phillips, 1999). However, most of the activities in these books are designed for learners to activate their language rather than focussing on new aspects of English. In spite of the fact that most of the activities have a clear aim, they do not have particular language focuses. Then, what learners really benefit in using them is the practice of speaking. The functions of drama in other aspects of learning are ignored. However, if the students have a text, it is possible to practise other language skills. In her book Holden (1981:61) **claims**, "using text might impede any kind of movements or gesture and constant reference to it will destroy concentration on the interaction". I would like to suggest that if the teachers have a meticulous plan in using a text, students might benefit more than by practicing oral skills. The acquisition of vocabulary and grammatical rules and the improvement of listening and reading skills are all possible benefits from the use of texts. [YSW:F:16]

Hunston (1993) classifies *claim* as a verb of arguing where there is in certain cases an implication of a difference in attitude between the writer and the sourced author. She points out in a later publication, however, that this is largely dependent on the context of use of the verb. In particular, we need to consider whether the text 'itself constitute[s an] argument, with the writer of the text (as attributor) as a participant in the argument' or whether the text 'simply reflect[s] upon or report[s] the argument' (Hunston, 1995, p. 150). In Example 5, the verb ***claim*** *is* used to indicate a difference in attitude between the sourced author and the writer. As we can see, the paragraph contains an argument about the effectiveness of using resource books to teach language in a drama classroom, and the student writer is himself/herself a participant in that argument, attributing a position to the sourced author Holden, and then counter-proposing.

There are, however, examples of the use of ***claim*** in the data where there is no clear signal of writer opinion. Consider the following example:

Example 6

Hall (1996) suggests that studies of punctuation use in children do not show clearly enough how they learn to punctuate and how they move to other punctuation marks in specific situations. Hall mentions that teaching punctuation in the classroom is always applied in content-based teaching. The students have a limited knowledge of punctuation at all levels, as their teachers feel less secure about teaching it than teaching spelling. Hall ***claims*** that, "To judge from the reaction of current-day politicians, people in commerce and industry as well as many parents, the failure to write English correctly are failures of contemporary education ... the complaints about standards of written English, and about punctuation ... are nothing new.' (Hall, 1996: 168). [UY:F:13]

We see here an example of a student who is, in Hunston's (1995, p. 150) terms, 'simply ... report[ing] the argument' made by Hall (1996). The verb *claim* in Example 6 thus does not clearly imply any disagreement between the student writer and Hall. In fact, the verb could be replaced with the verb *say* (which is clearly neutral) with little loss of meaning.

The extent to which the reporting verb *claim* then is able to increase academic visibility depends on how it is used. If it is used in a context where it prospects the writer's assessment of the sourced author or the cited information, then it would be reasonable to suggest that this verb does create a heightened academic visibility for the writer.

3.1.4 Point out

The verb *point out* is a strong indicator of agreement between the writer and the sourced author. According to Hunston (2000), the choice of this verb closes down any option of the writer disagreeing with the proposition being reported. Consider the following examples:

Example 7

Nevertheless, it could be argued that there is gradient in the behaviour of uncount nouns. Whilst there are typical uncount nouns such as *advice, furniture* or *information* that never occur with an article (CCGP2, 1998:4) there is also a wide range of uncount nouns which behave like count nouns and whose behaviours vary: some nouns combine with article *a/an* (e.g. *gloom/a gloom*), and others with plural suffix-(e)s (e.g. *discontent/discontents*). As to the unusual behaviors of uncount nouns, Hunston and Francis (1991:180) *point out* that 'some uncount nouns are associated with a slightly different patterns of behaviour which differentiates them from the typical members of the class', and that 'one can either say that they are uncount nouns which share some of the behaviours of count nouns or form a class of their own' (ibid.). [GDL:F:9]

Example 8

Hunston and Francis (2000:253) *point out* that patterns are related to meaning in that patterns play a central role in the meaning of the word, enable students to reform their meaning from them, and help students to effectively learn language …. Therefore, patterns can be said to be seen as useful points for student to notice grammar points among many lexical items in textbooks, so teachers and textbooks need to provide patterns as grammatical aspects for students in terms of language pedagogy. [YJK:F:6]

Both Examples 7 and 8 are typical of the ways in which the verb *point out* is used in my data. Use of the verb implies agreement with the views of the sourced author. In Example 7, the student clearly quotes from Hunston and Francis in a bid to support and expand on the proposition that he/she has just averred in the previous sentence. In Example 8, we see that the sentence containing the ideas attributed through the reporting verb *point out* to the sourced authors Hunston and Francis is followed by a sentence beginning with the logical connector *therefore*, indicating that what is to follow is premised on an acceptance of the ideas contained in the previous sentence. Because *point out* is a verb that inherently carries evaluation, I suggest that it contributes significantly towards the academic visibility of writers.

   In this section, we looked at a few examples of how reporting verbs influence writer visibility in the text depending on the type of evaluation carried by the reporting verb and the source of that evaluation. The next section will consider how the interaction of reporting verbs with other linguistic elements may impact academic visibility. I focus on 'as' structures and modifying adverbs, as these commonly occur in the data.

3.2 The use of 'as' structures and modifying adverbs

In Example 9, a reporting verb is used within an 'as' structure.

Example 9

As Hervey and Higgins (1992) suggest, claquing can also cultivate a sense of exoticism. In the case of the translation of The True story of Ah Q, the claquing of the literary

references and quotation in the ST do give the TT a sense of cultural foreignness ...
[SMY:F:52–53]

The reporting verb *suggest* was earlier analysed as a verb which signals a neutral stance on the part of a writer. However, when writers use the reporting verb *suggest* with the conjunction *as*, the evaluative quality of the citation changes. The writer now wishes to be included in the view contained in the proposition suggested by the sourced author. The above example is typical of how *as* is used in citations in the current data and it would be reasonable to suggest that such 'as' structures boost the academic visibility of a writer because of the positive evaluation they carry.

The examples that follow show some of the different ways in which modifying adverbs are used with reporting verbs in my data. In some cases, the modifying adverb itself carries an evaluation of the proposition being reported, as in this next example:

Example 10

However, as Aixela **aptly** points out the difficulty of this definition is that "in a language ..." (1996:57). [SMY:F:5]

Here, *aptly* signals a positive evaluation. The writer is in agreement with the sourced author's view, and there are in fact three indicators of agreement – the 'as' structure, the verb *points out*, and the modifying adverb *aptly*. The presence of multiple indicators of agreement makes the academic visibility of the writer much stronger than it would have been if there had been just the reporting verb *points out* to show agreement.

In the following example, the modifying adverb is used in a slightly different way. The adverb itself signals neither agreement nor disagreement, but rather describes the writer's interpretation of something that the sourced author has done:

Example 11

Phillipson (1992) also **critically** analyses Wardhaugh's views as expressed in the book, 'Language in Competition' as follows: 'Wardhaugh regards English as 'neutral and divorced from cultural associations .... His approach is typical of a native who uncritically applaud the spread of English. There is a strong element of the triumphalism of apologists of dominant languages.' (Phillipson 1992: 102–103). [TS:F:9]

The use of the adverb *critically* displays the writer's interpretation of how she thinks Phillipson has analysed Wardhaugh. Without the adverb, the verb *analyses* does not reflect anything more than the student writer's reporting of an action performed by the sourced author. It is the modifying adverb which gives us a glimpse of the writer, showing us how the writer reads and interprets the sourced author's analysis.

Another example of a modifying adverb showing a writer's interpretation can be seen in Example 12:

Example 12

Tsuda (1990) **strongly** suggests that the English language is a device to rule and discriminate against minor languages and dominates them. [TS:F:10]

As highlighted earlier, the reporting verb *suggest* carries a non-committal position from the sourced author and no evaluation from the citing writer. The use of the adverb *strongly*, however, changes the evaluative status of the citation. Not only is the sourced author now represented as having a heightened commitment to his own proposition, the writer is seen as being the one who has evaluated the reported work and ascribed this strong commitment to the sourced author. The use of the adverb thus heightens the visibility of the writer.

3.3 Summary: citations and academic visibility

To sum up, then, the main visibility choices in a citation are:

- choices between different kinds of reporting verbs,
- choices between using and not using an adverb in a citation and
- choices between using and not using an 'as' structure in the citation.

The main choices and their impact on writer visibility are presented below.

(a) Where we find citations with a reporting verb that carries no indication of author or writer evaluation, but only an indication of relevance, the writer has low visibility.
(b) Where we find citations with a reporting verb that carries a signal of sourced author evaluation, the writer is visible in the text.
(c) Where we find citations with a reporting verb that carries an evaluation from the writer, the writer is visible in the text.

(d) Where we find citations with reporting verbs modified by adverbs, the writer is visible in the text.
(e) Where we find citations within 'as' structures indicating a writer's alignment with the sourced author's proposition, the writer is visible in the text.

It is tempting to want to place the citations on a visibility cline – from citations which make a writer less visible to ones that make the writer more visible in a text. However, as we have seen in the above examples, visibility is quite often affected by a combination of different phenomena, and a cline would over-generalise how a writer's visibility in a text is affected through citations. Also, different writers may use the same reporting verbs differently (see, for example, my examples of the verb *claim* in Examples 5 and 6) and a cline would inaccurately represent the use of reporting verbs in the data. Having said this, it is nonetheless worthwhile for a second language writer to be made aware of these choices and to see how their citation choices could impact their academic visibility in a text. In the next section, I turn to some of the pedagogical applications of what I have discussed here so far.

4 Pedagogical Applications: A Focus on the Revision Process

The issue of academic visibility is complex (John, 2005, 2009). It is not always the case that more visibility leads to a better text. However, writers, and L2 writers in particular, need to be aware of the impact of their rhetorical choices on the identities they project to their readers. In an informal interview with students, I found that students rarely think about their choices when using citations. In fact, my impression was that they 'recycled' their reporting verbs and chose verbs based on how often they had used it previously rather than on what the verb reveals about their evaluation of the quoted author or quoted proposition. The next example, which compares excerpts from the draft and final versions of a dissertation by one of the writers in this study, illustrates this point. In the example, there are two sentences involving citations which underwent revision between the draft and final versions. The first instance of revision does not affect the visibility of the writer or the scholarly argument in the text, but the second affects both visibility and argumentation. The differences in the two versions are in bold.

Looking at the first point of difference between the two drafts, we see that the writer, in the draft version, uses the verb *points out*, which I earlier classified as a verb which enhances writer visibility because it shows agreement between the

Example 13

Draft [MD:D:1]	Final [MD:F:5]
Clearly, contrastive approach is a dominating approach in the investigation on learner corpora. However, **Granger (1998:12) points out** that the contrastive approach is different from the conventional CA (contrastive analysis), which involves 'comparing / contrasting what non-native speakers of a language do in a comparable situation' (Pery-Woodley 1990:285). Granger calls this type of CA as CIA – Contrastive Interlanguage Analysis, which includes two types of comparisons.	Clearly, the contrastive approach is a dominating approach in the investigation of learner corpora. **Granger (1998:12) distinguishes** the contrastive approach from the conventional CA (contrastive analysis), because it involves 'comparing/ contrasting what non-native speakers of a language do in a comparable situation' (Pery-Woodley 1990:143). Granger refers to this type of CA as CIA - Contrastive Interlanguage Analysis which includes two types of comparison:
(1) NL vs. IL, i.e. comparison of native language and interlanguage (2) IL vs. IL, i.e. comparison of different interlanguage.(Granger 1998:12)	(1) NL vs. IL, i.e. comparison of native language and interlanguage. (2) IL vs. IL, i.e. comparison of different interlanguages. (Granger 1998:12)
As Granger (ibid:13) puts in, 'NL/IL comparison aims to uncover the features of non-nativeness of learner language'.	**Granger (ibid:13) claims that**, 'NL/IL comparison aims to uncover the features of non-nativeness of learner language'.

writer and the sourced author. In this case, it would signal that the writer agrees with Granger's viewpoint that there is a difference between the 'contrastive approach' and the 'conventional CA'. With the verb *distinguishes* used in the final version, however, the element of agreement is no longer present. Rather, the writer is telling the reader that she has read what Granger has written, interpreted it and noticed the distinction that Granger makes between these approaches. Although the element of agreement is not present in the revised version, however, we could argue that the visibility of the writer is unaffected since a different kind of evaluative work is implied. The writer now presents herself as being the source of the interpretation of Granger's actions and ideas. Both verbs thus could be considered high visibility verbs, and I suggest that the scholarly argument after the revision also remains unaffected.

In the second area of difference, we note that the draft version contains an 'as' citation structure along with a non-idiomatic reporting verb *puts in*, whereas the final version contains a reporting verb structure without the *as* conjunction and with a different verb, *claims*. The revision here is significant for the meaning that is conveyed by the citation and the subsequent impact on the argument being made by the writer. The 'as' structure implies that the writer agrees with the sourced author and wishes to be seen as aligned with the sourced author's view. However, the reporting verb *claims*, used in the final version, does not show agreement with the sourced author. It does not show disagreement clearly either, in this particular case. With a loss of the signalled evaluation and alignment, it appears that the visibility of the writer has been affected by this change, and the writer could be said to be less visible in the final version than in the draft.

More importantly, if we look more closely at this revision, further observations can be made about the argument being constructed. I suggest that this writer was quite accurate in her initial use of an 'as' structure to signal alignment since, judging from the overall findings of her research, which was about how learner corpora can be used to teach writing, she does subscribe to Granger's distinction between CA and CIA. However, possibly because of her initial use of the expression *puts in*, which is non-idiomatic and which may have been highlighted to her as something she needed to amend, she revised her initial citation structure to an entirely different one in her final version. The revised citation unfortunately did not carry with it the same meaning and alignment as the structure used in the draft.

This example highlights important pedagogical implications. In our attempts to sort out issues of language, it is possible that other larger and perhaps even more important issues like stance, which is an important contributing factor to the construction of a scholarly argument, may be affected. The writer in this example intended to show alignment with the sourced author but in the final version did not do so and this affected the argument she presented.

For second language writers, guided revision during the supervision process and heightened awareness of the ways in which citations are used in academic writing might be helpful. This particular example illustrates one of the common problems for L2 writers - a lack of awareness of the meanings of reporting verbs and reporting structures. L2 writers need to understand the evaluative meanings behind different citation structures, the impact these can have on the scholarly argument being constructed and the subsequent impact on academic visibility. Revision provides dissertation supervisors and writers an opportunity to reflect on the intended evaluative meaning of citations in a text. It allows for careful consideration of the argument being constructed and gives writers an opportunity to think about the evaluations carried in their citations, and the corresponding visibility this affords for their academic identities.

5 Closing Reflections

This chapter has illustrated how a writer's visible academic identity in a text can be represented without using the first person pronoun. I have highlighted how citation sequences can affect the visibility of the writer in the text. This is a valuable lesson for writers as it brings into focus issues of evaluation through citation, which in turn affects the construction of academic arguments and academic visibility. If writers are made aware of how citations can reveal their understanding of their sources and the extent of their alignment with sourced authors, they can then be made aware of how citations can be used to construct a good academic argument with the optimal level of writer visibility. For second language writers, this awareness is fundamental as they face the challenge of developing an appropriately visible academic identity in their writing.

References

Bartholomae, D. (1995). Writing with teachers: A conversation with Peter Elbow. *College Composition and Communication, 46,* 62–71.

Bitchener, J. (2010). *Writing an applied linguistics thesis or dissertation.* London: Palgrave Macmillan.

Bizzell, P. (1992). *Academic discourse and critical consciousness.* Pittsburgh, PA: University of Pittsburg Press.

Casanave, C. P. (2002). *Writing games.* Mahwah, NJ: Lawrence Erlbaum Associates.

Charles, M. (2003). 'This mystery ...': A corpus-based study of the use of nouns to construct stance in theses from two contrasting disciplines. *Journal of English for Academic Purposes, 2*(4), 313–326.

Charles, M. (2006). The construction of stance in reporting clauses: A cross-disciplinary study of theses. *Applied Linguistics, 27*(3), 495–518.

Chubin, D. E., & Moitra, S. D. (1975). Content analysis of references: Adjunct or alternative to citation counting? *Social Studies of Science, 5,* 423–441.

Coffin, C., Curry, M. J., Goodman, S., Hewings, A., Lillis, T. M., & Swann, J. (2003). *Teaching academic writing: A toolkit for higher education.* London: Routledge.

Creme, P., & Lea, M. (1999). *Writing at university.* Buckingham: Open University Press.

Elbow, P. (1995a). Being a writer vs. being an academic: A conflict in goals. *College Composition and Communication, 46,* 72–83.

Elbow, P. (1995b). Interchanges: Responses to Bartholomae and Elbow. *College Composition and Communication, 46,* 87–92.

Groom, N. (2000). Attribution and averral revisited: Three perspectives on manifest intertextuality in academic writing. In P. Thompson (Ed.), *Patterns and perspectives: Insights into EAP writing practice* (pp. 15–26). Reading: Antony Rower Limited.

Hacker, D. (1999). *A writer's reference* (4th ed.). Boston: Bedford/St Martin's.

Harwood, N. (2005). 'I hoped to counteract the memory problem, but I made no impact whatsoever': Discussing methods in computing science using *I. English for Specific Purposes, 24*(3), 243–267.

Harwood, N. (2009). An interview-based study of the functions of citations in academic writing across two disciplines. *Journal of Pragmatics, 41*(3), 497–518.

Hewings, A., & Coffin, C. (2007). Writing in multi-party computer conferences and single authored assignments: Exploring the role of writer as thinker. *Journal of English for Academic Purposes, 6*(2), 126–142.

Hirvela, A., & Belcher, D. (2001). Coming back to voice: The multiple voices and identities of mature multilingual writers. *Journal of Second Language Writing, 10*(1/2), 83–106.

Hunston, S. (1993). Evaluation and ideology in scientific writing. In M. Ghadessy (Ed.), *Register analysis* (pp. 57–73). London: Pinter.

Hunston, S. (1995). A corpus study of some English verbs of attribution. *Functions of Language, 2*(2), 133–158.

Hunston, S. (2000). Evaluation and planes of discourse: Status and value in persuasive texts. In S. Hunston & G. Thompson (Eds.), *Evaluation in text* (pp. 176–207). Oxford: Oxford University Press.

Hunston, S., & Thompson, G. (Eds.). (2000). *Evaluation in text.* Oxford: Oxford University Press.

Hyland, K. (1996). Writing without conviction? Hedging in science research articles. *Applied Linguistics, 17*, 433–454.

Hyland, K. (1999). Academic attribution: Citation and the construction of disciplinary knowledge. *Applied Linguistics, 20*(3), 341–367.

Hyland, K. (2001). Humble servants of the discipline? Self-mention in research articles. *English for Specific Purposes, 20*(3), 207–226.

Hyland, K. (2002a). Authority and invisibility: Authorial identity in academic writing. *Journal of Pragmatics, 34*, 1091–1112.

Hyland, K. (2002b). Options of identity in academic writing. *ELT Journal, 56*(4), 351–358.

Ivanič, R. (1998). *Writing and identity.* Amsterdam: John Benjamins.

Ivanič, R., & Camps, D. (2001). I am how I sound: Voice as self-representation in L2 writing. *Journal of Second Language Writing, 10*(1/2), 3–33.

Ivanič, R., & Simpson, J. (1992). Who's who in academic writing? In N. Fairclough (Ed.), *Critical Language Awareness* (pp. 141–173). London: Longman.

John, S. (2005). The writing process and writer identity: Investigating the influence of revision on linguistic and textual features of writer identity in dissertations. (Unpublished doctoral dissertation). University of Birmingham, UK.

John, S. (2009). Using the revision process to help international students understand the linguistic construction of the academic identity. In M. Charles, D. Pecorari & S. Hunston (Eds.), *Academic writing: At the interface of corpus and discourse* (pp. 272–290). London: Continuum.

Kuo, C. H. (1999). The use of personal pronouns: Role relationships in scientific research articles. *English for Specific Purposes, 18*(2), 121–138.

Lillis, T. (1997). New voices in academia? The regulative nature of academic writing conventions. *Language and Education, 11*(3), 182–199.

Lillis, T. (2001). *Student writing.* London: Routledge.

Lillis, T., Hewings, A., Vladimirou, D., & Curry, M. J. (2010). The geolinguistics of English as an academic lingua franca: Citation practices across English-medium national and English-medium international journals. *International Journal of Applied Linguistics, 20*(1), 111–135.

Matsuda, P. K. (2001). Voice in Japanese written discourse: Implications for second language writing. *Journal of Second Language Writing, 10*, 35–53.

Moravcsik, M. J. & Murugesan, P. (1975). Some results on the function and quality of citations. *Social Studies of Science, 5*, 86–92.

Myers, G. (1989). The pragmatics of politeness in scientific articles. *Applied Linguistics, 10*(1), 1–35.

Petric, B. (2007). Rhetorical functions of citations in high- and low-rated master's theses. *Journal of English for Academic Purposes, 6*(3), 238–253.

Phan Le Ha. (2009). Strategic, passionate, but academic: Am I allowed in my writing? *Journal of English for Academic Purposes, 8*(2), 134–146.

Ramanathan, V., & Atkinson, D. (1999). Individualism, academic writing, and ESL writers. *Journal of Second Language Writing , 8*(1), 45–75.

Salager-Meyer, F. (1994). Hedges and textual communicative function in medical English written discourse. *English for Specific Purposes, 11*(2), 93–113.

Shaw, P. (1992). Reasons for the correlation of voice, tense, and sentence function in reporting verbs. *Applied Linguistics, 13*(3), 302–319.

Sheldon, E. (2009). From one *I* to another: Discursive construction of self-representation in English and Castilian Spanish research articles. *English for Specific Purposes, 28*(4), 251–265.

Stapleton, P. (2002). Critiquing voice as a viable pedagogical tool in L2 writing. *Journal of Second Language Writing, 11*(3), 177–190.

Starfield, S., & Ravelli, L. (2006). 'The writing of this thesis was a process that I could not explore with the positivistic detachment of the classical sociologist': Self and structure in *New Humanities* research theses. *Journal of English for Academic Purposes, 5*, 222–243.

Stott, R., Snaith, A., & Rylance, R. (2001). *Making your case: A practical guide to essay writing*. London: Longman.

Swales, J. M., & Burke, A. (2003). 'It's really fascinating work': Differences in evaluative adjectives across academic registers. In P. Leistyna & C. F. Meyer (Eds.), *Corpus analysis: Language structure and language use* (pp. 1–18). New York: Rodopi.

Tadros, A. (1993). The pragmatics of text averral and attribution in academic texts. In M. Hoey (Ed.), *Data, description, discourse* (pp. 98–114). London: HarperCollins.

Tang, R., & John, S. (1999). The 'I' in identity: Exploring writer identity in student academic writing through the first person pronoun. *English for Specific Purposes, 18*, S23-S39.

Thompson, G. (2001). Interaction in academic writing: Learning to argue with the reader. *Applied Linguistics, 22*(1), 58–78.

Thompson, G., & Ye, Y. (1991). Evaluation in the reporting verbs used in academic papers. *Applied Linguistics, 12*(4), 365–382.

Varttala, T. (2003). Hedging in scientific research articles: A cross-disciplinary study. In G. Cortese & P. Riley (Eds.), *Domain-specific English: Textual practices across communities and classrooms* (pp. 141–174). New York: Peter Lang.

Vassileva, I. (2001). Commitment and detachment in English and Bulgarian academic writing. *English for Specific Purposes, 20*, 83–102.

Zamel, V., & Spack, R. (Eds.). (1998). *Negotiating academic literacies*. Mahwah, NJ: Lawrence Erlbaum Associates.

Chapter 11

Two Sides of the Same Coin: Challenges and Opportunities for Scholars from EFL Backgrounds

Ramona Tang

1 Introduction

For several years now, I have been teaching young EFL postgraduates. Novice academics in the early stages of their academic careers in universities in their home countries, they come to Singapore to pursue a postgraduate degree (specialising in English Language Teaching and/or Applied Linguistics) as part of their professional and personal development and in many cases to enhance their career advancement prospects in their home universities. It is as a result of teaching them, supervising their research projects, and interacting with them that I have come to see something of how they view and position themselves within the professional academic community.

I listen to the stories of these scholars, the histories that motivate them to work as hard as they do and to pursue particular research topics, and I realise that they have such interesting voices and perspectives that the wider community in ELT and Applied Linguistics would certainly be interested to listen to. And yet, the research that emerges in the fields of Academic Literacies and EAP has largely focused on the *difficulties* that EFL scholars face in writing for publication and getting their voices heard in the international academic arena (e.g. Cargill & O'Connor, 2006; Cho, 2009; Flowerdew, 1999, 2007; Gosden, 2003; Li, 2006a, 2006b, 2007; Li & Flowerdew, 2007; Lillis & Curry, 2006; Uzuner, 2008).

In one sense, it is not surprising that Academic Literacies and EAP researchers and practitioners have tended to focus on the problems facing EFL writers. It is the very nature of our discipline to try to understand and address the challenges faced by academic writers, so empowering them to function in more effective ways within the academic context. But it is possible to empower particular groups both by highlighting the privileged practices and cultural capital that they do not yet possess and hence may choose to acquire, *and* by highlighting the useful cultural capital (sometimes latent and hence not utilised) that they do already have. To my mind, we have focused much on the former and too little on the latter. I want, in this chapter, therefore, to enact a shift from our 'tendency to emphasize problems' to 'a focus on possibilities' (Phillion, 2002, p. xxii), to balance the largely negative tenor of our conversations in this area thus far with a more positive message.

Certainly, there are many challenges that all writers face when they write and seek academic publication. And for someone who is embarking on this undertaking in a language which is not his/her L1, there are likely to be additional hurdles. Striving for not just linguistic accuracy but also idiomatic language use, having to learn the rhetorical and interactional conventions of a different academic tradition, learning to engage appropriately with the 'key texts' of a different academic tradition (which includes getting access to those texts to begin with and then reading them in a foreign language) – these and other difficulties have all been highlighted in the literature and can prove frustrating to academics writing in a foreign language, especially when their native speaker peers do not seem to appreciate the 'invisible benefits' (Lillis & Curry, 2010, p. 1) that they have simply by virtue of their native speaker position. But I would suggest (and I'm certainly not the first to do so) that where there are challenges associated with being 'different' in some way, there are also additional opportunities for precisely the same reason. This chapter has been born out of a desire on my part to provide a richer and more encouraging picture of EFL scholars writing for publication and contributing to the international academic community, to highlight that even as the endeavour is fraught with challenges, it is also filled with possibilities.

In this chapter, I start by discussing some of the work already done in this area, and go on to focus on a few new narratives offered by 8 EFL researchers at different stages of their academic careers, to highlight some of what they encounter as they negotiate their way through the research and publication process, and how they make sense of and make use of the unique cultural and linguistic capital that they possess.

2 Already in the Literature: The Unique Cultural and Linguistic Capital of EFL Scholars

It is now hardly contentious any longer to say that English has emerged as the international lingua franca of academic research and scholarship.

(See, for instance, Canagarajah, 2002; Flowerdew & Li, 2009; Hyland, 2009; Lillis & Curry, 2010.) And because academic publication is not only the primary means by which academics construct, negotiate and disseminate knowledge (e.g. Becher & Trowler, 2001; Hyland, 2000, 2009) but is also now increasingly central to the status, prospects and employability of academics (Becher & Trowler, 2001; Burgess & Martín-Martín, 2008; Chen, Gupta & Hoshower, 2006; Curry & Lillis, 2010; Flowerdew & Li, 2009; Lillis & Curry, 2010; Nir & Zilberstein-Levy, 2006; Uzuner, 2008), this 'global anglicization of academic publishing' (Flowerdew & Li, 2009, p. 2) has meant that many EFL scholars are finding themselves under pressure to write in English, a language not their own, if they wish to participate in academic conversations beyond their country's borders. We see this in recent research on contexts as varied as China (Cargill & O'Connor, 2006; Flowerdew & Li, 2009), Italy (Giannoni, 2008), Korea (Cho, 2009), Sudan (ElMalik & Nesi, 2008), and Hungary, Slovakia and Spain (Curry & Lillis, 2004). [It should be noted, however, that the extent to which English is privileged over local and national languages in publication is dependent on various factors, and varies considerably by country, institution, and even discipline. See, for instance, Lillis and Curry's (2010) rich ethnographic study of the publishing practices of scholars from four countries in Europe, Polo and Varela's (2009) cross-disciplinary survey in one university in Spain and Casanave's (2002) case studies with young bilingual Japanese faculty.]

While many have focused on the difficulties faced by EFL scholars seeking publication in English, I wish in the rest of this chapter to focus on the other side of the coin – the fact that the cultural and linguistic capital (Bourdieu, 1973; Bourdieu & Passeron, 1990) that EFL scholars possess, which is in many respects so different from that possessed by their Anglophone counterparts, offers them unique opportunities to contribute to and enhance the research in their fields.

Canagarajah has been one of the most outspoken on this subject. In his 2002 work, *A Geopolitics of Academic Writing*, he writes about what 'periphery' scholars have to offer to the international community, and implies that they have a duty to engage in the academic conversations of the 'center':

> [Periphery scholars] should retain the power of the restless/vibrant 'margin' to offer a critical and constructive contribution to the often conservative/stable 'center'. ... They have a part to play in the constant reexamination and reformulation of established knowledge. ... [T]hey cannot abdicate their responsibility to interrogate knowledge related to periphery concerns in international academic fora. Ghettoizing periphery

scholars will only prove advantageous for the mainstream in making its own knowledge about the periphery suit its own interests. (Canagarajah, 2002, p. 268)

Canagarajah's conviction that periphery scholars have a unique contribution to make to the academic conversation of their disciplines is clear. What is more, he emphasises that the value of their contribution stems precisely from the fact that they are able to offer a different perspective. His is not a call for an accepting homogenisation. Instead, he underscores the need for periphery scholars to enter the academic conversation on their own terms, '*maintain[ing] their critical detachment from the mainstream*, while productively interacting with center scholars through their publications' (p. 268, my emphasis).

Some element of just such a simultaneous detachment from and interaction with the mainstream can be seen in Pavlenko's (2003) narrative account of her journey from being a Jewish student discriminated against in her native Ukraine to being a research-productive tenure-track academic in America. From the vantage point of someone who was by then well on her way to becoming the prolific researcher she is now, Pavlenko was able to write, '[An] advantage of my refugee background is the inside perspective on the immigrant experience, second language (L2) socialization, and bilingualism that allows me to walk back and forth across the divide that in the field of Second Language Acquisition (SLA) often separates "us" (academics) from "them" (L2 learners and users)' (p. 182).

Pavlenko reports that she found herself 'rebelling' against and questioning what she read in mainstream linguistics and SLA because

> [t]he scholarship simply did not reflect me nor anyone I knew, living, breathing individuals, at the nexus of multiple power relations that often determined what – and how much of it – gets or does not get acquired. Nor did it recognize the fact that more than half of the world population was multilingual which made monolingualism and monolingual-like competence an exception rather than the rule. (Pavlenko, 2003, p. 184)

She writes of her need 'to do something *to* and *in* the profession' (an expression she borrows from Matsuda, 2003), and says: 'I was bursting – and still am – with points to be made, new intersections between various areas of research to be created, and new studies to undertake, all of which would reflect second language learning in context, happening to real people' (p. 191).

Pavlenko's narrative is an inspiring account of how she capitalised on her own cultural and autobiographical background, and saw a way to use the perspectives that she had because of her history to make an impact on the discipline she was seeking entry into. And in the face of the dominant discourse on the disadvantages associated with being an EFL scholar, what is worth highlighting, I feel, is the sentiment that Pavlenko expresses towards the end of her account:

> In all of these years, the issue of my nonnative speakerness never surfaced in any but the most trival manner (typically, in corrections of those pesky articles and tenses). Consequently, I find that calling myself a 'non-native' or 'peripheral' writer does not reflect the reality of my own academic existence. I feel pretty involved in some of the key conversations in my two fields and am also very aware that *my own multilingualism positions me at a very privileged angle.* (Pavlenko, 2003, pp. 191–192, my emphasis)

The privilege of being able to draw on a familiarity with multiple languages and multiple cultures is also evident in Li's (1996) cross-cultural study of what constitutes 'good writing'. Li, who grew up in China and subsequently attended graduate school in America, chose to explore the complexities surrounding articulating the criteria for 'good writing' from two perspectives which are 'as different from [each other] as one can imagine' (Li, 1996, p. 3) – Chinese and American. Her study looks at the verbal and written feedback of American teachers and Chinese teachers responding to the same set of student papers, and she likens her study to 'a pair of bifocal glasses' (Li, 1996, p. 9), suggesting that it is often in seeing a phenomenon through the lens of a different cultural tradition that we come to a better understanding of our own tradition. This is a crucial point that she makes because it highlights yet another important reason for working to ensure that as many culturally and geographically different voices as possible are included in the academic conversations of our discipline. It is not simply that our perspectives are broadened when we learn about another context or culture, but that an appreciation of what happens in another culture often deepens our understanding of our own.

Recognising the value that an 'outsider' perspective can bring to collective understanding, Li says that 'the multiplicity of truth is often brought to light by outsiders' and that '[t]he reason why outsiders are more perceptive is not that they are more objective ...; rather, they bring new perspectives to objects that are often too familiar, too much taken for granted by the insiders' (p. 3). What makes Li's work particularly intriguing to me in this respect is her revelation in the preface of the English version of her book (published by State University of New York Press) that a Chinese version of her book was being published in China. We can see how the value of her cross-cultural study would be evident to readers in two very different parts of the world. For the one, China is the outside perspective; for the other, America is.

It is clear then that for Suresh Canagarajah, Aneta Pavlenko and Xiao-Ming Li, the potential that they see for EFL scholars having an impact on their disciplines is significant. The contributions that they envision are *transformatory* in nature, resulting in:

- established knowledge being reexamined through an outsider's eyes, and reformulated, and
- research foci that go beyond the 'mainstream' to more accurately reflect the concerns and the reality of experience of people from a diversity of linguistic and cultural contexts.

This is certainly a very optimistic outlook, but it is worth noting that although Canagarajah, Pavlenko and Li started out from the 'periphery' (Sri Lanka, Ukraine, and China respectively), they were, by the time of writing the works discussed above, operating from privileged bases in the US, with every likelihood of their future careers staying firmly within the 'center'. I raise this not to discount the validity of their views but to suggest that the realities facing different sorts of EFL scholars may not necessarily be the same. A researcher who studies and works his/her whole life in a periphery country is not the same as one who is born in Thailand, for example, studies in the UK and subsequently stays there to work. And neither is the same as the one who is born in Thailand, studies in the UK, and returns to Thailand to work, or the one who is born in Thailand, studies in the UK, and subsequently works in a variety of different EFL countries around Asia. These very different kinds of EFL scholars may face different realities in terms of access to materials, opportunities to network, opportunities to participate on a regular basis in the international academic conversations of their discipline, pressures to publish in local/national languages, opportunities to converse in English about their research, and so on. *All* are likely to have perspectives that are to some extent influenced by their unique personal and professional histories, and thus will have valuable insights to contribute to the international community. But, even though I have always tended towards the idealistic, I would recognise that the kind of transformatory contribution highlighted above may not be equally attainable for all, and that it may be easier or more difficult for some to get their voices heard.

This is a reality that Canagarajah (2002) himself recognises, and Cho (2004), too, has suggested that although 'local knowledge' of particular cultures is an asset that NNSE scholars have over their monocultural, monolingual counterparts, it may be easier to capitalise on 'local knowledge' in some types of research than others, and 'local knowledge that is complementary, additional, or compatible to Center-based established knowledge may be more acceptable to the established research community' as compared to 'local knowledge that may confront and transform established disciplinary knowledge' (p. 66).

Whether transformatory or complementary in nature, the contributions of scholars from diverse linguistic and cultural backgrounds have the potential to enrich the discussions in their disciplines, and this is something the journal editors interviewed in Flowerdew's (2001) study clearly recognise. Flowerdew interviewed the editors of 12 international journals from the fields of ELT and Applied Linguistics in order to find out their attitudes towards contributions from non-native speakers of English (NNSE). Although focusing largely on the editors' general attitudes and problematic aspects of NNSE contributions noticed by the editors and their reviewers, the article does touch briefly (2½ pages in a 30-page article) on some of the positive attributes of NNSE contributions, as highlighted by the journal editors. According to Flowerdew's informants, NNSE contributors:

- Show an awareness of aspects of language such as cross-cultural pragmatics.
- Display the objectivity of an outside perspective.
- Possess native speaker (NS) knowledge of other languages.
- Are essential to the international nature of international journals.
- Can test theories of the dominant centre.
- Can investigate issues that might not occur to researchers in the centre or investigate these issues in different ways, using different data.
- Have access to research sites where NSs would be intrusive.
- Can alert the centre to research undertaken in other scholarly traditions.

                                                        (Flowerdew, 2001, p. 127)

Flowerdew's study is interesting in that it is one of the few in existence which explicitly attempts to spell out precisely what EFL researchers have in their favour. Conducted from the perspective of outsiders (i.e. the editors, the gatekeepers, the *recipients* of texts written by EFL scholars), Flowerdew's study also forms an interesting counter-balance to the works by Canagarajah,

Pavlenko and Li discussed earlier, which were written from the insider perspective of someone from an EFL background.

In this chapter, I continue to look into what EFL researchers have in their favour and how they see themselves participating in the discussions of their discipline.

3 The Methodology

Eight EFL researchers at different stages of their academic careers graciously participated in this study. Four have doctoral degrees and are either Assistant Professors or Associate Professors now working in universities in Asia. They range from having 6 years to 25 years of teaching experience in higher education. The other four EFL participants are concurrently lecturers (on study leave) from universities in Asia and postgraduates enrolled in either a Master's or PhD programme at a university in Singapore. As a convenient way of indicating group membership for the purposes of this study, I refer to the first group using the title 'Dr', and the second group without a title. All the names used in this chapter are pseudonyms.

The narratives for seven of the eight participants that I discuss in this chapter were elicited through a written survey distributed via email. Participants were told that I was interested in exploring the personal and professional narratives, experiences, and views of EFL academics at various stages of their academic careers, and that I was keen to read as detailed an account of their experiences as they had the time to give. There were some slight differences in the phrasing of the questions emailed to the different participants, to take into account differences in their background and their current status (working or studying). However, by and large, the main questions asked in the survey were:

- What are your research interests at the moment?
- What made you decide to choose this/these as your area(s) of research?
- Do you publish in English only, in English *and* in your L1, or in your L1 only? What motivates your choice as to the language and the types of journals/books in which to publish your work?
- In your journey as an academic researcher and writer thus far, have you experienced any successes or encountered any opportunities which you feel are the direct result of your EFL background? Do you have any specific examples or stories to share?

- To what extent do you think it is possible for researchers from an EFL context to use their backgrounds (linguistic, cultural etc.) to their advantage in the world of international academic research and publication?

Working with the belief that our histories influence our current perspectives, I asked questions which I hoped would encourage the participants to share specific stories of their own experiences, rather than simply general opinions about the topic at hand. From studies such as Flowerdew (2001), we know, in theory, what EFL researchers are able to bring to the international academic community. I was interested here in exploring specific ways in which real EFL researchers are contributing or could contribute to their niche areas of research, actual instantiations of what we may already know in theory.

One of the eight participants, Dr Bencsik, originally from a Central European country, but now working in Asia, preferred to be interviewed. We followed roughly the same set of questions as those found on the written survey. The interview was recorded and I later transcribed relevant portions of it.

As I read through the responses, I tried to pull out from the narratives ways in which my eight participants' histories, motivations, postgraduate work, research and consultancy work, publications, linguistic expertise, and cultural knowledge position them in unique ways to enhance the academic conversation within ELT and Applied Linguistics. I also read with the aim of identifying common threads in the narratives. In doing so, I was mindful of Webster and Mertova's (2007) observation that '[n]arrative is not an objective reconstruction of life – it is a rendition of how life is perceived' (p. 3). Thus, even as we aim to gather insights from the experiences of my eight participants, we need also to bear in mind that all their narratives are shaped from 'chosen parts' (Webster & Mertova, 2007, p. 3) of their lives, and the one telling the story has already edited his/her experience through various filters. With this study, there is of course yet another layer to the storytelling – *my* shaping of my participants' stories into a meta-narrative of my own. Coles (1989) has said that 'as active listeners we give shape to what we hear, make over [others'] stories into something of our own' (p. 19). I hope that in my attempt to paint a more positive picture of the realities of EFL scholars' contributions to the academic community, I have not distorted their stories, but have managed to capture some of the complexity and richness of their experiences.

4 The Benefits (and Burdens) of Insider Knowledge

Based on the responses of my informants, it emerges that one of the most obvious ways in which EFL researchers contribute to the academic conversation within ELT and Applied Linguistics is by drawing on their insider knowledge of their home cultures to offer a different perspective to the issues being discussed by their discourse communities. Although Li (1996), as discussed above, has suggested that there is the potential for our collective understanding to be expanded when the behaviours of members of one culture are studied through the lens of a different culture, a number of my participants point out that there is at the same time the potential that any investigation of culture-dependent phenomenon through the lens of a different culture may give rise to misinterpretations, and that it takes an insider perspective to minimise the potential of the behaviours under investigation being misconstrued.

The ability of a researcher who is a 'cultural insider' to empathise with his/her research subjects and to offer to the discourse community a picture of the phenomenon under investigation which takes into account often unspoken cultural attitudes and traditions is something which Dr Jiang, the most senior member of the group of EFL informants in this study, highlights in the extract below.

Dr Jiang, Associate Professor, 25 years of teaching in higher education, originally from China but now working in another Southeast Asian country
My EFL background gives me a privileged vantage point from which to research language teaching and learning in China. Because of my own experience as an EFL learner in China, I'm capable of empathizing with Chinese EFL learners like myself. As a member of the same cultural group, I have much in common with participants in my research – shared assumptions, attitudes, beliefs, self-perceptions, strategies, motivations, culturally-based conceptions of learning, and so on. This allows me to interpret what they do and why they do something from an insider's perspective, an emic perspective. This is crucial to developing understandings of language learning and learners in their sociocultural context and to minimizing the all too frequently occurring problem of (mis)interpreting the behaviors and cognitions of members from one culture through the lens of a different culture. This is, I believe, the unique contribution that a researcher from an EFL context and conducting research in that context can make.

[For example, if we look at] the promotion of communicative language teaching in China, not so long ago, many Western researchers tended to regard CLT as an autonomous methodology that should work in every context. However, drawing on my own experience of learning and teaching English in China and my culturally shaped understandings, I made a case against a blind transplanting of CLT in the Chinese context by drawing attention to fundamental beliefs, perceptions, attitudes, relationships, and assumptions rooted in a time-honored Chinese culture of learning that are potentially inimical to CLT principles and practices.

Another example concerns Chinese teachers' on-the-job professional development work. Some Western scholars have few positive things to say about such development work in China. My insider knowledge accumulated from my own working experience, numerous school visits and many collaborative projects with school teachers has enabled me to view many activities teachers engage in on a routine basis (e.g., collective lesson planning; end-of-semester work report; lesson observation) in a different light and identify the dynamics and benefits of such activities. ...

I would say it is not only a possibility but a strength of researchers from an EFL context to capitalize on their sociocultural knowledge and own language learning experience in their research and publication. Their situated, insider knowledge and experience can provide a privileged, emic perspective that is not available to an outsider. This is a chief reason why much of my research has focused on English language teaching and learning in China, the EFL context I come from.

Liu Chun, a lecturer at the early stages of his academic career, has similarly recognised that his insider knowledge of his culture positions him to have a different viewpoint on some of the issues discussed in his field of research. For him, 'setting the record straight' is something which drives his research in the area.

Liu Chun, postgraduate student in Singapore (on leave from his post as lecturer at a university in Northwest China)
The reason why I'm interested in the issue of plagiarism is that I took an academic writing course back at college, in which our English teacher from Britain introduced the topic and taught us some skills aimed at avoiding it. The notion of plagiarism seemed to echo my science background at that time, which, to me, emphasized precision and accuracy ..., and more importantly, my belief in fairness (being credited for what and only what one has done). This interest was heightened after I read the article by Flowerdew and Li (2007) about how novice Chinese scientists reuse language in writing English journal articles. ... [The practice of language reuse] documented by Flowerdew and Li ... was so reminiscent of my English learning experiences back at college, i.e., noting down useful expressions in a notebook and using them in my speaking and writing. Another thing was my interaction with a PhD student back at college who was trying to publish an article in a prestigious medical journal in America. I helped her check her English writing and I still remember in our discussion how she kept referring to her notebook, in which she kept expressions she thought would be useful to

her. While reading Flowerdew and Li's article, all these rang the bell, and I immediately liked the study and set out to find out more similar studies.

[The topic is] interesting to me on both personal and professional counts. I feel very strongly about what the literature claims about the role of Chinese culture in the seeming propensity or acceptability of plagiarism among Chinese learners and the scarcity of research by Chinese scholars working in mainland China (at least in applied linguistics) in international journals. First, I do believe that some cultural and educational practices may contribute to a different perception of the notion of plagiarism, but I do not think it is accurate, and even appropriate to claim that the Chinese culture is accept[ing] of plagiarism. I think some views in the literature seem to be essentialistic in that they are largely based on the assumption of the cultural acceptability of plagiarism rather than solid evidence. In my study, I attempted to look at attitudes towards plagiarism with reference to awareness of it because I feel, as also suggested by some literature, it is perhaps not that the students accept plagiarism but that they may perceive plagiarism differently.

Chinese English learners constitute the largest EFL population in the world, but the research in that context, particularly by researchers working in that context, is disproportionately represented in the international TESOL publications. … As an insider in that context, I feel a need to do my little bit to address those issues.

5 Access to Research Sites and Participants

Related to the 'insider knowledge' discussed above is the clear advantage that EFL scholars have in terms of their comparatively easy access to research sites and participants which may be difficult for an 'outsider' to gain access to.

Liu Chun, the postgraduate student that we heard from in the previous section, recognises that his ability to speak to potential research subjects at particular research sites, to collect data from them, and then to analyse and discuss his findings through cultural lenses appropriate to his research subjects represents a unique form of social capital that can be used to his advantage. He also recognises that the relative scarcity of English-medium published research that addresses his particular context represents an opportunity for him to make a real contribution to the field.

Liu Chun, postgraduate student in Singapore (on leave from his post as lecturer at a university in Northwest China)
I think the reason why I could investigate perceptions of plagiarism among university students in mainland China was partly attributable to my status as a

university teacher in China, which made it easier for me to gain access to the research sites and the participants. As an insider, I'm more likely to know people in that context, which is very important to get things done in China because I guess the Chinese society puts far more emphasis on connections than many other societies. In China, it is very hard to gain access to schools unless you know some people there or you are very powerful. Otherwise, it is likely that no one will trust you.

The very fact that not many studies conducted in the EFL contexts have been published in English-medium publications poses an opportunity for EFL researchers. For one thing, [as mentioned,] EFL researchers have access to what NES researchers may not - the sort of connections, an awareness of the appropriate ways to do things. [For example,] you don't have to pay people who go to the school to collect the data for you if they are your students, friends or subordinates … but you may need to pay or at least treat the principal or other powerful people of that school if you hope things will go well.

6 Access to Research and Resources from a Different Scholarly Tradition

Besides access to research sites and participants, EFL scholars also have the advantage of possessing linguistic knowledge that allows them to consult and draw upon academic resources from a scholarly tradition that may be completely different from that typically accessed by a mainstream English-speaking academic discourse community. While English is now undoubtedly the international lingua franca of academic scholarship (e.g. Canagarajah, 2002; Flowerdew & Li, 2009; Hyland, 2009; Lillis & Curry, 2010), it would be a naïve English-speaking academic who imagines that research in his/her niche area of research does not take place and get published in many other languages in the world. One of the great contributions that EFL scholars can make to the international English-speaking academic community is to introduce and distil the research published in other languages into the disciplinary conversation.

The following comment from Chang Yu, a PhD candidate in a university in Singapore, shows the potential for EFL scholars to significantly open up and enrich a field of study.

Chang Yu, PhD candidate in Singapore (on leave from his post as lecturer at a university in Northwest China)
[W]hen I was writing about the use of hedges and boosters in English and Chinese academic papers, it was imperative to consult the Chinese literature because there is very little relevant literature in English covering the Chinese language. The

metadiscourse model proposed by Hyland (2005) was entirely based on English language, my question was how to operationalize it in Chinese. That's why I spent quite some time to review relevant Chinese literature and try to work out a taxonomy which can be applied to Chinese text. Thus I searched the Chinese online databases published in mainland China, and I went to the Chinese library of this university (fortunately there is one here!). Finally, I located some literature including a PhD thesis (Li, 2006) on metadiscourse in Chinese language and some sporadic literatures about relevant aspects such as Chinese modal verbs (Lu, 2004), how modality (Xu, 2007) and evidentiality (Chen, 2009) are conveyed in Chinese language etc. Based on these literatures, I was able to compile a working taxonomy for my own study. [Here is a selected list of the Chinese literature I reviewed:]

Chen, Y. (2009). *Hanyu chuanxin fanchou yanjiu [A study of the evidentiality in Chinese]*. Beijing: China Social Sciences Press.

Li, X. M. (2006). *Hanyu yuanhuayu biaoji yanjiu [A study of metadiscourse markers in Chinese]* (Unpublished doctoral dissertation). Fudan University, Shanghai, China.

Lu, X. K. (2004). *Xiandai hanyu jiben zhudongci yanjiu [A study on modal auxiliaries in contemporary Mandarin]*. Beijing: China Social Sciences Press.

Xu, X. J. (2007). *Xiandai hanyu kenengqingtai yanjiu [A study on modality of possibility in contemporary Chinese]* (unpublished master's thesis). East China Normal University, Shanghai, China.

Chang Yu's discussion of these Chinese sources in the literature review and discussion sections of his own work (in English) offers a window into the research of a scholarly tradition that English-speaking researchers would have no other way of accessing, and I would suggest that EFL scholars are able to greatly enhance disciplinary conversations because their linguistic capital often allows them to participate in the discourse communities of two (or more) different cultures, if they so choose.

7 Personal Histories which are Brought to Bear on Research

Like other academics, many of the EFL researchers in this study are engaged in research which has particular resonance for them by virtue of their personal histories and backgrounds. It follows that such research has the potential to provide important insights into the geographical contexts and cultural communities from which these EFL researchers come, insights which might never otherwise be surfaced or given voice within a wider community. We have already seen from the narrative slices offered above by Dr Jiang (the Associate Professor with 25 years of teaching experience in higher education) and postgraduate Liu Chun that their personal histories are closely connected to the research areas they have chosen, and that in their work, they seek to provide insights into, and even challenge prevailing mindsets about language learning and learners in the Chinese context. The following account by Dr Naing, originally from Myanmar and now an Assistant Professor at a university in another Southeast Asian country, offers another example of an EFL researcher whose personal history informs the work that she does. It is clear from her account below that this work serves to deepen the discourse community's collective understanding of cultural practices in Myanmar, and also, more generally, of her chosen research areas – folktales and oral storytelling.

Dr Naing, Assistant Professor, 6 years of teaching in higher education, originally from Myanmar, now working in another Southeast Asian country
I decided to choose folktales as my area of research for my MA dissertation at [X university] because at that time "Selected Myanmar Folktales" was the prescribed English textbook for high school students in Myanmar. These are Myanmar folktales translated into English. I wanted to become an English language teacher, and initially wanted to find out the pedagogical significance of using these tales as a prescribed textbook (e.g. how it helps to develop reading and writing skills as well as to enrich vocabulary). But after getting feedback from my supervisor on my research proposal, I realized that it was more viable and interesting to examine the narrative features of these translated tales, which can be said to have survived translation or paraphrase unlike the linguistic features. ... Since there was enough to say about the narrative features within the scope of an MA dissertation, I decided to leave out the issues on pedagogical significance in the end.

After my MA, when I had to find a topic for my PhD research, my first proposal was to do a comparative study of narrative structures in folktales from south-east Asian nations. But after doing some literature review, I realized that I needed to go deeper into south-east Asian studies if I wanted to continue working on this topic. So I ... decided to look at how these tales are actually told. It led me to my second area of research interest, oral storytelling. Personally, I had fond memories of listening to storytelling on the radio as a kid. Professionally, I thought ... I could look at verbal, vocal and visual features and how these features work together to represent meanings as the narrative develops ....

At present, I am trying to relate my work on oral storytelling performances to language teaching in [name of country] primary schools .... I am also trying to expand my scope of narrative studies to include conversational storytelling, and study it in relation to oracy development, especially the development of interactional and narrative competence in ESL/EFL students. This choice, I would say, is largely due to professional reasons. I see the need to make my work as relevant as I can to the institution I am now working at.

In professional terms, the direction that Dr Naing takes in her research is pragmatically influenced by what she feels are the demands and interests of her graduate programme, the institution in which she works, and the discourse community. But we note that the motivations and history behind her research interest are uniquely hers, born out of her familiarity with the high school students in Myanmar, her fond memories of listening to storytelling on the radio as a child, and so on. It is this personal history and cultural familiarity, intersecting with mainstream research theories on narrative structure and oracy development, which characterise Dr Naing's research and give it its particular flavour.

Although it is quite clear that insider knowledge of their home cultures, access to particular research sites and participants, access to research from a different scholarly tradition, and a personal history of growing up in an EFL country may constitute general forms of cultural capital for EFL researchers to draw on as they negotiate a place for themselves in the international academic discourse community, it is not my intention here to suggest that the unique contributions of EFL researchers must necessarily relate directly to the EFL countries they come from. Certainly, many EFL researchers *do* choose to turn the research lens on their own culture in some way (Dr Jiang, Dr Naing, Liu Chun and Chang Yu all fall into this category), but there are many others who do not and who choose instead niche areas of research which may not require them to explicitly draw on or reference their home cultures or EFL backgrounds.

Perhaps, in such cases, it may be more important to keep in mind that the 'autobiographical self' (Ivanič, 1998) will always to some extent mediate the meanings that we make. Even if researchers do not explicitly refer to their personal histories and cultural backgrounds in their research, those histories invariably give them uniquely-tinted glasses through which they view their research field, topics, participants and findings. What we make of the canonical literature in our field, what we find worth investigating and reporting, and how we interpret and discuss our findings are all matters that are at least partially influenced by the values and assumptions that we bring with us to our research. This is true of *all* researchers, not just EFL researchers, and one might argue then that it is in fact *all of us* (English L1, ESL, EFL speakers), each drawing on our unique personal histories to bring our own particular take on our own particular research interests, who enrich the discourse community's collective understanding.

The idea that an individual's unique personal history, more than his/her status as a native or non-native speaker of English, is what determines the nature of the contribution that he/she might make to an academic field was also raised by Dr Bencsik, an Assistant Professor originally from Central Europe but now working in Southeast Asia. When asked about the extent to which EFL scholars might be able to use their backgrounds to their advantage, he made the point that it is not one's linguistic background which ultimately matters, but one's personal history, and how one chooses to capitalise on that.

Dr Bencsik, Assistant Professor, 16 years of teaching in higher education, originally from Central Europe but with experience of language teacher education programmes in many countries, and currently working in a university in Southeast Asia

[In terms of making a contribution to the international academic community,] I don't think it makes any difference whether I come from an EFL background or an L1 background. I don't think it's got anything to do with EFL. I think it's personal contribution. And if you have something to say, I think you can say it. I don't believe [young EFL scholars] don't have chances of publishing in international journals. They just have to write it up and send it. And if it's up to the standard, they can get published. It's got nothing to do with whether you are Chinese, or Indonesian, or Hungarian. ...

What [EFL scholars] can bring in [is] maybe a different point of view. Because of our cultural background, seeing things slightly differently and understanding the world slightly differently. I think it's important because even if you take the same issue, there might be differences between how an American or an Australian sees the same problem .... They went probably slightly different routes to higher education, and that definitely shapes their beliefs and values, and usually we see the world through our different filters, so we pick out things that are important for us and we don't notice other things that are not that important. So we focus on certain things and ignore other things. Otherwise we just go mad. You can't notice everything. And I think it's not the issue of being EFL, ESL, [or] L1, but *what kinds of experiences shaped you as a person.*

... [My background is] a little bit of a pick and mix of different things and different experiences. I never planned that I would be working [where I am now]. It happened. And I don't know where I'm going to work next or how long I'm staying here. And that definitely gives me a perception of the world which may be different from someone who is more stable and settled down in one context.

8 Sowing for the Next Generation

As increasing numbers of EFL students travel abroad to study in English-dominant countries, it becomes imperative for the Anglophone academic community (certainly within the fields of ELT and Applied Linguistics) to understand at least some of the cultural, intellectual and discoursal heritage that their international students bring with them. EFL scholars who are themselves from those contexts and who have already successfully navigated their way through an Anglophone academic system are perfectly positioned to offer research insights that will help both novice EFL students and the university academics who have to teach them.

All four of the EFL postgraduates who participated in this study were working in the area of academic writing research, and it was clear from their responses to my questionnaire that their development as researchers in the field was paralleled by a growing self-awareness of themselves as EFL academic writers. Research interests were often driven by their own personal struggles with academic writing in the past, and there was often a strong desire to plough research insights back into the teaching of academic writing to the 'next generation', their own students. This account by Wei Ying is a case in point.

Wei Ying, just completed her second Masters degree (MA in Applied Linguistics) in Singapore, returning to her lecturer post in southern China
During the writing of my [first] MA dissertation [in China], I had a feeling of utter helplessness. … One of my coping strategies was just to follow structures of other people's dissertations. For example, I noticed that there were generally introduction and summary sections in each chapter of a dissertation, and there was a literature review section in a dissertation in most cases. Thus I simply followed suit, without clearly knowing what literature review was actually for. I think if I had obtained more and better knowledge about academic writing, genre-specific features, rhetorical moves in various sections of a dissertation and possible expectations of English discourse community, I would have had a much easier, more pleasant and fruitful writing experience at that time.

To do research about academic writing, I believe, would empower myself as well as others …. To be more specific, for example, carrying out a study with regards to the use of hedging in academic texts seems to have helped me gain increasing knowledge about its functions and potential rhetorical differences between Chinese and English. This would help me to be more aware of the use of hedges in my own academic writing. Furthermore, the findings of such a study and tentative conclusions may also inform current academic literacy pedagogy and implicate instructional practices, which would benefit student academic writers as a whole. … From my past writing experience, I believe many student writers (in China and similar situations) need guidance in their academic writing practice and from my current writing experience at Singapore, I came to realize (happily) that doing research in this area could benefit myself, and other writers, particularly novice academic writers from similar sociocultural backgrounds.

We see similar sentiments in the account below. Like Wei Ying, who feels that her research into hedging not only helped her in her own writing but could also benefit future students, Chang Yu, a PhD candidate and lecturer at the start of his academic career, sees that his research into metadiscourse not only helps him to participate more fully within his discourse community but could also feed into the future training of EFL students in China.

Chang Yu, PhD candidate in Singapore (on leave from his post as lecturer at a university in Northwest China)
I feel this area [metadiscourse used in scholarly writing] is very much relevant both to me as a teacher researcher and my students as EFL learners. … For me, further exploring this topic in academic writing can enable me to better understand the underlying mechanisms of scholarly writing. … Some knowledge [in this area] is very helpful for someone like me who is trying to participate, though only peripherally, [in] the discourse community. By participation, I mean the process of moving from the periphery towards the center of a discourse community. In other words, I began as an apprentice of the discourse community. Gradually, through taking part in a variety of "tribal" activities such as seminars, publication, conference etc. I would become a full member of the community. Metadiscourse is important because it is an integral part of the scholarly communication ….

I don't think I'm the only beneficiary, many novice researchers like me may share the benefits from such a research. For my students, this topic is also very important because as EFL learners, their use of metadiscourse in academic writing could be quite different from those [of] native-speakers of English. …

[According to a British Council report,] Chinese EFL test-takers … have been very weak in speaking and writing as compared with students from other East Asian and South East Asian countries. So academic writing in English seems to be an area which needs more attention in English language teaching in China. Even for English major students, academic writing is not given enough attention …. Take my university for example, only two hours of writing is devoted to writing classes every week for two semesters in the second year for undergraduates major[ing] in English. Students are supposed to learn from the basic use of mechanics in writing to the writing of a few hundred words passages which are coherent and well-organized. However, they don't have any other assignments in English except those from the writing class. How can you expect a great leap forward of their English composition within such a short period of time and with insufficient input? Let alone the final year 5000-6000 words dissertation in English …. Many students barely even know what the constitutive parts are of a dissertation or why they have to cite from others. But the policy in China all over the country is to require all English major undergraduates to submit a paper in English before they can get their degrees. … [I]t becomes imperative for teachers and researchers alike to devote more attention to help students to improve their academic writing ability and meet such requirement.

We see from these accounts that there is immense potential for these postgraduate researchers from China to bring something very valuable to the international community of academic writing researchers, to offer research insights that will help both novice EFL students from China and the university academics who may have to teach them.

9 Contributions from EFL Scholars Necessary for Sustaining Growth in Disciplines

A number of my EFL participants also see that they have a role to play in ensuring the continued growth and sustainability of their niche areas of research in the long term. If academic sub-fields want to flourish and develop, they need to be open to new voices – both voices which confirm theories in the field which were perhaps formulated in the 'centre', as well as voices which challenge, question and reformulate dominant theories where necessary, in the light of new evidence emerging from different contexts.

Liu Chun, one of the postgraduate scholars we heard from earlier, highlights the importance of having 'diversity' in his field:

Liu Chun
I think there are many ways Chinese EFL researchers can contribute [to the international academic literacies discourse community]. One obvious way is the diversity they can bring into [this] discourse community. I believe diversity is essential to countries, communities, and individuals alike. I guess one of the many reasons why America is the strongest country in the world is its relative tolerance towards diversity. This kind of diversity facilitates creation and invention, which is the source of its development and prosperity. Accordingly, it's hard to imagine that a community with a universal voice (say, the international academic literacies discourse community with a dominating Anglophone voice) can prosper in the long run. I feel the kind of diversity the Chinese EFL researchers bring along can benefit the international academic literacies community.

PhD candidate Chang Yu also recognises that he is able to bring diversity to his chosen field. However, he also shrewdly recognises that the ability to offer a different voice does not in itself guarantee that that different perspective will be worth the consideration of others in the discourse community. Research, regardless of who conducts and reports it, still has to be of sufficient quality for it to be accepted into academic circulation.

Chang Yu
Diversity is key to the continued growth and development of the international academic community and I think there is need for researchers who are from different cultures and backgrounds so as to enrich the ecological environment.

So my status and presence as an EFL researcher is necessary to maintain such diversity in international discourse community. [However] I don't intend to over-stress the uniqueness of my background as an EFL researcher from China. A Chinese background only cannot guarantee the quality of research.... For example, some of the best work on Chinese culture and classics were done by those excellent sinologists from other countries (e.g. Fairbank, Waley). But I think if there are more EFL researchers from China joining the ELT research [field], and each tried to offer their little piece of contribution, the whole picture in China would become more explicit. ... I agree with Canagarajah (2002) that there are still voices of 'the periphery' that are unheard of by 'the center' in our field. So one thing many of us from 'the periphery' could do is probably to help to bring those marginalized voices to the international community.

One of the obstacles to getting more diverse voices into mainstream English publications, according to some of my EFL participants, has to do with how the research has to be 'packaged' and the publication endeavour negotiated. Chinese postgraduate Liu Chun, for instance, is confident of the potential that he and others like him have for making a meaningful contribution to the international academic scene. However, he pragmati-cally acknowledges that they need to learn the rules of the 'writing game' (Casanave, 2002) in order to improve their chances of being allowed to 'play':

Liu Chun

As Chinese EFL learners' academic writing is inevitably situated in or influenced by the Chinese socio-cultural contexts, our insider knowledge of the socio-cultural contexts, the Chinese language and literacy practices may help us make unique contributions, if we can be proficient enough in English academic discourses in applied linguistics and thus get our voices heard in international publications.

In order to use their backgrounds to their advantage, the EFL researchers need to learn about both the discourse conventions and the politics of publica-tion (e.g., negotiating with the reviewers and the editor, etc.) widely endorsed by English-medium publications. Otherwise, no matter how interesting their studies are and how unique their perspectives are, they may not get them heard by the international academic community.

But even as scholars from a different academic tradition strive to learn the 'rules' of the 'game' of international English-medium academic publica-tion, and strive through their discourse practices to give 'a tangible and public demonstration that [they have] legitimacy' (Hyland, 2000, p. 10), there is the possibility that the increasing participation of such scholars in the international academic conversation may, over time, result in an open-ing up of the community mindset to allow for different kinds of norms to be deemed viable. As Ridley (2004) has asserted, 'Genres and discourses of academic disciplines are ... in a constant state of flux, in that their purpose, content and form are both constituted by what has gone before and constitute what is to come in the future' (p. 92). Just as the social practices of a discourse community influence the kinds of writing and interactions that are produced in a particular discourse community, so the kinds of writing and interactions that become increasingly evident in a community are likely to shape the future practices of that community. This is a hope that one of my participants expressed:

> **Li Lianfeng, just completed her masters degree in Singapore, returning to her post as lecturer in eastern China**
> [A]s more value is put by journal editors on the content issues EFL researchers deal with that are situated in their EFL contexts, the writing conventions those researchers practice in their own cultures are more likely to be accepted. Following the diverse voices in the international academia will be a diversity in writing conventions. Possibly in the future the Anglo-American conventions may not be the only acceptable yardstick by which to determine whether a research article is good or not and deviations from the Anglo-American norms will also be allowed.

These young EFL scholars, we see, are optimistic that the increasing presence of their diverse voices in their field will not only contribute to the growth and sustainability of their niche areas of research, but also slowly transform the discourses through which disciplinary interactions are allowed to take place.

10 The Importance of Actively Seeking Opportunities to Contribute

From the narratives that have been highlighted thus far, it is clear that there is significant potential for EFL scholars to make valuable contributions to the academic community, and EFL scholars themselves are able to recognise this. However, just because the potential is there, it does not mean that the opportunities to do so will come easily. Opportunities are made; they do not usually drop into one's lap.

The literature has highlighted the importance of establishing contacts wherever possible. Casanave (2002) has written about the importance of 'effective networks of professional relationships' (p. 204) in the Japanese academic context. And the multilingual scholars from Europe participating in Lillis and Curry's (2010) study highlighted networks and relationships of various kinds that were important to their research and writing. These included links with other scholars, connections to different departments, disciplines and institutions, links with people in other countries, and so on.

The participants in my study who were further along in their academic careers also emphasised the importance of establishing networks of contacts. Dr Bencsik, for instance, was very vocal about actively developing professional contacts and seeking opportunities to work and publish.

Dr Bencsik, Assistant Professor, originally from Central Europe, currently working in a university in Southeast Asia
[It's important to] work. I didn't get invited to [British Council] meetings or to these opportunities because I was sitting in my office lamenting on my bad fate to be born on the wrong side of the fence. I just carried on with my work, and people noticed it. Also I think what people like me need is a very extensive network of contacts, because that helps. So I think EFL people, and basically anybody, I mean, they need to work on expanding their professional contacts and using them. In Europe, in South East Asia, I think I can go to any country, and I will find somebody or a couple of people I have worked with in the past. So if I want to go to Vietnam, there are a couple of people I can email right away. If I want to go to Thailand, there will be a few people; [so also in] Malaysia, Philippines. And that's the same for Central Eastern Europe, Britain, Mexico, Brazil, and those kinds of professional contacts really help you to move your career along ...

Dr Yang, another of the Assistant Professors in my study, also highlighted the importance of personal contacts for EFL researchers, although she recognises that, for *all* researchers, it is in fact a whole slew of factors and circumstances working together which ultimately determines whether or not a particular researcher's voice is heard in an international publication.

Dr Yang, Assistant Professor, 7 years of teaching in higher education, originally from mainland China and now working in Hong Kong
The fact that I could access the target 'tribes' – using personal contacts, relying on sincerity and driven by some perseverance, with the facility of my 'cultural and linguistic background' and some familiarity with the local context, did help [me in my research]. ...

I'm afraid in anyone's case, the 'unique' contribution [that one can make to the international discourse community] is perhaps largely a result of the 'unique' personal connections the researcher has, the contingencies, the restrictions, and the researcher's personality and intellectual competency.

I guess in general it takes time for [our cultural and linguistic] advantage to be taken out more fully than we've seen so far - if I think of the applied linguistics teacher-researchers in mainland China for example. ... [T]hose who want to (or have a chance to) get published internationally is only a tiny percentage of the large population of the researchers. It's good if everyone just does what is called for in their context and does what they can to contribute to whatever community they're in or can reach.

Dr Yang's sentiment at the end of the above quote is reminiscent of Dr Bencsik's view discussed earlier in this chapter – that *all* researchers have their own unique contributions that they can make to their fields. The only way that an academic field can develop is through the contributions of a diverse community of individual researchers, all bringing something to the table which the community recognises and can engage with, but which at the same time bears their own unique stamp.

11 The Attraction of Publishing in English

Despite the wealth of literature that highlights the struggles that EFL scholars face in publishing in English, some of the responses from my younger participants also suggest that publishing in English was a personal challenge that they relished.

Li Lianfeng, completed her masters degree in Singapore, returning to her post as lecturer in eastern China
[P]ublishing in English means greater recognition by the world and can bring a greater sense of self-fulfillment. By self-fulfillment, I don't simply mean more international recognition. It is something related to the realization of an ideal. Being an English major, I aspire to produce and publish something in English, which is more of a symbol of having achieved a goal after many years of learning and using English.

Wei Ying, another postgraduate we heard from earlier, gives more reasons for why publishing in her L2 holds such an attraction.

Wei Ying
[If given a choice,] I would choose to publish in English only. First, I have much confidence now in my academic writing ability, after the two years [in Singapore], especially after I have undergone efficient training in the academic writing course as a MA student. Second, I think English publication would have much more circulation and wider readership. One thing I've noticed is that English articles or books seem to be more frequently cited than literature in Chinese. After all, English is being used as an international lingua franca; whereas Chinese is just used as a

regional lingua franca. … There is a third consideration, that is, as I am now better informed about English academic writing conventions …, I seem to be more willing to accept and get more used to English ways of thinking and writing. For instance, I would unconsciously use a lead-in sentence at the beginning of a paragraph to introduce the topic explicitly and directly. I've also get more and more used to using "I", rather than the collective personal pronoun "we", to express my personal views and indicate my writer ownership. I think this is [a] more westernized way of writing, which I seemed to struggle with almost one year ago. … For the past two years of studying at Singapore, I have produced a number of academic written work for the fulfillment of course requirements and they are all in the English language. …[I]f I have to switch back to write in Chinese, I may need to shift back to an oriental way of writing, in a conscious way and I am afraid there may be some difficulty for me to translate certain English terms into Chinese, terms like "authorial voice" or "writer identity", whose original flavor may get lost once they are translated into Chinese.

Furthermore, I believe that relatively, there might be more chances for novice academic writers' work to get published in English-medium journals than a limited number of key Chinese-medium journals of applied linguistics in China. I noticed that most authors who had their work published in core Chinese-medium journals were already established Chinese professors with a very few published work by PhD students. I am afraid that it would be extremely hard to enter into the discourse community of applied linguistics in China, especially if you are not well known in the Chinese academia or [have no] 'guan xi' (connections).

It is interesting to note Wei Ying's comment that, having become used to writing in English for her postgraduate coursework, it would in fact prove difficult to write academic papers in Chinese, her L1. Not only would she have to find the appropriate terms in Chinese to refer to academic concepts she has only ever read and thought about in English, but the discoursal patterns she has worked so hard to learn and internalise in order to succeed in her English-medium postgraduate studies would have to be 'unlearned' again. Much research has focused on the challenges that EFL scholars face in producing academic work in a language which is not their native language, but it is worth noting that EFL scholars whose formative years in academia were spent in English-speaking countries may in fact find it easier to produce academic papers in English, rather than their L1 (which they continue to speak and use with no difficulty in every other context). The following quote from Dr Naing highlights exactly the same phenomenon.

Dr Naing, Assistant Professor, originally from Myanmar, now working in another Southeast Asian country
I publish in English only. English has been the medium of instruction, especially throughout my post-grad studies. All the theories, concepts, terms, etc. which I

was exposed to and which I have leant from the courses I did were taught and discussed in English. Both my MA and PhD theses are written in English as well. It would be quite difficult (if not awkward) for me to explain or discuss in my L1, Myanmar, e.g. "What is narrativity and how do we specify it in oral storytelling?" I could use some examples from my L1, but the explanation or discussion as a whole would still be in English. It would be pretty hard for me to write in my L1 about my research accurately.

Even as we discuss the unique contributions that EFL scholars can make to the disciplinary conversation through publishing their work in English, then, we need to bear in mind that not all EFL researchers have a real choice in terms of which language they use to write about their research.

12 Conclusion

It is clear to see, from the narratives shared by my eight EFL participants, that 'challenges' and 'opportunities' are indeed two sides of the same coin. Where there are challenges associated with being 'different' in some way, there are also additional opportunities for precisely the same reason. The cultural and linguistic heritage of EFL scholars may present them with a few obstacles as they seek to participate in the international discourse community. For instance, they may have to learn the discoursal practices valued by an English-speaking disciplinary community. They may have to find ways of presenting what may be culture-specific concerns to a wider audience in a way that invites their intellectual engagement. They may have to find a balance between drawing upon the scholarly tradition and canonical literature that their Anglophone counterparts would be familiar with, and introducing key research from their own scholarly traditions which may not be well-known beyond the boundaries of their home countries and/or language community, but which may be crucial to informing their own studies.

But at the same time, the background and heritage of EFL scholars can be a tremendous advantage to them for precisely these same reasons. They have the opportunity to enrich and expand their disciplinary communities, both through the introduction of alternative and often equally viable ways of representing meaning, as well as through the introduction of new perspectives developed in diverse academic and cultural contexts. They have the opportunity to bring to the academic discussion new concerns and issues. They have the opportunity to showcase research done in their own scholarly traditions and in their own languages in international

English-speaking arenas, thus expanding the reach of one academic community and the understanding of another at the same time.

All researchers have unique contributions that they can make to their field. I hope this chapter has gone some way to highlight some of the reasons why there is rich potential for EFL researchers to use their linguistic and cultural capital to their advantage, and to be a vital part of a thriving international disciplinary community.

References

Becher, T., & Trowler, P. (2001). *Academic tribes and territories*. Milton Keynes: SRHE and Open University Press.

Bourdieu, P. (1973). Cultural reproduction and social reproduction. In R. Brown (Ed.), *Knowledge, education, and cultural change* (pp. 71–112). London: Tavistock.

Bourdieu, P., & Passeron, J.-C. (1990). *Reproduction in education, society and culture*. London: Sage.

Burgess, S., & Martín-Martín, P. (2008). Introduction. In S. Burgess & P. Martín-Martín (Eds.), *English as an additional language in research publication and communication* (pp. 7–15). Bern: Peter Lang.

Canagarajah, A. S. (2002). *A geopolitics of academic writing*. Pittsburgh, PA: University of Pittsburgh Press.

Cargill, M., & O'Connor, P. (2006). Developing Chinese scientists' skills for publishing in English: Evaluating collaborating-colleague workshops based on genre analysis. *Journal of English for Academic Purposes, 5*, 207–221.

Casanave, C. P. (2002). *Writing games: Multicultural case studies of academic literacy practices in higher education*. Mahwah, NJ: Lawrence Erlbaum.

Chen, Y., Gupta, A., & Hoshower, L. (2006). Factors that motivate business faculty to conduct research: An expectancy theory analysis. *Journal of Education for Business, March/April*, 179–189.

Cho, D. W. (2009). Science journal paper writing in an EFL context: The case of Korea. *English for Specific Purposes, 28*, 230–239.

Cho, S. (2004). Challenges of entering discourse communities through publishing in English: Perspectives of nonnative-speaking doctoral students in the United States of America. *Journal of Language, Identity, and Education, 3*(1), 47–72.

Coles, R. (1989). *The call of stories: Teaching and the moral imagination*. Boston, MA: Houghton Mifflin.

Curry, M. J., & Lillis, T. (2004). Multilingual scholars and the imperative to publish in English: Negotiating interests, demands, and rewards. *TESOL Quarterly, 38*(4), 663–688.

Curry, M. J., & Lillis, T. (2010). Academic research networks: Accessing resources for English-medium publishing. *English for Specific Purposes, 29*(4), 281–295.

ElMalik, A. T., & Nesi, H. (2008). Publishing research in a second language: The case of Sudanese contributors to international medical journals. *Journal of English for Academic Purposes, 7*(2), 87–96.

Flowerdew, J. (1999). Problems in writing for scholarly publication in English: The case of Hong Kong. *Journal of Second Language Writing, 8*(3), 243–264.

Flowerdew, J. (2001). Attitudes of journal editors to nonnative speaker contributions. *TESOL Quarterly, 35*(1), 121–150.

Flowerdew, J. (2007). The non-Anglophone scholar on the periphery of scholarly publication. *AILA Review, 20,* 14–27.

Flowerdew, J., & Li, Y. (2009). English or Chinese? The trade-off between local and international publication among Chinese academics in the humanities and social sciences. *Journal of Second Language Writing, 18,* 1–16.

Giannoni, D. S. (2008). Medical writing at the periphery: The case of Italian journal editorials. *Journal of English for Academic Purposes, 7,* 97–107.

Gosden, H. (2003). 'Why not give us the full story?': Functions of referees' comments in peer reviews of scientific research papers. *Journal of English for Academic Purposes, 2,* 87–101.

Hyland, K. (2000). *Disciplinary discourses.* London: Longman.

Hyland, K. (2009). *Academic discourse.* London: Continuum.

Ivanič, R. (1998). *Writing and identity.* Amsterdam: John Benjamins.

Li, X.-M. (1996). *"Good writing" in cross-cultural context.* Albany: State University of New York Press.

Li, Y. (2006a). A doctoral student of physics writing for international publication: A socio-politically-oriented case study. *English for Specific Purposes, 25,* 456–478.

Li, Y. (2006b). Negotiating knowledge contribution to multiple discourse communities: A doctoral student of computer science writing for publication. *Journal of Second Language Writing, 15,* 159–178.

Li, Y. (2007). Apprentice scholarly writing in a community of practice: An 'intraview' of an NNES graduate student writing a research article. *TESOL Quarterly, 41,* 55–79.

Li, Y., & Flowerdew, J. (2007). Shaping Chinese novice scientists' manuscripts for publication. *Journal of Second Language Writing, 16,* 100–117.

Lillis, T., & Curry, M. J. (2006). Professional academic writing by multilingual scholars: Interactions with literacy brokers in the production of English-medium texts. *Written Communication, 23*(1), 3–35.

Lillis, T., & Curry, M. J. (2010). *Academic writing in a global context.* London: Routledge.

Matsuda, P. K. (2003). Coming to voice: Publishing as a graduate student. In C. P. Casanave & S. Vandrick (Eds.), *Writing for scholarly publication* (pp. 39–51). Mahwah, NJ: Lawrence Erlbaum.

Nir, A. E., & Zilberstein-Levy, R. (2006). Planning for academic excellence: Tenure and professional considerations. *Studies in Higher Education, 31*(5), 537–554.

Pavlenko, A. (2003). The privilege of writing as an immigrant woman. In C. P. Casanave & S. Vandrick (Eds.), *Writing for scholarly publication* (pp. 177–193). Mahwah, NJ: Lawrence Erlbaum.

Phillion, J. (2002). *Narrative inquiry in a multicultural landscape.* Westport, CT: Ablex.

Polo, F. J. F., & Varela, M. C. (2009). English for research purposes at the University of Santiago de Compostela: A survey. *Journal of English for Academic Purposes, 8,* 152–164.

Ridley, D. (2004). Puzzling experiences in higher education: Critical moments for conversation. *Studies in Higher Education, 29*(1), 91–107.

Uzuner, S. (2008). Multilingual scholars' participation in core/global academic communities: A literature review. *Journal of English for Academic Purposes, 7*(4), 250–263.

Webster, L., & Mertova, P. (2007). *Using narrative inquiry as a research method.* Abingdon, Oxon: Routledge.

Afterword

Afterword

English Medium Writing for Academic Purposes: Foundational Categories, Certainty and Contingency

Theresa Lillis

1 Interests and Concerns in the Field of Writing for Academic Purposes

In writing this concluding reflective chapter I need to briefly position myself in relation to the chapters and writers' work in this book, as my reflections are obviously bound to my specific interests, experiences and concerns. I am a researcher and teacher whose principal empirical concern is writing, which for much of my research life has been academic writing. I have worked as a teacher in spaces designated institutionally as EAP, ESP, ESL, EAL, as well as in disciplinary marked spaces, such as humanities, education, linguistics, working with students across the age range. For the past 15 years I have been working as a teacher of language, linguistics and learning based in a UK university. My research focus has been on student writing and on professional academic writing, by people who use English as their main written academic language or as one amongst several. I share therefore many of the interests and concerns illustrated in the chapters in the book. Methodologically my main interest is ethnography and in how we can draw on and develop traditions in ethnographic research to explore what's involved and at stake in academic writing. Where it seems relevant to do so, I make explicit connections with my research interests and findings.

The chapters in this book reflect the interests and concerns that have been at the centre of pedagogically oriented research on academic writing in English as a second or foreign language for some considerable time. These include the following:

- A recognition of the pressures faced by scholars – students and professional academics – around the world to write academic texts in English. This is evident in all the chapters but foregrounded in Chapters 2, 6, 8, 9, 10 and 11.

- The need to learn about these academic texts by identifying the linguistic and rhetorical features of English medium academic target texts, such as research articles, postgraduate dissertations and undergraduate assignments. Identifying key features of such texts has been, and continues to be, a core descriptive goal in this field and is most strongly represented in this book in Chapters 3, 7, 8 and 10.

- The epistemological and pedagogical position that making language visible is a key way of ensuring access to and participation in the successful production of academic texts. This is an implicit position in all the chapters but sharply outlined in Chapters 2, 4, 5, 9 and 10.

- The commitment to engaging in research which aims to be useful to writers. This commitment is seen in the carrying out of basic descriptive research – mostly on texts but also on writers' perspectives and experiences – and in the devising of pedagogic and intervention strategies, drawing on such research, to help facilitate writers' success. All the chapters reflect this commitment.

- A belief in the importance of getting language on the agenda in debates around the production of written academic knowledge and, in line with this, a commitment to finding ways to work with (in) academic disciplines and their specialists in higher education, by, for example, designing ways in which 'language specialists' can work with 'content specialists' such as lecturers, journal editors etc. to support students' or professional academics' writing. Efforts to work with 'content specialists' are explicitly discussed in Chapters 2 and 5.

The chapters acknowledge, build on and extend traditions of inquiry of some thirty years to confront specific challenges and questions. Across the chapters, we find a combination of reference to established works and frameworks alongside a welcome engagement with works less well known in this Anglophone-centre dominated field of research. Examples include reference to the works of Flowerdew alongside those of Cho and Li, in discussions of professional academic writing; Hyland alongside work by Campoy-Cubillo et al. and Lewandowska-Tomaszczyk and Melia, in relation to corpus studies; Ferris, Hyland and Leki alongside more recent work by one of the chapter authors, Hu, and Zhang on peer feedback practices; Duszak and Samraj alongside Apanowicz and Mendel in research on PhD theses. There is also a welcome attention to work not usually drawn on in this predominantly verbal oriented field. This includes reference to work by Jewitt and Kress on multimodality in the focus on visuals in undergraduate academic writing, and to Ivanič and Lea and Street on non-textual dimensions, such as the significance of identity in and for academic writing. Identity has been a key focus in all fields concerned with communication practices and is of growing interest in this particular research tradition of academic writing in English, the nature of which I discuss in more detail below. Methodologically, the chapters illustrate the tools currently in use in researching academic writing in English: diverse text analytic frameworks such as move analysis, discourse analysis, a range of linguistic and corpus tools; and writer/participant oriented analysis using interviews and survey data, reflective diaries (as e-logs or hard copy) and commentaries by writers and researchers.

The chapters are drawn from around the world, and whilst their disciplinary home might be labelled differently according to where you/I/the writers are located geographically and institutionally, I think that for the most part they sit within a disciplinary and ideological space which is most easily recognisable as an overlapping of 'Applied Linguistics', EAP (English for Academic Purposes) and 'Second Language Writing'. The most obvious framing evident from Applied Linguistics is the approach to the study of language phenomena as one of problem identification and effort after (re)solution, captured in the widely-quoted definition of Applied Linguistics below:

> The theoretical and empirical investigation of real-world problems in which language is a central issue. (Brumfit, 1995, p. 27)

Thus the chapters reflect the imperative not just to do research but to do research which will have a (relatively) immediate impact on a specific 'problem' in the world: in this book, the problem involves defining the nature of English medium academic texts, the obstacles and issues faced by users of English as a 'second' or 'foreign' language seeking to produce such texts and developing ways to support successful text production. (Of course, EFL/EAP is not merely one key strand in Anglophone-centre based Applied Linguistics but has been a core empirical focus, so much so that AL is often used as synonym for concerns about EFL and EAP). From the field of EAP/ EFL we find the powerful textual imperative that pervades this book, that is the drive to get at and unpack the nature of the texts that users of English around the world want to, or are expected to, produce (reflected in the considerable work by for example Swales, e.g. Swales, 1990, and Johns, e.g. Johns, 1997). Much invention and energy has gone into devising analytic tools for identifying features of texts and the ways these work. From 'Second Language Writing' which has emerged as a specific area of study predominantly from the US, we can see the importance of exploring academic writing as a particular high stakes communicative practice and, in particular, the need to create space for exploring academic writing from a 'second' or 'foreign' language perspective in institutional contexts where attention to writing in a first language is usually taken as a given (see for example, Matsuda et al., 2006).

What gets to be counted as a disciplinary field is complex and relates not least to specific geo-historical relations of ideas, people, institutions, languages and nation states. Trying to label (or re-label, depending on your starting position) a disciplinary field can be seen as a partisan, even imperialist, activity – 'this is part of my field not yours', 'these are the key people, ideas and works in our field', etc. etc. But I think it's worth trying to identify the boundaries of our working academic fields, using 'field' in a more explicitly Bourdieu sense (see Bourdieu, 1991), that is to signal historically situated and structured knowledge-making practices, and to be aware of the constant need for greater reflexivity about the academic categorisations and boundaries with which we are working. One advantage of working in a field where a myriad of dimensions and therefore categories seem potentially significant – including writing as text, writing as learning, writing as identity work, writing as networks of production etc. – means that perhaps our intellectual borders are less tightly boundaried or policed and that we are well placed to engage in the kind of reflexive work that will help us engage with the uncertainty and complexity necessary for future thinking and research ...

The contours of this specific disciplinary/ideological space which I will call 'EWAP' (English medium writing for academic purposes) become more evident if we compare it with fields which are, if not cognate, certainly relevant to the key empirical focus of the chapters, *writing* and *English*: thus *writing* is a key focus in research and pedagogic fields such as composition and basic writing (US), and academic literacies (e.g. in the UK, South Africa); *English* is a prime focus in fields such as world Englishes, politics of English, English as a lingua franca. I suggest that the foundational categories of these latter fields stand in some contrast to, and indeed disrupt, foundational categories in EWAP that for the most part remain stable (and staples) in the chapters and the disciplinary space they reflect and constitute. This is not to say that the foundational categories are left wholly untouched. In some places they are explicitly challenged. But for the most part these categories – which I discuss below – are used, even when, I would suggest, they are at the same time being implicitly undermined or questioned. Overall, therefore, the chapters lead the reader to be both reassured and unsettled. The chapters as a whole I would suggest bring into relief the way in which foundational categories are both prevailing and at the same time being problematised in EWAP. They thus illustrate well the nature of this field as it is currently configured.

2 Foundational Categories and Routes Through EWAP

Whilst the chapters cover different contexts in terms of geography, age group, institutional contexts and specific targets or genres of academic writing, they have in common, for the most part, core foundational categories and framings central to the disciplinary/ideological space of the field of EWAP that they occupy. These categories relate not only to the phenomena under study but also, as significantly, to the *framing* of the phenomena under study and thus shape how we come to make sense of what it is we are looking at.

2.1 Route 1 ...

Thus, one route we travel across the chapters in this book is through a world of certainty – about what we are looking at, how and why. So *English* is used as a bounded language, in the singular rather than the plural, the key challenge being to identify which bits of this language are important, or salient, in specific predetermined text types. The terms *native, nonnative, foreign, first* or *second* are also for the most part treated as straightforward categories, with students and scholars construed in a dichotomous ways as *either* L1 *or* L2, as *either* native *or* non-native. The certainty in such dichotomous framing of first/second, native/foreign is not separate, of course, from the certainty surrounding the notion of the language of English, and indeed these dichotomous framings help to ensure that the bounded category of English continues to be meaningful and powerful. *Writing* is for the most part construed as verbal, in one medium, and envisaged as a final text or product. This writing is furthermore construed as being produced by an individual *writer* who, it is assumed, through careful attention (for the most part) to details of the type of texts she/he is writing will develop sufficient competence to produce texts appropriately. The rationale and purpose of research on texts is also presented for the most part straightforwardly; such research aims to identify key features of target texts and genres and make knowledge about these features available to those wishing to write academic texts. Attention is paid to teasing out empirically those aspects of texts which are significant (a challenging task indeed) but, for the most part, such analysis takes place against an *a priori* notion of what these texts, and indeed, at a more abstract level, genres, are, and therefore, how they should be. Likewise the specific *community* which enacts and determines the nature of these texts and genres figures as a clearly identifiable social space in which people are either less or more central, expert or novice, already in or travelling towards. Community, tied in to genre, is therefore construed as relatively easily recognisable, and *multiple* – that is, different academic communities appropriate to different groups of scholars – rather than *diverse* and problematic, in terms, for example, of geography, power, historical differences. Perhaps a good case in point here is that whilst multiplicity has been strongly taken up in writing research (not least through taxonomies of salient features, e.g. Hyland, 2000), the more evocative yet equally useful notion of 'disciplinary conversations' (Bazerman, 1988) and the ways in which such disciplinary texts and conversations are constructed, enacted and fragmented translocally have been less well discussed (see discussion in Lillis & Curry, 2010, chapter 1).

This world of certainty through which we travel across most of the chapters signals a strong continuity of the project with not just what I am calling here EWAP but of course with the larger project of teaching English globally, within which EWAP is closely nested, that is as English as Foreign Language (EFL), historically associated with Anglophone centre institutions, funding and interests. And this brings us to another foundational framework I would suggest of EWAP. Across this vast project there is a strong *normative imperative*, what I, with Mary Scott, have called elsewhere the imperative to 'identify and induct':

> the emphasis is on identifying academic conventions - at one or more levels of grammar, discourse or rhetorical structure or genre - and on (or with a view to) exploring how students might be taught to become proficient or 'expert' [in those conventions] and developing materials on that basis. (Lillis & Scott, 2007, p. 13)

The normative pedagogic imperative driving much work in EWAP is underpinned by the foundational categories discussed above. And language here takes on a curious position, for while a key goal of EWAP is to make language visible so that its resources can be learned and used by writers for their purposes, it is also made curiously invisible, in line with the Enlightenment goals of language as clarity, something to look through, rather than work with (for a recent, interesting overview and discussion, see Turner, 2011). This happens at a number of levels, an obvious example being that in the process of holding still (or idealising) the conventions of 'academic English' so as to make them visible and reproducible, little attention is paid (for the most part) to the shifting, changing and contested nature of such conventions or indeed this particular language, English. Thus the messy 'stuff' of language(ing) and the way it is nested in knowledge making practices, including text evaluation as well as production, is mostly ignored. This Enlightenment ideology of language is most evident in the overarching thrust of the book, that 'good science will out', that is, knowledge will be made and shared with the world, if the language problem is sorted.

The certainty route evident in the book is the one which, I would suggest, is the most clearly signposted and, again I would suggest, is the most common route in EWAP currently.

2.2 Route 2 ...

Yet it is not the only route travelled in EWAP. And indeed there are some signposts across this book – some clearly marked, others sometimes a little hidden – which readers can follow if they/we wish a less comfortable journey. And a key starting point is, most obviously, the chapter by Okada and Casanave. In their chapter, challenging rather than reassuring, some of the foundational categories discussed above are problematised; thus, categories such as *L1, L2, native, non-native, minority, standard, non-standard* are held up for explicit questioning by both the writer/participant and teacher/researcher, challenging any easy use of dichotomies that as teachers and/or researchers we may find comfortable to work with.

A clear challenge is also made, in the chapter by Paltridge and Woodrow, to the notion that the problem – used here to mean 'phenomenon' – we are exploring is a language one, and can therefore be addressed by focusing on language alone. Their explicitly non-textualist framing signals that whilst language-as-text is clearly important in the study and teaching of academic writing, dimensions ranging from 'students' insecurities' to 'time management' need also to be taken into account. So that, in answer to the question of whether being successful in English medium academic writing is always about knowing about language, their answer is, 'well, yes and no'. But exactly when 'yes' and when 'no', and how and with what consequences for whom is not pursued (I would like to have heard more). This position is also evident, albeit more implicitly, in the chapter by Cargill and O'Connor, where the significance they attach to involving expert 'insiders', senior scientists, in their workshops on academic writing for publication signals that insider knowledge of the practices of academic text production (which

is usually implicit) is at least as significant as explicit attention to the micro
details of texts.

A strong critique is also made by Tang of the (predominantly Anglophone
centre) tendency to frame debates around the writing of scholars 'from
EFL backgrounds' in negative terms. Her chapter foregrounds the cultural
capital that such scholars possess and their potential contributions to disciplinary communities. In pointing to and illustrating this capital, Tang not
only challenges any deficit stance on writers/writing positioned as being
from the 'periphery', but points to the transformative potential of such
writers/writing to transnational knowledge making.

Stirrings which signal that the foundational categories are not quite as
robust as might first appear are evident across other chapters, albeit in less
straightforwardly explicit or critical ways. Thus the fact that the text-based
studies are strongly situated at intersections of time, space and discipline
reflects a concern to engage with specificities of language and text production which goes well beyond a straightforward or boundaried notion of
English, academic English or even a particular subject specialist register of
English. Texts are connected to users as much as idealised use, albeit often
implicitly, raising questions about the status attributed to both. Thus for
example, the careful attention to the description of shell nouns by Nesi and
Moreton in a corpus of undergraduate writing implicitly challenges assumptions about which kinds of use and users are considered more appropriate
and on what grounds. In the same way, I think, the writers' reference to the
long-claimed categorical difference between writing and speaking implicitly opens up the space for some consideration of the status of such a claim,
including a much needed debate about what kinds of registers, genres,
modes and language(s) should or should not be currently and translocally
acceptable or useful in and for academic writing.

Contingency of the foundational categories is evident across the chapters,
even if such contingency itself is not explicitly signposted. Thus the categorical distinctions between L1 and L2, native and nonnative, are undermined
by the references to 'near-native' speakers of English that we find in some
chapters, the qualification implicitly signalling the limits of the categories
and the act of categorisation itself. Other examples reflecting the need to
engage with contingency through attention to situated practice are as
follows. 1) The attention to one specific academic journal when conceptualising and empirically exploring 'writing for publication', which implicitly
problematises the meaning of 'international' and – again implicitly I think
– categories such as 'community' and 'genre' (Cargill & O'Connor). 2) The
attention to the specific English medium dissertation practices of a group of

Polish writers in their local contexts, and on their own terms, rather than such locality being construed as a contrast to Anglophone centre English medium practices (Lewkowicz). 3) In a similar non-deficit way, the attention to the English medium rhetorical practices of Chinese writers is used to highlight the potential rhetorical and intellectual value of such practices to all students at a time of the increasing use of multimodalities in young people's everyday e-communication practices (Leedham).

There are also indications from the data presented that emphasis on individualised competence might not be the only or most meaningful way of focusing on successful text production. Whilst not signposted at all, I think that some data usefully directs our attention to the ways in which English can be usefully conceptualised as a resource, connected with a range of people and practices and which can be drawn on by others at specific moments in time, rather than a good or commodity (necessarily) to be owned by individuals. I'm thinking here in particular of the data in the chapter by Hu and Ren on peer review practices which seemed to echo, in part, findings from other studies showing that students prefer teachers rather than peers to give feedback on their writing. However Hu and Ren's data also show that students perceived peer feedback positively where this was viewed as one source of information alongside others, such as teacher feedback. Rather than concluding that students need to be encouraged to view peer review more positively, drawing on my research with Mary Jane Curry on scholars' practices, I would consider that the students are probably right to want a range of commentators or brokers (Lillis & Curry, 2006) commenting on their writing, including key gatekeepers, in this case the teacher. I would, therefore, read the documented resistance to peer feedback as reasonable, and more in tune with the ways in which people often work to produce texts, that is by drawing on and connecting with resources that are differentially available (Curry & Lillis, 2010). And this for me connects with an important point made by Okada, that the foundational categories in EWAP tend to make more sense, hold more authentic weight, where the users in question are construed as *learners* taking part in formal education or institutional practice, rather than as people used to using language(s)(ing) to engage, to do something, in this case, produce an 'acceptable' written academic text. So, by construing the people we work with only, or predominantly, as 'learners', our attention may be (mis)directed towards resistance to a pedagogic practice, rather than towards the ways in which people routinely work with language as a resource to get something done.

3 Reflexivity, Epistemology and Strategy

Foundational categories enable us to hold a phenomenon still, examine it and reach towards those useful conclusions that are so eagerly sought after and so important to us, as teachers, scholars and students, in our academic work. The broad questions seeking such conclusions are well illustrated in this book, including the following: What does a successful English medium research article/dissertation/thesis introduction etc. look like? What specific features (linguistic, generic, discourse, rhetorical) are essential in order to produce a successful academic text? What can teachers of academic writing in English most usefully focus on, when, where and how? In what ways do people's previous and current experiences, expectations and practices shape how they engage in writing and learning? Who do writing and 'EAP' teachers need to work with in order to ensure that participation in the production and dissemination of texts is more accessible and inclusive?

The chapters and 'two routes' (I'm sure there are more) through the book illustrate the power of foundational categories in exploring such questions, but also some of the tensions and ambivalence at the heart of such categories with which researchers, teachers and writers have to contend.

Teachers and researchers in EWAP are familiar with the kinds of issues I am raising here. I guess what I am doing is articulating these from my specific perspective and interests. And a key concern of mine here is normativity, which I think frames much of EWAP work. To be clear about what I'm saying here – a key goal must be to share any insider information we have which may help people to write in ways which satisfy institutional demands, expectations, conventions etc. And in a world where the Anglophone centre continues to hold much sway, and where there are strong desires to access centre based practices, efforts around facilitating peripheral access to such powerful knowledge is central. But. My own position is that to adopt a strictly normative position is neither valid scientifically nor ethically. Scientifically, categories such as English L1 and L2, verbal and visual are always provisional and contingent ... useful for as long as they are useful but must always be contingent upon questions such as: Whose English are we talking about? What is being read as English or not English here, by whom, with what consequences? When writing is approached in this way (and here I find the works of Canagarajah (e.g. 2002) and Lu (e.g. 1994) evocative), the categories that underpin this normative framing look far less straightforward and compelling.

To conclude I would like to briefly suggest how we can approach our use of foundational categories (often necessary in engaging with institutional policy and practice) whilst at the same time always reminding ourselves of their contingent status.

3.1 Reflexivity: Making visible the categories we work with

Reflexivity, the continual questioning of the fields and categories with(in) which we explore phenomena, is a highly valued intellectual tool in some traditions and disciplines, such as anthropology, and closer to EWAP, linguistic ethnography (see for example, Rampton et al., 2004), and should be part of our ongoing work as teachers and researchers. By drawing on a critical ethnographic gaze, the procedures and practices – the often taken-for-granted 'tools of the trade' – become as much a part of our intellectual work as the phenomena we think we are studying (see also Lillis & Scott, 2007; Lillis, 2008). In broad terms this means that we adopt an anthropological stance towards any dimension of 'language as culture', that is, always as phenomena to be explored rather than taken as given. The value and significance of any categories we use will therefore always be open to questioning and contingent upon their value and significance in any specific use and context. There are specific analytic tools and frameworks from critical ethnographic traditions that I think are particularly relevant currently to the focus on English medium academic writing: these include attention to the significance of the mobility of people and resources discussed in detail by Blommaert (see for example Blommaert, 2005) and the more longstanding debates on the politics of style, as explored in detail in theoretical and empirical work by Bourdieu (e.g. 1984).

3.2 Epistemology: Conceptualising English as a networked resource

There is much work, in fields already mentioned, which problematises what is meant by 'English' and the monolingual and static assumptions underpinning our naming of language(s) as compared with, for example, the notion of 'languaging' (e.g. Phipps & Gonzalez, 2004). With specific reference to written academic text production, particularly high status texts such as academic journal articles, an important epistemological shift is to construe the 'English problem' not in terms of increasing individual competence in managing linguistic, rhetorical and discoursal features, but in terms of the 'the capacity to access English as a resource attached to other key resources – such as centre academics, centre based networks' (Lillis & Curry, forthcoming). The importance of conceptualising English as a networked resource has become particularly clear in longitudinal research that I have been involved in on academic writing for publication, where complex texts are forged for varied audiences and institutions across several geographical and linguistic contexts (Lillis & Curry, 2006, 2010). We have been exploring how different dimensions to networks – local and

transnational, formal and informal, strong and weak, durable and temporary – support and constrain English medium academic publishing (Curry
& Lillis, 2010), but I think that, given the increasing awareness of the need
to start from a position of mobility and multilingualism, considering such
dimensions is as important in educational and indeed all other contexts.

3.3 Strategy: Working with tensions across institutional and epistemological framings

In terms of strategy, such as engaging institutions in discussion about the
significance of language work in the academy, we will probably find that we
have to use some foundational categories, at least some of the time. This may
mean that in order to ensure that resources are made available we have to
argue for specific needs and interest of specific groups of people, however
configured. In discussion with colleagues over curriculum and pedagogy, we
may often have work to with available discourses and judge when and where
we can problematise these. We cannot, Alice-in-Wonderland-like, simply step
outside of prevailing discourses. At least not all of the time. But we do need
to remind ourselves that strategy and epistemology are not the same and
that as language workers we need to keep our eye on epistemology. A good
example here is the way in which *academic literacies* is often used currently:
used normatively to signal a taxonomy of different kinds of writing practices
in the academy and, at the same time, used to signal a specific epistemological stance, that is writing as social practice (Lillis & Scott, 2007). The same
can be true for *English* or *writers* or *language*: we can work with these categories as long as we also remind ourselves of their limitations and the ways in
which they may, sometimes, be clouding our efforts after understanding.

References

Bazerman, C. (1988). *Shaping written knowledge*. Madison, WI: University of
    Wisconsin Press.
Blommaert, J. (2005). *Discourse: A critical introduction*. Cambridge: Cambridge Uni-
    versity Press.
Bourdieu, P. (1984). *Distinction: A social critique of the judgement of taste*. (R. Nice, Trans.).
    London: Routledge and Kegan Paul.
Bourdieu, P. (1991). *Language and symbolic power*. (G. Raymond & M. Adamson, Trans.).
    Cambridge: Polity Press.
Brumfit, C. (1995). Teacher professionalism and research. In G. Cook & B. Seidlhofer
    (Eds.), *Principle and practice in applied linguistics* (pp. 27–42). Oxford: Oxford Uni-
    versity Press.

Canagarajah, A. S. (2002). *Critical academic writing and multilingual students*. Ann Arbor: University of Michigan Press.

Curry, M. J., & Lillis, T. (2010). Academic research networks: Accessing resources for English-medium publishing. *English for Specific Purposes, 29*, 281–295.

Hyland, K. (2000). *Disciplinary discourses*. Harlow, England: Pearson Education.

Johns, A. M. (1997). *Text, role and context: Developing academic literacies*. Cambridge: Cambridge University Press.

Lillis, T. (2008). Ethnography as method, methodology and 'deep theorising': Closing the gap between text and context in academic writing research. *Written Communication, 25*(3), 353–388.

Lillis, T., & Curry, M. J. (2006). Professional academic writing by multilingual scholars: Interactions with literacy brokers in the production of English medium texts. *Written Communication, 23*(1), 3–35.

Lillis, T., & Curry, M. J. (2010). *Academic writing in a global context*. London: Routledge.

Lillis, T., & Curry, M. J. (Forthcoming). English, scientific publishing and participation in the global knowledge economy. In E. J. Erling & P. Seargeant (Eds.), *English and international development*. Bristol, UK: Multilingual Matters.

Lillis, T., & Scott, M. (2007). Defining academic literacies research: Issues of epistemology, ideology and strategy. *Journal of Applied Linguistics, 4*(1), 5–32.

Lu, M.-Z. (1994). Professing multiculturalism: The politics of style in the contact zone. *College Composition and Communication, 45*(4), 442–458.

Matsuda, P., Ortmeier-Hooper, C., & You, X. (Eds.). (2006). *The politics of second language writing: In search of the promised land*. West Lafayette, IN: Parlor Press.

Phipps, A., & Gonzalez, M. (2004). *Modern languages: Learning and teaching in an intercultural field*. London: Sage.

Rampton, B., Tusting, K., Maybin, J., Barwell, R., Creese, A., & Lytra, V. (2004). UK linguistic ethnography: A discussion paper. Available at http://www.uklef.net/documents/papers/ramptonetal2004.pdf

Swales, J. (1990). *Genre analysis*. Cambridge: Cambridge University Press.

Turner, J. (2011). *Language in the academy: Cultural reflexivity and intercultural dynamics*. Bristol, UK: Multilingual Matters.

Index